Ingredient Branding

Philip Kotler · Waldemar Pfoertsch

Ingredient Branding

Making the Invisible Visible

 Springer

Professor Philip Kotler
Kellogg Graduate School
of Management
Northwestern University
Evanston, IL 60208, USA
p-kotler@kellogg.northwestern.edu

Professor Waldemar Pfoertsch
China Europe International
Business School
699 Hongfeng Rd.
Shanghai 201206, China
wap@ceibs.edu

ISBN 978-3-642-04213-3   e-ISBN 978-3-642-04214-0
DOI 10.1007/978-3-642-04214-0
Springer Heidelberg Dordrecht London New York

Library of Congress Control Number: 2010926489

Cover design: WMXDesign GmbH, Germany

Printed on acid-free paper

Springer is part of Springer Science+Business Media (www.springer.com)

Foreword by Bayer

CDs and DVDs, water bottles, sports eyewear, binoculars, helmets, storage boxes for food, car headlights, automotive roof glazing – these are just some of the everyday products that benefit from the unique properties of Makrolon®, **a plastic manufactured by Bayer MaterialScience AG**. To draw the attention of trade and consumers to this high-tech material, many of the consumer goods made from it now bear the quality mark "made of Makrolon®", which has transformed Makrolon® into a world-famous brand.

"Ingredient Branding" is the technical term for this strategy of taking the product – originally a business-to-business product – to the consumer marketplace, where it gains global **recognition**. Bayer MaterialScience is exploiting the benefits of a brand strategy to make its high-tech polycarbonate Makrolon® stand out from its competitors. This cooperation between Bayer and selected Makrolon® processing companies began in 2000. Through this arrangement, the consumer is related the message that not only is the product manufacturer committing himself to the quality of the product but so too, is the supplier of the most important constituent – the material used to make it.

Since its invention in 1953, this plastic has been regarded as a **versatile** material with many positive properties. With its customizing ability for transparency/opacity, impact strength, temperature-independent dimensional stability, exceptional flow properties and light weight, the application potential for Makrolon® is virtually unlimited. As far as brand strategy is concerned, it is an enormous benefit to Bayer MaterialScience that the plastics industry has known and worked with Makrolon® for several decades. A new aspect, however, is the targeting of other groups. The aim is that not only product designers, buyers and engineers should be made familiar with the material but also the tradesmen and consumers. Since plastic is a **key component** of the consumer product and bears considerable responsibility for its function, but cannot be directly "seen", **Ingredient Branding** makes an important contribution.

Some examples of consumer products that bear the quality mark "made of Makrolon®":

- Our Latin American partner Videolar, uses this seal of quality to show which plastic guarantees optimum storage quality and data security for its writable CD-Rs and DVD-Rs.

- Sheffield Plastics Inc., a Bayer MaterialScience Company, produces Makrolon® polycarbonate sheet products for a variety of markets, including architectural, security, specialty vehicle glazing and sign applications. Manufactured to offer attractive protection in areas subject to high traffic, vandalism or burglary, and tough enough to withstand severe weather, Makrolon® sheet products provide unsurpassed quality and performance.

- The UVEX Sports GmbH & Co. KG, headquartered in Fuerth, Germany and its worldwide agencies extending from the United States to Japan utilize the benefits of Makrolon® for their branded cycling, skiing and sports goggles, UVEX Supravision® visors in motorcycle helmets and Microshell outer shells in cycle helmets. This form of **Ingredient Branding** is currently unique in the sporting goods segment.

- Steiner Optik GmbH in Bayreuth uses Makrolon® to manufacture the body of its high-quality binoculars and thus give the optical system the necessary protection.

- The German manufacturers of the Alurunner® high-tech sled and the American manufacturers of the Makboard transparent snowboard both draw attention to aspects of the product experience that are enhanced by Makrolon® plastic – the seat on the Alurunner® and the basic material in the case of the Makboard.

- The Asian company Zhongshan C&C Luggage Manufacturing Co., Ltd. uses the "made of Makrolon®" tag as a marketing tool for its Crown hardtop cases, as does the Japanese company Matsuzaki Industry Co. Ltd. for its Maruem brand.

- Last but not least, Makrolon® has in recent years also made a name for itself in the field of designer lamps. The Italian company Luceplan is another marketing partner that uses Makrolon® to manufacture and promote its classical Constanzina range of lampshades.

All these **established partnerships** that are part of the **strategic marketing** of Bayer Material Science's high-tech polycarbonate promote the Makrolon® brand. As a result, the end user can better identify with the product.

This book gives managers and future decision makers useful information on this interesting marketing tool that helps consumers to look not only at the product itself but also at the materials used in its manufacturing when making a **purchasing decision**.

Jürgen Hohmann   Spring 2010
Bayer Material Science
Business Unit Polycarbonates
Global Branding Makrolon®
Leverkusen, Germany

Foreword by Microban

During my 30-year career, which includes being a consultant with McKinsey & Company and senior executive at IBM, I've thought long and hard about how to strengthen various businesses. However, it has only been in recent years, as CEO of Microban, that I have fully appreciated the amazing power of Ingredient Branding. So, when I learned that Philip Kotler and Waldemar Pfoertsch were writing a book focused on this subject, I was only too happy to help. As far as I know, this is the only comprehensive, scholarly, yet very practical book on Ingredient Branding.

I've found that business leaders are constantly searching for new, important ways to strengthen their businesses. Most leaders are looking to grow share, raise prices, broaden distribution or improve their product mix – e.g., sell more of their premium products. They deploy many "conventional strategies", such as driving greater awareness through advertising or offering temporary price reductions. Ingredient Branding is not a substitute for these "tried and true" strategies. Rather, it's another strategy to add to the arsenal. It's like adding another arrow to a quiver. And the business leader with more arrows – more firepower, is more likely to win in the marketplace.

Ingredient Branding: Making the Invisible Visible is on the mark. This book provides helpful frameworks to understand Ingredient Branding, when it should be used, and how to get the most value from it. It also provides examples and case studies that bring the conceptual frameworks to life. It is both scholarly, and yet almost a "how to" guide for people with a charter to make things happen.

Of course, leveraging an Ingredient Brand is not going to be the right strategy for every business all the time. However, it's constantly surprising to me how often I speak with sharp business leaders, and they haven't even considered this important strategy.

If nothing else, this book will enhance your knowledge of Ingredient Branding and make you a better well-rounded business leader. And of course, it may also lead you to drive stronger business performance in the marketplace through Ingredient Branding.

David J. Meyers   Spring 2010
President and CEO
Microban International, Ltd.
Huntersville, NC, USA

Foreword by Bitrex

My career has taken me in a few directions, but I could never have predicted that I would be actively involved in something, which Philip Kotler and Waldemar Pfoertsch refer to as "Ingredient Branding". However, this is exactly what we have been doing here at Macfarlan Smith for almost thirty years. The preparation of this foreword has also made me realise what an interesting journey our product Bitrex® has personally taken me on.

Having started my career as a chemical analyst, I have responsibility for overseeing both sales and marketing of Bitrex® globally. The challenge, as encountered by my predecessors, was how to take a product ingredient, which has no effect on the performance of the product, and make it the reason for the consumer to purchase the product. Simply put, I have relied on the fundamentals of Ingredient Branding.

As the most bitter substance ever discovered, our key selling points of Bitrex® are safety, innovation and credibility. Bitrex® has a wide and varying use. Its primary use is to render a product unfit for human consumption. This started with the use of Bitrex® in denaturing industrial alcohol, and has lead to preventing children from ingesting a range of household chemicals, and deterring dogs from eating common garden pesticides. It is in applications such as these latter two markets in which we see Bitrex® gain its full potential as an Ingredient Brand.

My experience of product category managers is that they are constantly looking for new means of selling their products to the consumer. It is our job to educate them that Bitrex® is an option. Once informed, these managers can confidently develop new marketing strategies, not only connecting their products closer to the customer, but also enhancing their own personal knowledge of a unique marketing tool. When a Bitrex® partner utilises the Bitrex® brand, they have a number of options to communicate this to end consumers. Done efficiently, this message can have many positive outcomes for our partners such as innovation, product improvement, market leadership, and caring for the customer. All of which reflect well on our partners. Crucially, we ensure that the message from Bitrex® inclusion is clear and easily understood by the consumer. I'm sure this is the same for most Ingredient Brands.

A fundamental part of our business model is to work with highly regarded experts in the field of safety. In addition, our dedicated technical service ensures our credibility, and of course, efficient use of Bitrex® in our partners products. We, as I'm certain are the case with other Ingredient Brands, face fierce competition. It is the ability to offer something more, something motivating and inspirational, which separates successful Ingredient Brands from cheaper generic imitators. This also ensures that Bitrex® continues to move forward as a brand.

To summarise, Ingredient Branding has been our line of business for a long time. Maybe only now are the strategies employed fully recognised as a unique marketing tool. This educational book will help readers to develop their personal marketing skills, and hopefully lead to the Ingredient Brands of the future.

Cameron Smith   Spring 2010
Bitrex® Business Manager
Macfarlan Smith Limited
A Johnson Matthey Company
Edinburgh, Scotland, United Kingdom

Preface

The explosion of high-tech products, from PCs and mobile phones to modern textiles and household appliance has made it increasingly difficult for customers to make purchasing decisions. In order to process all the information that is available to them, one could say that they need the help of a "translation key"[1]. An example of such a key could be a strong brand name which communicates special features and advantages of a product, thereby simplifying the decision making process for customers. This "key" is especially important for Ingredient Brands – brands within brands; they make the invisible component visible in the minds of the final user.

Starting back in the 1960s, a few companies have been very successful in developing a strong Ingredient Brand and making their logos icons in the consumer minds (see Fig. 1).

Now in the new millennium, hundreds of component suppliers have discovered the power of Ingredient Branding. There is a worldwide rush of suppliers in various industries to reach the minds of the final consumer. The success stories of companies such as **Intel Corporation, WL Gore & Associates, Bayer AG, The NutraSweet Company** and **Dolby Laboratories,** have revealed the potential advantages of Ingredient Branding and shown many component suppliers that they can realize better return on investment with new

---

[1] Kevin Keller (2008): Strategic Brand Management Building, Measuring, and Managing Brand Equity; Third Edition, Upper Saddle River, p. 294; and Simon, Hermann; Sebastian, Karl-Heinz (1995): Ingredient Branding in: Absatzwirtschaft, Vol. 38, 1995, No. 6, pp. 42–48.

Fig. 1. Logos of well-known Ingredient Brands
(All rights reserved by the logo owners)

marketing strategies. Today we find companies that consciously choose to employ the Ingredient Branding concept and others that do it without knowing the principles and terms. Some seem to have attained success, some are struggling. From our research and practical insights, we know Ingredient Branding is a complex Branding concept involving integrated, multi-level marketing.

One cannot find a better example to support the Ingredient Branding concept than the largest soft drink manufacturer of the world. Neville Isdell, Chairman, Board of Directors and CEO of The Coca-Cola Company in Atlanta, expanded the Branding strategy for his products in 2005 by drawing more attention to an ingredient, the artificial sweetener, than the drink itself. The new product, promising zero calories and amazing taste, is called "Coca-Cola Zero™" and it is produced with a mixture of Aspartam and Acesulfam Potassium, among others. Interestingly, the sweetener brand is not explicitly mentioned in their marketing campaign and the reason for this is given later in this book. This innovative strategy was the beginning of a new era for Coca-Cola, with the sweetener ingredient at the center of all marketing activities. This marks a general new trend: repositioning of product groups in relation to their ingredients.

For those of you who are new to Ingredient Branding, this book will provide tips and guidance from experts in the field, empowering you with the necessary knowledge to embark on the road to transform your brand into an Ingredient Brand, also referred to in this book as an "InBrand". The concepts and methods which are introduced in this book were developed jointly around the globe: in the United States (Chicago), Germany (Pforzheim), and China (Shanghai), and summarize the newest findings and experiences from many companies. We present a fresh selection of case studies and give the reader insights into the most current research results.

This effort was achieved through the help of many academics and practitioners. First, we would like to thank the deans of our business schools: Dipak C. Jain from Kellogg School of Management, Rolf Cremer of China Europe Business School (CEIBS) and Rudi Kurz from Pforzheim University for giving us the support and opportunity to work on such an interesting topic. They kept us focused on the big picture of the practical application of our research. We also would like to thank many of our colleagues for their support and encouragement during the five-year-long effort to get our insights on paper.

We had many important and challenging discussions with researchers around the globe. Great thanks to John Quelch from Harvard Business School, Roland Mattmüller from the European Business School (EBS), Stille Lee from the Antai College of Economics & Management at Shanghai Jiao Tong University, Stephen L. Vargo, University of Hawaii at Manoa, and many more. In particular, we would like to mention Ralph Olivia, Professor of Marketing and Executive Director at the Institute for the Study of Business Markets (ISBM), from Penn State Smeal College of Business. He set up various meeting and seminar with companies to help us discuss our findings in real business settings. In his current function he is supporting the importance of B2B and B2B2C marketing and branding, because he knows first hand from his former job at Texas Instruments (TI), where he was involved in the early stages of the In-Branding concept development of DLP for Texas Instruments.

Special thanks go to Juergen Hohmann, Bayer Material Science AG Global Brand Manager, who supported our research efforts through insights and generous support. Due to his contributions we could actually conduct secondary and primary research in Europe and China. Some of his Chinese Bayer managers also helped us understand the specific conditions for InBranding in this market. In particular, we would like to mention Jeffry Pi, CEIBS MBA alumni and Brand Manager at Bayer (China) Ltd. Martin Godetz, Export Director of UVEX Sports and license partner of Bayer AG Makrolon, who helped us to get a better understanding of the effects and impediments of Ingredient Branding at the Original Equipment Manufacturer level, thank you for the extensive discussions and long nights at various bars during the joint InBranding promotion with Juergen Hohmann.

We also had long discussions with David J. Meyers, President and CEO, Microban International, Ltd. and Michael Demmler, former General Manger of Microban, Germany. These gentlemen are good examples of gifted entrepreneurial leaders who sensed the power of InBranding and had the guts to apply the concept, even before it was fully understood by academics. By convincing hundreds of enterprises to add ingredients (antibacterial protection) to their end user products, they not only made their companies successful, but also helped create marketing concepts and case studies to be used for teaching.

In this context we would like to thank Cameron Smith, Manager at Bitrex Division of Macfarlan Smith Limited, Edinburgh, Scotland who saved the lives of many children by applying the InBranding concept to prevent poisoning accidents. We would also like to mention Florian Hingst, the German Bitrex representative who dedicated his career to protect children's lives through the promotion of Bitrex.

We have to thank many students from our business schools, particularly the CEIBS MBA classes 2005, 2006, 2007, 2008 and 2009, and the students that wrote masters and diploma thesis on this innovative marketing concept. They challenged our thinking and identified many new applications. Special thanks to research assistants Christian Linder, Hendrik Scheel (Pforzheim University) and Lu Ma (CEIBS, Shanghai), who helped us to write and edit the various drafts. Also thanks to Sabrina Bitzenhofer who designed all the graphs, and to all the logo owners who granted us permission to reprint them, and to Marion Park, who spent countless hours editing the numerous manuscript versions.

We probably could not mention all the people who helped us finish this book, but would like to praise the talented staff at Springer Heidelberg for their contribution, in particular Martina Bihn.

The authors are solely responsible for the content of this book.

Philip Kotler   Spring 2010
S. C. Johnson & Son Distinguished Professor
of International Marketing at the
Kellogg School of Management, Northwestern University,
Evanston, IL, USA

Waldemar Pfoertsch
Professor International Business,
Pforzheim University, Germany
Associate Professor of Marketing,
CEIBS China Europe International Business School,
Shanghai, PR China

Contents

CHAPTER 1

Branding Ingredients

The fact that consumers are willing to pay more for a branded product is a well-accepted phenomenon in the business to consumer (B2C) industry. Whether it is for long-lasting quality, superior workmanship, or merely as a status symbol, brands like Mercedes-Benz, Chanel, and Sony command premium prices and exclusive reputation for their products.

The advantages of a strong and attractive brand may long be taken for granted in consumer goods, but a recent phenomenon has emerged; that of branding the ingredients contained in the end product. (See Fig. 2: Logos of selected Ingredient Brands and the complete list of Ingredient Brands in the Appendix). After all, what makes up the end product but the sum of its ingredients? Why not advertise and use to advantage the very things that contribute to the desirable end result?

If implemented and pursued intelligently, branding ingredients could be a win-win situation for manufacturers of both ingredients and final products. For the consumer, there could be no doubt that becoming a more powerful and intelligent shopper, i.e., having the power to demand quality ingredients in the products he/she buys, is a good thing. In an economy where consumers are satisfied with their purchases, business is brisk for manufacturers, who in turn, strive to offer better and better products to continue to satisfy the consumer … and thus, the wheel of a healthy market economy keeps turning.

P. Kotler and W. Pfoertsch, *Ingredient Branding: Making the Invisible Visible*,
DOI 10.1007/978-3-642-04214-0_1, © Springer-Verlag Berlin Heidelberg 2010

Fig. 2. Logos of selected Ingredient Brands

Branding in general may have reached a saturation point, even leading to the emergence and popularity of "Unbrands", but the emergence of Ingredient Branding is lending a whole new dimension to the power of brands. Let's get started in learning all the ins and outs of Ingredient Branding.

1.1 What Is Ingredient Branding?

In today's market environment, characterized by intense competition, increasing globalization and established customer preferences, current marketing approaches implemented by component companies have some limitations. Rising customer sophistication makes it increasingly difficult to market to consumers, but it also opens up different ways of reaching the customer, giving producers more opportunities to sell their products. Ingredient Branding is one of these ways.

Many studies have demonstrated that educated customers appreciate products with branded ingredients[1] and are willing to pay a higher price for an Ingredient Branded product.[2] Intel, for example, owes its corporate success to their "Intel Inside" campaign.[3] In the early 80s however, when they created the Ingredient Branding concept, it seemed like a gamble. At the time they had a mere $500 million in sales, and yet they invested $110 million in their Ingredient Branding campaign over a period of three years and drove both their concept and the business forward.[4] Intel hired experienced professionals from other companies, such as NutraSweet®[5] and DuPont® (Teflon, Stainmaster Carpets, Lycra, etc.), who had previous management experience with the Ingredient Branding concepts at those companies. Many industry insiders predicted that they had gambled too much, but history shows that they knew what they were doing.

The Intel logo became so well-known that Intel now dominates the computer processor market. In 2006, Intel modified its Branding concept from Ingredient Branding to a concept driven to a master brand, letting the product brands become the pulled ingredient. Ingredient Branding, however, was and is not an easy way to get your product offering to the market. If your product is one that you market directly to the consumer, there are various channels you can use. If your product, on the other hand, is a component or ingredient in another company's product offering, the relationship with the customer lies with the other company, the OEM (Original Equipment Manufacturer)[6] and this company may not be interested in helping you contact their customers. This is a situation in which Ingredient Branding may be able to help increase a company's supplier power and/or create consumer demand, thereby increasing sales. In many cases, a company cannot Ingredient Brand due to lack of resources. There are various conditions required for an In-Branding concept. These include:

- The component or ingredient has to be highly differentiated and must create sustainable value for the customer, like Microban® with its anti-bacterial protection or Gore-Tex® and its water resistance outdoor clothing line.

- The component or ingredient is central to the functional performance of the final product, as in the Brembo brakes used in high performance cars or the Shimano gear system used in quality racing bikes.

- The downstream company also supports the Ingredient Branding efforts made by the component manufacturer because it has made significant investments in the brand specific to the OEM offerings.

- The final product itself seeks a high-branded value and can differentiate their product offering. Examples here are Perkins Diesel Engines for Chinese heavy construction equipment and 3M's Scotchlite or Scotchguard for textile manufacturers.

- The final products are complex, assembled from components supplied by multiple firms, who may sometimes sell the "ingredients" separately. You can find this sort of ingredient/component in the automotive aftermarket with Recaro car seats.

It is important to keep in mind, however, that these conditions are not set in stone; they are continuously changing. Big changes have occurred over the last years. Brands such as **Microban**, antibacterial protection; **Ingeo** from **NatureWorks**, environmentally-friendly plastics; **CoroWise**, naturally sourced cholesterol reducer from Cargill; DLP from Texas Instruments; **Cable and Wireless Systems**, network applications; and many more, have managed to put their brand perception in the minds of consumers.

There are many more examples of companies that are currently operating with the Ingredient Branding concept. In this book, we analyze their offerings and various market approaches and integrate these to give you a clear and concise approach to implement your own Ingredient Branding concept. A complete list of these companies can be found in the Appendix.

Ingredient Branding is a marketing concept that has been around for a long time, but has only recently started to take flight. In the first half of the 20th century, **Hoechst AG** and **BASF AG**, successful chemical corporations, had already begun to market well-known dyestuffs (**Indanthren**) and synthetics (**Hostalen**)[7] as independent brands to buyers in the next part of the value chain.[8] DuPont had similar success in the U.S. with **Teflon** in the 1960s. However, the sales potential of Ingredient Branding was revealed by the huge success of the "Intel Inside" campaign, launched by the microprocessor manufacturer at the beginning of the 80s.

Ingredient Branding provides advantages for both component manufacturers as well as OEMs, the manufacturers of finished goods. Numerous suppliers have tried to implement their own Ingredient Branding marketing concepts, modeled on the Intel case, in order to escape the anonymity and substitutability of supplying a part or component. Since the advent of Ingredient Branding, more and more companies have discovered the advantages it has to offer. They have also discovered what works and what doesn't work in terms of having a successful Ingredient Brand.

1.2 A New Brand Strategy?

Considering that brand value sometimes makes up a major portion of total company value, brand management is an essential part of future-oriented management. By implementing strong brand management, businesses are prepared to adapt to ever-changing competitive conditions. Brand management also contributes indirectly to the individual success and failure of these businesses. The fact that Intel managed to rise to one of the most successful companies worldwide after implementing its Ingredient Branding strategy inspired many. This success story highlights impressively the potentials and possibilities of InBranding for businesses.

The brand policy, as the central element in marketing, is especially important as the brand stands for the performance of a business and its products in customers' minds.[9] Figure 1 shows the Ingredient Brands Intel and Microsoft as two of the most valuable brands as published by Interbrand. It compares their brand value between 1999 and 2008.

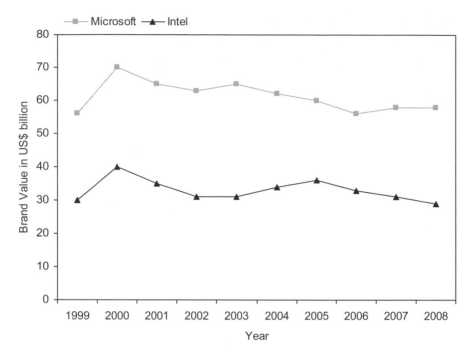

Fig. 3. Interbrand brand values over time of InBrands Intel and Microsoft

Both companies market products to the end user (B2C) and to the business client (B2B) by using Ingredient Branding to various degrees. In the first case study of this book we will describe and analyze Intel's way to the top. We will also shed some light on the Branding concepts of many companies.

The scale and speed of change in the global economy have combined to force industrial businesses to use more proactive marketing measures and to implement focused brand strategies. This enables them to be faster and more flexible in response to the changing competitive conditions, and to both supplier's and customer's constantly changing needs. Still, many companies are at a loss when it comes to the topic of Ingredient Branding, and fail to make use of it in marketing their products. Although the application of **brands for industrial products**[10] has, for decades, been the topic of discussion in various industries, with numerous examples of success, the concept of a strategic brand for industrial goods has still not received much attention. These concepts have only recently been recognized under the designation "Ingredient Branding", and been incorporated into a strategic brand strategy for industrial goods.[11]

This book is about Ingredient Branding, the basics, the success stories and the "how-to-do" of the Ingredient Branding concept for implementation in your company. The term **InBrand** or **InBranding** is used in this book in order to simplify the term, Ingredient Branding. Also, it is important not to make the mistake of mixing up In-Branding, with co-Branding or brand extension. We will explain in detail the difference in the various Branding strategies and activities, which are possible. **David A. Aaker**, Professor of Marketing, Emeritus, brought another possibility for Ingredient Brands to our attention. An end user oriented company can expand the reach of its current product offering to other (new) customer groups and applications by using an Ingredient Brand developed by them. For example, **General Motors** has used its **Northstar Racing Cars** experience[12] to sell to younger customer groups who are active in racing sports[13]. Sony markets Trinitron[14] for televisions and computer monitors.

Small and medium-sized businesses should not miss the chance to differentiate and market themselves internally as well as externally with a consistent and coherent brand. In this way, they not only offer customer orientation, but they also gain a competitive advantage. It is also easier for small and medium-sized companies to profit from Branding because their decision process is shorter and easier than that of large companies. Additionally, small and medium-sized companies are more aware of their unique strengths and weaknesses. With the current changes in the relationship and structure of supplier pyramid (e.g. Tier 1, Tier 2, etc.), the need for brand management will become far more apparent.

It is an outdated idea that Branding is simply the equivalent of an advertising campaign; to our knowledge, this is only one aspect of external communications. These days, it is not enough to set up a colorful advertising campaign in order to guarantee brand success. Over the course of a strategic brand strategy, customers must be provided with a multi-sensory brand experience.[15] Brand management is too challenging for many advertising agencies to achieve solely with their ad campaigns, which have become increasingly short-termed and one-dimensional. Successful brand management needs more: design/composition and management competence with all relevant marketing-tools; for instance, corporate design, trade fair concepts, multi-channel-management etc.

Many companies offer not only components but also final products. In the case of GE, they sell washing machines and dishwashers to end users as well as medical equipment to hospitals and jet turbines to airlines. This demonstrates how difficult it can be to determine the Branding strategy of a particular company. It may help to look at divisions of companies, but unfortunately, such data is hard to get.

The majority of suppliers seem to want to avoid the cost and trouble of an Ingredient Branding strategy. Classical marketing instruments, however, such as product improvements and pricing conditions, may not be enough as they are unable to significantly differentiate and fail to ensure company success. In the past, suppliers have concentrated their marketing efforts on their direct customers, who might also be the supplier for another company. The end user, the traditional concept of consumer, is at least two or three steps away from them. This results in undesirable anonymity in the following stages of the value chain, a situation in which suppliers are not known by end users.

Ingredient Branding can create consumer demand (pull effect). When a company can demonstrate the superior performance of an ingredient or component in the final product, the customer is more likely to request the ingredient or component in their potential purchase of the product. Consumers may even force the OEM to use the component as a result of its perceived quality.[16]

Not using an Ingredient Branding concept can result in substitutability of the ingredient or component and a situation in which the direct customer-supplier relationship is reduced. One important thing that Ingredient Branding can offer is increased strategic differentiation from the competition. **Recaro**, Germany, a successful supplier of car seats, is a perfect example. Through their "aftermarket" service, and the successful sponsorship of various car races, customers created a pull-effect that induced manufacturers of sport cars to start cooperating with Recaro.

Besides increasing differentiation potential, Ingredient Branding also helps to rebalance the power between supplier and OEM in the favor of the supplier. It decreases the limitations and dangers of a narrow and one-sided customer-supplier relationship. One example of how InBranding can push beyond these boundaries is **Microban**. They provide manufacturers of spas and whirlpools – like Kohler, Toto, and American Standard – an additional way for differentiation. Additionally, there is Rubbermaid Kitchen utensils, Dirt Devil vacuum cleaner and countertops from Cosentino, with the intention and means to advertise its brand Microban directly to end customers.

With product improvements and innovations, as well as the offering of additional services, and a more rapid and more reliable delivery policy, in addition to ever lower prices, businesses try to create preference in the eye of the consumer and to differentiate themselves from the customer – often in vain. The average profitability of most suppliers has not increased over the last decade. InBranding is a promising way out of this dead end street.

1.3   What Can You Expect from This Book?

After this introductory chapter, you can expect the following to be covered in this book:

Chapter 2 has been dedicated to the theoretical **basis of Ingredient Branding.** This chapter identifies the various influential factors and introduces the basic aspects of marketing in the business-to-business-to-consumer (B2B2C) markets. Furthermore, it explores the risks and opportunities that Ingredient Branding can provide to suppliers, as well as downstream markets. We elaborate on single-level and multi-level Branding and develop the stages of Ingredient Brand development. The book also explores here on the principles of Branding and the requirements for Ingredient Branding. It gives advice how to distinguish between co-Branding and Ingredient Branding. It introduces the Push-Pull principle and illustrates a framework for conceptual thinking. At the end, we describe conditions and requirements for Ingredient Brands in various industries.

In Chapter 3, we visit the most famous Ingredient Branding example – the Intel Inside Ingredient Branding success story. We analyze in detail the success story of "Intel Inside" as a classic example of successful Ingredient Branding. Although many articles and books have been published about this concept and the company, an in-depth analysis of the impact of its brand management has never been discussed to our knowledge. We give you information and insights on how the company explored and nurtured the concept of InBranding.

In Chapter 4, the implementation of the Ingredient Branding principles within a company is displayed; we highlight the significance of the Branding concept at the beginning and then direct the focus on Ingredient Branding and its strategic options and give hints for the implementation including the communication policy.

In Chapter 5, success stories in various industries will be presented. This Ingredient Branding in action with several real life examples from a wide variety of industries, including **automotive, fibers in the textile industries, glass,** and examples from the **food industries** are examined regarding their applicability for multi-level Branding. This analysis is especially important for medium-sized suppliers to get a better picture of their Branding activities, as well as to provide suppliers with workable strategies.

In Chapter 6, we go into details on various Ingredient Branding business cases:

Teflon: Basics of Ingredient Branding

Dolby: Leading an Industry with Innovation

Tetra Pak:	A Machine Builder becomes a Household Name
Bitrex:	Implementing the Network Approach
Shimano:	Implicit Ingredient Branding
Makrolon:	The High-Tech Material
DLP:	Pampering the Customer
Schott Ceran:	Differentiating with Success
Microban:	Convincing and Measuring

In Chapter 7, we synthesize all of the examples and cases together in a clear, concise "user's manual" for managers who want to use the Ingredient Branding concept. Moreover, we present the future perspectives of the Ingredient Branding concept, and in order to provide the reader with a distinct system for valuating Ingredient Branding as a marketing tool, an **instrument of performance measurement** is introduced here, too. We also elaborate on the future perspective on Ingredient Branding and its role in the marketing world.

Summary

- Branding is a significant management tool used to achieve differentiation and create sustainable competitive advantage.

- Though it has been around for many years, Ingredient Branding is picking up in popularity in recent years due to Intel's success, among others.

- Co-Branding and Ingredient Branding is not the same thing.

- Ingredient Branding has developed into a powerful concept, especially for component and ingredient manufacturers.

- InBranding is a multi- versus a single-level marketing method.

- Brand extension is another way to capitalize on the power of Ingredient Branding.

Notes

1   Desai, K.K., and Keller, K.L. „The effects of ingredient branding strategies on host brand extendibility" *Journal of Marketing* 66 (2002): 73–93.

2   Havenstein, M. *Ingredient branding: Die Wirkung der Markierung von Produktbestandteilen bei konsumtiven Gebrauchsgütern.* Wiesbaden, 2004.

3   Some may argue it was leadership innovativeness or the rough lessons of their management approach, but competitors with innovative leaders who learned similar management lessons, like IBM, TI and many more, were not successful because they did not use the Ingredient Branding concept.

4   Dover, J. „Adding value through the 'intel inside' brand." In *Customer value: Moving forward – back to basics,* edited by B. Donath, 1997, p. 29.

5   Now owned by J.W. Childs Associates, a leading private investment company.

6   OEM could be defined in two ways, we are suggesting using the most recent definition:

   A) Originally, an OEM (original equipment manufacturer) was a company that supplied equipment to other companies to resell or incorporate into another product using the reseller's brand name. refrigerators like Frigidaire might sell its refrigerators to a retailer like Sears to resell under a brand name owned by Sears. A number of companies, both equipment suppliers and equipment resellers, still use this meaning.

   B) More recently, OEM is used to refer to the company that acquires a product or component and reuses or incorporates it into a new product with its own brand name.

   Aeronautical Industry

   OEM refers to the aircraft manufacturers. Examples of globally present OEMs in this industry are Airbus of Europe, ATR of France/Italy, Boeing of the United States, Bombardier of Canada, Embraer of Brazil, and United Aircraft Corporation of Russia.

   Automobile Industry

   OEMs are the industry's brand name car manufacturers, such as General Motors, Ford, Toyota, Volkswagen, Honda, Chrysler, etc. The OEM definition in the automobile industry constitutes a federally licensed entity required to warrant and/or guarantee their products, unlike the „aftermarket" which is not legally bound to a government-dictated level of liability.

7 BASF also brought Luran to the market.

8 Kemper, A.K. „Ingredient branding." *Die Betriebswirtschaft* 57 (1997): 271–274.

9 Bruhn, M. *Die Marke: Symbolkraft des Zeichensystems.* Bern, 2001.

10 Anderson, J.C., and Narus J.A. *Business market management: Understanding, creating, and delivering value.* 2nd ed. New Jersey, 2004.

11 Ludwig, W.F. „Branding erobert auch die Investitionsgüterindustrie." *Markenartikel* (2000): 16–25.

12 The Cadillac Northstar LMP was a series of Le Mans Prototypes built by General Motors' Cadillac brand for use in the American Le Mans series as well as an attempt to return Cadillac to the 24 Hours of Le Mans since they first entered in 1950. The Northstar LMPs were named after the Northstar V8 engines which powered them.

13 Kotler, P., and Bliemel, F. *Marketing-Management: Analyse, Planung, Umsetzung und Steuerung.* Stuttgart, 1999.

14 The Trinitron was first used as a TV tube, a type of CRT (cathode ray tube) developed by Sony Corporation. It differs from the standard tube types because it employs an aperture grille (wires stretched vertically down the screen) instead of the usual shadow mask (a metal plate with holes in it). Many observers believe that Trinitron tubes generate brighter, clearer images than those using the shadow-mask technology.

15 Formulated this way by Wilfried Leven in his initial lecture: „The power of industrial branding (Maidenhead Microbrew): The scope of branding, in: Kotler, P.; Keller, K., (2006): Marketing Management 12e, Upper Sattle River, p. 275.

16 Muehr, D. „Branding für Automobilzulieferer." PLEX Studie No. 07, 2001, www.plexgroup.com/cox_www/images/publications/path6/PLEXstudie_01_07_automotive.pdf.

CHAPTER 2

Basics of Ingredient Branding

Ingredient Branding has only started to thrive[1] since the late 1980s as an accepted marketing concept.[2] In the global economy, companies need to not only establish, but also maintain, their competitive advantage, as well as create commercial success in their market and provide criteria for their customers to differentiate them from their competition.[3] Until the early 80s, most companies were focused on tangible resources due to material or production technology restraints. Now, however, we see a considerable shift towards a focus on intangible resources such as brand management[4] and customer loyalty. Many current publications consider one of the most valuable assets for any firm as the intangible asset represented by its brands.

Companies and organizations are beginning to embrace Branding efforts that create value for both the consumer and the company. With the establishment of brand management, companies attempt to attract and retain customers by creating and promoting value for money, image, corporate social responsibility and other values important for the understanding and use of the product. Including brand identity in their offering enables companies to differentiate themselves in a continuously overcrowded market. With the entry of new participants in the market, existing manufacturers must continually search for new and better means of exploiting their existing brands.

According to recent publications, the two strategies, which are most commonly used in order to maximize brand potential, are **brand extension** and **co-Branding**.[5] As mentioned previously, Ingredient

P. Kotler and W. Pfoertsch, *Ingredient Branding: Making the Invisible Visible*,
DOI 10.1007/978-3-642-04214-0_2, © Springer-Verlag Berlin Heidelberg 2010

Branding is a more recent strategy, which fits under the umbrella of co-Branding. Early research in this area has shown both positive[6] and negative effects for the brands, which employ an InBranding strategy, as well as an impact on consumer product evaluations.[7]

The newest research, in contrast, illustrates that Ingredient Branding offers a potential for successful brand management and increased profits for companies along with product offerings that create added value for the customer.[8] If a customer knows and understands the function, features and benefits of a component (ingredient), he or she will pay more attention to this offering, and, if it creates a unique product offering, this can lead to loyal and profitable customer relationships.[9]

This approach surpasses the limitations and dangers of a too narrow and single-sided customer-supplier relationship.[10] The traditional B2B (Business-to-Business) brand strategy of marketing activities is only geared towards the next link in the OEM value chain, but Ingredient Branding can help to overcome this. The Intel Corporation demonstrated the marketing possibilities of Ingredient Branding for both component manufacturers, as well as the manufacturers of finished goods.[11] Since then, numerous suppliers have tried to implement their own marketing concepts modeled on the Intel case in order to escape anonymity and substitutability of supplying a part or a component.

2.1   Theoretical Basis for Ingredient Branding

In both theory and practice, InBranding is often defined as the **marking** or labeling of components or other industrial goods.[12] A more detailed view of the particular goods considered possible targets for InBranding is given in the following systematic classification approach for industrial goods. According to this approach, industrial goods can be distinguished according to the criterion "institutional whereabouts" in capital goods and consumer goods.

In general, **industrial goods** can be InBrands, depending on functionality and the importance to the end user. Hence, materials and parts, which enter the end product, unchanged or are fabricated, further are possible targets for InBranding.[13] Materials and parts, for instance, can be raw materials, e.g. wool (example **Woolmark**) or manufactured materials and parts, (bicycle gears **Shimano**, sweetener **NutraSweet** or microfiber **Gore-Tex**).[14] **Consumer goods**, on the other hand, serve as end products for the immediate satisfaction of human needs and are not considered as possible targets of InBranding. Examples of these goods are food, clothes, television, and private cars.

In addition to the Branding of materials and parts, it is also possible to brand the manufacturing company as an "institution". In this case the Branding approach is part of **corporate Branding**. InBranding and corporate Branding are not mutually exclusive so there is the possibility of an **overlap of both approaches**. An example is McNeil Nutritionals NutraSweet Inc. By labeling their products with the logos "NutraSweet", they market the contained materials and their company, at the same time.

Most businesses, however, develop independent brands for their products, making it rare to find a correlation of ingredient and corporate Branding. InBranding in the automobile industry is an exception to the rule and is covered in more depth in chapter 5 of this book.

Ingredient Branding is strategic brand management for materials, components, parts, services, etc.[15] In recent years the Branding efforts have increased and cover not only components, but also manufactured parts and services, Ingredient Branding applications lead to more sophisticated applications and they have gained more complexity (see Fig. 4).

For simplicity's sake, we will use the term "components" or "ingredient" synonymously. By labeling **single component parts** or **component systems**, a company can draw the attention of end users and customers to their InBrands within the manufacturer brands. The majority of suppliers and other preliminary product manufacturers form an essential part of the finished goods, yet become invisible to the following market stages.[16]

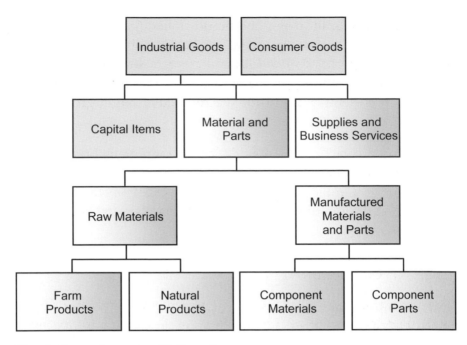

Fig. 4. General targets of InBranding

By the implementation of a multi-stage (multi-level) brand policy, component manufacturers strive for a significant **competitive advantage**. As suppliers, they want to escape the interchangeability of their products and develop, strengthen, and extend their market position.[17] InBranding also opens up opportunities to the manufacturers of finished goods – they can further enhance their products by using branded components. This form of Ingredient Branding is called "Inverse Ingredient Branding" in marketing literature. As mentioned previously, the Intel Corporation was one of the pioneers in the area of Ingredient Branding. Intel has defined InBranding briefly and concisely as the "...Promotion of a brand within a brand to the end user. "[18] Another possible definition of InBranding is focused on the increased brand value of the supplier component: "Pars pro toto". A part represents the whole: in some cases, an unknown (invisible) component of a product becomes more well-known (visible) than the product itself. Thereby **the part becomes the trigger for the buying decision** in favor of the final product.[19] A more comprehensive definition is found in the following:

> **Ingredient Branding** is the brand policy (goals, strategies, instruments) concerning a branded object (necessary condition) of materials, components, or parts (raw materials, component materials, or component parts) that represents a brand for the respective target group (sufficient condition).[20]

Some authors consider components as an Ingredient Brand when they cannot be sold separately, but we experience in practice that most of the InBrands did not followed this rule; instead most of them sold their products separately, particularly in the aftermarket for automobiles.

Stages of Development

After analyzing many of the existing Ingredient Brands, we developed an understanding of the likelihood of success for components or ingredients. As we mentioned earlier, the customers' perceived value of the benefits of the particular ingredient is the most important factor. Yet the customer must also be able to hear, see and/or feel these benefits. Therefore, the seller or producer has a chance to make their Ingredient Brand visible.

For new and innovative products, the chances for market success in the early phase of the product lifecycle are the most obvious. Consider, however, that the component could be part of a new application. Ingredient Branding can also start in a **later stage of the product life cycle**. Actually, the Ingredient Branding concept can be implemented over the whole lifecycle of a particular product. One example is the **Makrolon** brand, from **Bayer Material Science**. They only began Branding their product, polycarbonate branded as Makrolon, to the final user after fifty years of existence, and it worked very well. We discuss this case in more detail in chapter 6.

By examining the classic InBranding examples **Intel, Dolby, Lycra, Gore-Tex, CoroWise, Solae, Splenda**® and **NutraSweet** we can see that they began early in the product lifecycle. Various factors are important to create an InBrand, position in the product lifecycle is just one. Ingredient Brands can come and go; therefore it is crucial to **understand the strategic implications** of the possible development of an InBrand. With this purpose in mind, it is important to consider four stages over time (see Table 1). These stages indicate the movements that unknown InBrands have to run through on their way to **establishing brand equity**.

In the **first stage**, a component manufacturer enters into a **co-operative agreement** with the end product manufacturer as part of its Ingredient Branding strategy. Part of this cooperation is the agreement that the supplier's components are labeled on the end product. The supplier hopes to profit by the joint presentation of his new InBrand and the already established brand of the finished product. As trade-off, the manufacturer of the end product receives certain incentives like **price reductions** or **advertising expenditure subventions** from the supplier. This process step is referred to as building up credit and exploitation of well-known brands, respectively. As a result, the InBrand profits from piggybacking the reputation of the end product and becomes known by itself after some time.

In **stage two**, the **breakthrough** occurs. An Ingredient Brand can finally step out of the shade of its host product. In this phase, continual promotion to the end user and a careful cooperation with partners are necessary.

In the **third stage**, the **InBrand pays back** the "loan" to the host product manufacturer; the host is profiting now from the increased brand value. In this phase both brands are regarded as equally important.

In the **last stage**, the **brand value of the Ingredient Brand** has finally excelled the **brand value of the end product manufacturer**. As a result, the InBrand does not depend on brand awareness of the end product anymore. As a result of its own brand equity, it can choose the direct buyers in the B2B business, and is even in the position to dictate the market prices for products in their respective industrial area.

The main point in this 4-Stage-Model of Ingredient Branding (see Table 1) is that the **brand value of the InBrand will eventually exceed the brand value of the host product manufacturer brand** and, therefore, needs to be monitored critically. It is assumed that a long-term, equal partnership of both brands is rarely feasible. Hence, the danger in the statement of this theory is that a lot of end product manufacturers avoid cooperation with InBrands from the beginning, simply to avoid being on the losing end of such a partnership.

Table 1. Four stages of Ingredient Branding

	Stages	Description
1.	Building up credit, Exploitation of well-known brands	Unknown InBrand profits from piggybacking already established brands
2.	Breakthrough and market proven	Unknown InBrand becomes known or even famous
3.	Payback, Synergy	Known InBrand supports former partners and other users of their brand.
4.	Fiesco-Effect	Known InBrand is omnipresent and could not be used as a differentiator and is pushing former supporters into price wars.

Not every brand relationship has to end with a **Fiesco-Effect**[21]. Intel, for example, is present in more than 80% of all computers, and in 2006, they changed to a corporate master Branding concept and kept the Ingredient Branding on the product level (e.g. **Intel Centrino Inside**). Like Intel, Microsoft has achieved a similar position. However, it is important to keep in mind that many other factors, in addition to the brand, were important to achieve this.

Most companies with less powerful market positions have to take precautions. One rather illustrative example is **Gore-Tex**. After trying various Branding concepts with their partners, they developed a distinct set of criterion for partnership and joint Branding. Today, they limit partners to certain applications (cycling, sailing, etc.) and certain industries or regions. With these restrictions and regional limitations, they avoid weakening the partners' possibilities for differentiation.

When defining Ingredient Branding, it is common practice in marketing literature to include similar themes like **co-branding** and **inverse Ingredient Branding.** They are helpful to better explain and define the marketing partnership that emerges in the process of cooperation between the supplier and end product manufacturer.

Correlation to Co-Branding

The concept of Branding, including both InBranding and co-Branding, is built on the foundation of Information Integration and Attitude Accessibility theories[22]. The informational integration theory describes the process in which two stimuli, or in this case, brands, are combined to form consumers' attitudes toward a product. These attitudes are used in interpreting and evaluating specific brands and manifest themselves through consumers' purchase behaviors. The theory of attitude accessibility suggests that the more salient the brand attitude, the more likely that attitude will be used in the creation of a consumer's evoked set. The positive attributes of a brand in a co-Branding strategy can result in the consumer electing to include a particular product in his or her evoked set and ultimately lead to the purchase of that product.

Over the past 15 years, a considerable amount of research has shown that Branding can help consumers to recall important product advantages. For example, the associations between a brand name and a particular product benefit can help a person to understand the product's positioning; and the association between a brand name and a product category can help a person to **recognize potential usage situations**.[23] This conceptualization of a brand name as a recall prompt has been used to hypothesize how people create evoked sets, evaluate alternatives, and make decisions about the appropriateness of **brand extensions**.[24]

Co-Branding is defined as the combination of two brands to create a single, unique product. This association between the brands can be either long or short-term and can be represented by physically combining two or more brands or symbolically associating the brand names. The first strategy consists of associating the host brand with a secondary brand in order to give it **symbolic additional attributes**. The second strategy incorporates key attributes of one brand into another brand as ingredients.[25] The purpose of co-Branding is to capitalize on the equity of the brands and enhance the success of the product. Prior experience with these brands provides consumers with a certain level of quality assurance.

The following example of the computer and memory chip manufacturer Infineon Technologies shows, on the one hand, that the exact definition and differentiation of certain terms is not a priority for businesses in their day-to-day work, on the other hand, that the conceptual differentiation of Ingredient Branding from other forms of partner marketing is still very difficult. Under the auspices of "co-Branding" **Infineon** requests its business partner ... "to put the Infineon Technologies trademark into a product and/or its package and user manuals to signal that this product contains the semiconductor solutions of Infineon Technologies."[26]

This might give the (mistaken) impression that co-Branding and In-Branding are the same. This confusion has been nurtured by the fact that, in marketing literature, the same defining approach is used, in part, for both ingredient and co-Branding.[27] In one definition of co-Branding, for instance, it is enough if an already company-owned branded product or service is marked by an additional brand name.[28] Also, Brandchannel's online brand encyclopedia defines **co-branding** as "The use of two or more brand names in support of a new product, service or venture."[29] Nevertheless, these broad definitions are far too general, since they can also be used for paraphrasing the process of InBranding.

From our perspective, categorizing is important to determine the possible actions of the various players involved. In every co- or In-Branding activity, there are at least two companies involved, and, therefore, their Branding strategies determine the outcome of the approach. If there are two compounds with the same types of products involved, and both of them want to promote their product together, we recommend defining it as co-Branding strategy.

A good example of this is **Bentley Motors** luxury cars and **Breitling** watches. In one promotion campaign, they advertise both products together although they have two different products. The common denominator is the same image and similar messages, and together, they help each other **strengthen their respective brands,** while simultaneously remaining distinct from each other. It can be a bit complicated when the products are actually put together, like a club or bankcard with a credit or debit card function. The membership or the club works together with **Visa**® or **MasterCard**® and offers two products as one. If the product cannot be sold separately and/or is a component/ingredient of another product, such as a stereo system in a car, the Ingredient Branding strategy should be applied. We'd like to refer the reader to the example of Intel and Microsoft with Hewlett Packard (HP) computer to illustrate this point.

Some large manufacturers own product brands which they use to enhance their final product offerings, like **Trinitron** from **Sony**, **Quattro** from **Audi**, **Northstar** from **Cadillac** and many more. Here we talk about Ingredient Branding through **self-brands**.

It is especially interesting that according to this classical definition of co-Branding and Ingredient Branding, both strategies overlap at one point. Certain brand alliances of finished products and components can be assigned to both strategies at the same time. This correlation of both definitions is one of the most important reasons why both terms are used as synonyms in many discussions about brand strategies. We keep them separate, but consider InBrand as a form of co-Branding where the ingredient provider is approaching the final customer and help the other brand to become successful, too. It is a long-term relationship and can be terminated easily. Fig. 5 shows the possible dimensions of single/multiple product/brand combinations.

	Single Brand	Multiple Brand
Multiple Products	**Separate Brands**	**CoBrand**
Single Products	**Single Brands**	**InBrand**

Fig. 5. Dimensions of single/multiple product/brand combinations

Inverse Ingredient Branding

Another form of partner marketing, or InBranding, which is frequently mentioned in marketing literature, is inverse InBranding. It simply means that the impulse and incentive for a co-operation comes from the end product manufacturer. By enhancing the finished product with one or more well-known and established supplier/component brands, their actual market position is improved and strengthened.[30] This implies strong competition in the respective industrial sectors in which the performance and quality of the produced goods rarely differ from each other. In that case, the additional Branding of component brands offers end product manufacturers the attractive possibility to differentiate themselves from the competition. In contrast to Ingredient Branding, **the major driving force of Inverse Ingredient Branding is the manufacturer of the finished products**.

There are several good examples in the car industry to illustrate inverse InBranding. Some of the most well-known component systems in this industry are: the antilock brake system (ABS) and the electronic stability program (ESP), offered worldwide by **Bosch**, **Continental**, **TRW Automotive**, and **Delphi**. Their component systems provide a vehicle with features that represent a decisive factor in the buying decision of a customer.

For the purposes of inverse InBranding, **car manufacturers (OEM)** try to enhance the demand of their products by choosing product quality and brand strength of certain supplier and communicating this by labeling the component systems in their vehicles, thereby achieving a competitive advantage.[31] However, it is important to take into account when considering this example that the market leading OEMs of a particular market predominantly use component systems of the same brand or the same manufacturer, making product differentiation in terms of inverse InBranding almost impossible. In Europe, for instance, car manufacturers predominantly use the components systems of **Bosch** and **Continental** in their cars; while, in North America, companies such as **TRW Automotive** and **Delphi** dominate in this respect.

Push- and Pull-Principle: Basis of InBranding

The basic underlying market principles of Ingredient Branding are the **push and the pull**.[32] The pull principle takes effect when the manufacturers of the Ingredient Brand direct their communication efforts directly at the end consumers, bypassing the manufacturers of the finished product. The main idea is to create consumer demand for the ingredient at the retail level, so that they pull the product through the distribution channel, forcing middle stages to use this ingredient.[33]

A **push strategy** means that an ingredient manufacturer concentrates his marketing efforts on promoting his products to the next step in the value chain (e.g. manufacturers of the finished goods).[34] This approach is especially important if a supplier hasn't yet established a strong market position and the demand for his products is still low. By applying the pull strategy, on the other hand, component manufacturers leap one or several market stages in order to direct their communication and marketing efforts to the final customers.[35]

Ingredient Branding harnesses both principles within the scope of its multi-level marketing strategy. By applying the push principle on the one hand, the next level in the supply chain is convinced to buy those products; simultaneously implementing the pull principle on the other hand, directly to the end users, will result in a **demand pressure** making their components irreplaceable to the manufacturers of the end product. In order to support the branded ingredient most effectively, a manufacturer should always use a coordinated push and pull program as shown in Fig. 6.

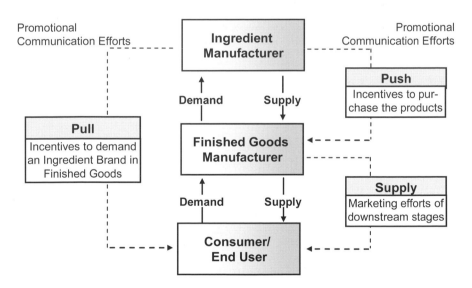

Fig. 6. Push- and pull-principle of Ingredient Branding

The potential of applying a **push- and pull strategy** depends heavily on the resources and products of the respective supplier. Many suppliers do not have the financial capabilities at their disposal to market a product brand at multiple levels across the value chain directly to end customers. The nature, composition, and exchangeability of the components can also prevent the successful application of a push- and pull strategy in the first place.

2.2   Principles of InBranding

Ingredient Branding is a special form of brand alliance, based on cooperative design and delivery of a product, with particular emphasis on the possibility to identify the components in the final product.[36] Ingredient Branding occurs when a component part or service is promoted to the final user. The promotion can be seen from two perspectives: the manufacturer or the supplier.

It is an advanced Branding concept that, if successfully implemented, can be beneficial to both partner brands. However, the motivation behind Ingredient Branding has traditionally been from the host brand's perspective. The host brand wishes to differentiate itself from the competition through the inclusion of the Ingredient Brand into the final product. The perspective of the host brand, using ingredients as brand extensions has been researched and documented as a proven concept.[37]

In manufacturing-initiated Ingredient Branding, the manufacturer usually chooses an ingredient with an existing brand that already has strong brand awareness. The manufacturer promotes the fact that this ingredient is part of the end product in the hopes of persuading end users that their product has certain positive attributes, which are associated with the Ingredient Brand: "The value of Branding has also been recognized by suppliers who produce ingredients or components that are incorporated into final products."[38]

Supplier-initiated Ingredient Branding occurs when a supplier of a component part or service initiates the promotion of its ingredient, which is part of the end product, to the final user in an effort to create brand awareness. The supplier hopes that their investment in brand awareness will result in the consumer's request or "pulling" the Ingredient Brand from the manufacturer. This supplier-initiated Branding is what the authors of this book refer to as "InBranding."

The concept of InBranding has received minimal attention in literature on the topic of Branding. The distinguishing factor between InBranding and traditional Ingredient Branding is the motivation behind the strategies. The motivation behind traditional Ingredient Branding revolves around the host brand and usually extends or modifies an attribute of the host brand in an effort to enhance consumer brand evaluations.[39] The motivation behind InBranding revolves around the Ingredient Brand or component brand forming an alliance with a **product manufacturer** in an effort to create brand awareness for the Ingredient Brand and generate pull effects through the value chain. It is the distinction between consumer and manufacturer behavior that separates them. Consumer behavior creates pull and manufacturer behavior creates push. Consider push and pull effects as parts of marketing mix decisions. Supporting pull and push increases the probability of coordination. The combination of the **push and pull creates synergy** for the complete marketing mix. The supplier offers a component or service to his customer, the OEM. Thus, the supplier has a **B2B relationship** with the producers of such products as automobiles and electronic products. The OEM produces a product that is to be used by their customer, the final user. The final user buys the product or service in a pure **B2C relationship** with the OEM.

According to this principle, there are two **separate stages of customer relationship**: supplier with OEM, OEM with final user. With InBranding, the two stages are interconnected: Step (2) follows step (1), and step (3) occurs, where the supplier informs the final user that a particular ingredient is part of the product offering, which makes the final user choose this product over competitive offerings.

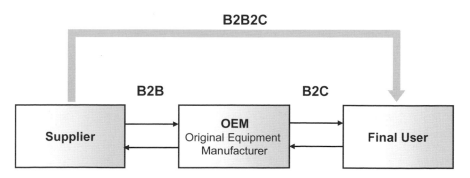

Fig. 7. InBranding framework

In this step (4), the final customer "pulls" the product because the particular ingredient component is desired. This is a continuous process of push and pull, with a high success rate if done appropriately. The following InBranding model illustrates these processes (see Fig. 7).

Even companies with strong consumer brands can use InBranding to enhance or protect their competitive position, as Chevron does with TEXTRON, and GM with Northstar, to power up its Cadillac brand for the performance-oriented customer segments[40] with racing components in their luxury cars. In Fig. 8 we show four possible stages for Ingredient Branding in a real-life example. **LION Apparel** provides functional apparel for firefighters, with branded fibers and laminates that provide superior protection. DuPont and 3M deliver base materials for suppliers and together with branded suppliers like **Gore-Tex**. In this and many other cases, we have to consider more stages: components, modules, systems, integrations with

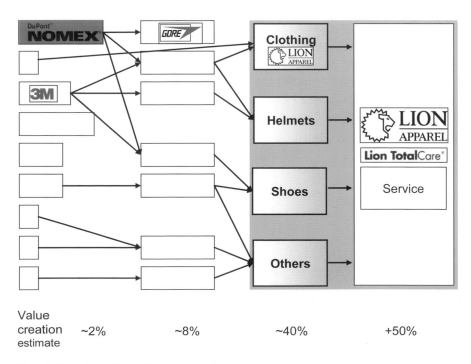

Fig. 8. Textile InBranding example

software and services, etc. This means that all up-stream markets have to be considered, including the end customers who are being included in the marketing of the component. As opposed to multi-stage Branding, single-stage Branding only promotes the brand to the player at the next stage in the value chain.[41]

Another important aspect to mention is the position of the ingredient in the value chain. Due to various factors, InBranding can occur in an early or later stage of the value chain, depending on the importance of the particular functionality to the end user, or the situation in the industry.

This can be illustrated with the example of an end user who needs a high-performance outdoor jacket that is very light but also water-resistant but breathable. Sports enthusiasts with this kind of requirement are often cyclists or sailing fans. The preferred vendor for sailing clothing is **MURPHEY** and **NYE**, sponsors of the America Cup team[42].

W. L. Gore & Associates (Gore) supplies to a module or system supplier. They manufacture inlays or part of the jackets, as well as supplying directly to the jacket manufacture or supplying the final product to the retailer where it is possible for the end user to purchase it. **Gore** illustrates the possibility of a 5-layer approach to In-Branding throughout the value chain. This is shown in Fig. 9. Therefore, Gore needs to inform all the players in the value chain about the high performance of their product offering.

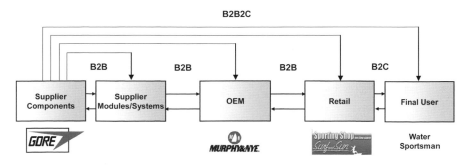

Fig. 9. Multiple layers of InBranding

Single-Level and Multi-level Branding

Ingredient Branding is a form of multi-level Branding of industrial manufacturers of parts and/or components. This means that all downstream markets including the end customer are being comprised in the marketing of the component. Contrary to multi-level Branding, single-level Branding is only addressed to the next following stage in the value chain. To avoid confusion, it is necessary to mention that the terms of **multi-level Branding** and multi-level marketing as well as **single-level Branding** and single-level marketing are used synonymously in marketing literature.

On closer examination, the following differences can be detected between these terms: while the concept of Branding is only focused on

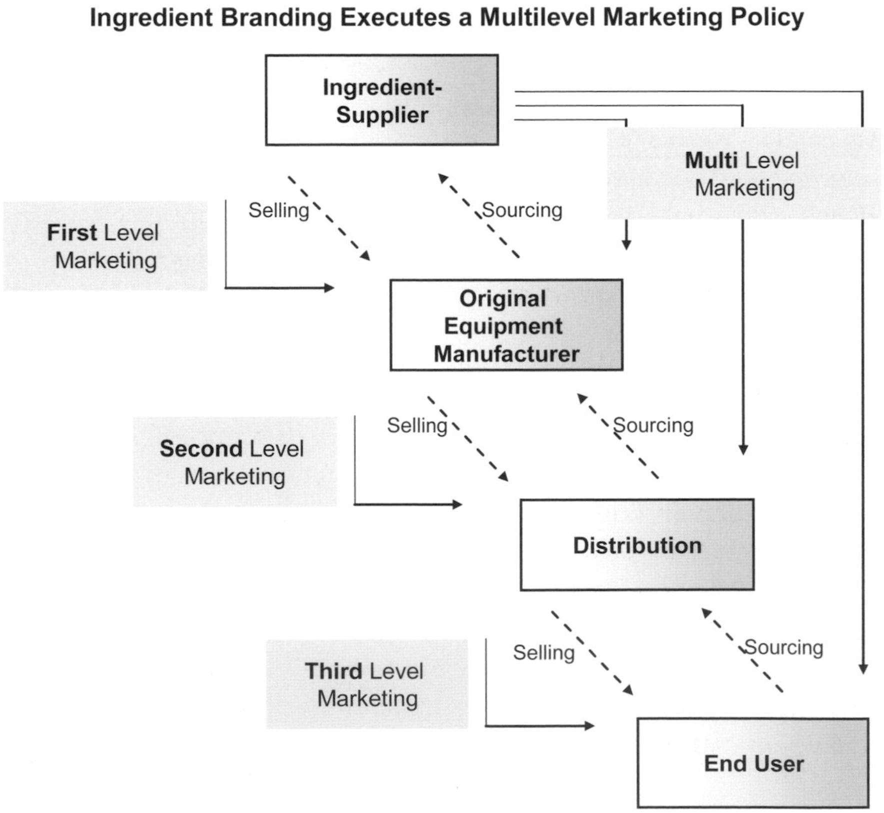

Ingredient Branding Executes a Multilevel Marketing Policy

Fig. 10. Single-level and multi-level branding

the brand itself and brand value of the product, the marketing concept embraces all possible marketing instruments. Depending on the brand strategy, companies can follow different objectives for increasing their sales numbers. The multi-level brand strategy uses the pull-strategy to create consumer demand, so that the product is pulled through the distribution channel, forcing middle level to use this ingredient. Single-level Branding, on the other hand, employs the push-strategy with the intent to create a demand pull through the request of the customer and distributor, which will then necessitate the final product manufacturer to put the ingredient or component inside. Single-level and multi-level Branding are shown in Fig. 10.

2.3 Requirements for InBranding

Today's economy is affected, above all, by a strong **division of labor** in the production of products and services. Thus, it is common practice that the majority of goods have to go through numerous market stages, starting from the first production stage until the final consumption/use, and as they progress along this chain, they continuously increase in value.[43] Primarily, component manufacturer/supplying companies, demanders of preliminary products and the private end users are involved in this process of added value.

Component manufacturers are private businesses whose products and services are designated for industrial markets only. This means that their goods have to pass another market or processing stage before reaching – as final product – the private end user. Therefore, businesses demanding those preliminary products are not private consumers but **organizational customers**. These are categorized again into private businesses, state facilities, and public institutions. State facilities are military and police; while churches, hospitals, schools, and colleges/universities are assigned to the public institutions. Their own performance depends on the goods and services of component manufacturers.[44]

Private companies, on the other hand, can generally be classified into three groups: users, OEMs, and middlemen. Users, for instance, are businesses that demand machines to use in the production of their own goods and services. OEMs, on the other hand, incorporate the purchased materials, parts or components into their final products. In the automotive industry, for example, many parts of a car – sometimes even the whole assembly – are out-sourced by the car manufacturers. Therefore, the essential difference between them is the fact that OEMs enhance the value of the demanded goods before passing them on to the users at the end of the value chain. It is interesting to note, however, that manufacturers of preliminary products must also purchase the necessary resources for their production on the same market. Thus a component manufacturer can be – in contrast to a finished product manufacturer – supplier and customer at the same time.

A well-known OEM market is the computer industry. The **Intel Corporation** produces microprocessors, which are the centerpiece of every computer. Nevertheless, the actual computer manufacturer appears on the market as the sole manufacturer of the computer, although different suppliers produced numerous components of the PC. The automobile industry represents another well-known OEM market. Here, as well as with car manufacturers and the production of their vehicles, OEMs depend on components and other preliminary products from their suppliers.

Nevertheless, the **built-in components** are not usually mentioned in the marketing and sale of the vehicles, because car manufacturers only want to associate their own brand with the car. In addition to the OEM market, there is also a spare part market (**aftermarket**) for components. OEMs or their respective suppliers usually serve this market directly.[45]

The last group, industrial middlemen, is essentially composed of distributors, retailers, and wholesalers who distribute industrial goods *unmodified* from the manufacturers to users, to OEM's, and to other middlemen. They form the last part of the value chain. Although, they create **added value for customers** in this process, they are not valid targets for an Ingredient Branding strategy.

As already mentioned, companies only purchase on B2B markets in order to process these goods and services in their production and distribution of goods and services. The goods marketed in the business-to-business arena have to pass through at least one subsequent stage of processing, transformation, or retailing, before they reach in modified or revised form private customers.[46]

Therefore, in relation to the marketing of their products and services, component manufacturers face an **entirely different business environment** than manufacturers of finished products, whose marketing efforts are directed mainly at private consumers.

The marketing activities of component manufacturers are usually directed exclusively at the next market stage, which is composed of other private businesses, state facilities, and public institutions. This kind of component manufacturer single-level marketing is usually called industrial marketing or business-to-business marketing.[47] The kinds of customers in industrial marketing are shown in Fig. 11.

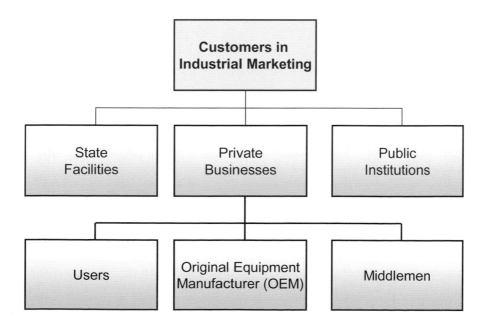

Fig. 11. Customers in industrial marketing

InBranding starts with this kind of single-level B2B marketing and expands it to a multi-stage marketing strategy. Therefore, the implementation **of an Ingredient Branding strategy** requires an **extensive reorganization** of the present marketing strategy for component manufacturers.

In an Ingredient Branding strategy, marketing efforts are no longer solely directed at the companies in the next market stage, but also at subsequent stages of the value chain, leading up to the end customers. In this way, the previously mentioned pull-effect is achieved: the demand for products containing the respective components increases.

Supply Industry

The supplier business in the B2B market differs from other commercial business relations (business type) in that there is a much stronger emphasis on the **continuity of the business relationship** between supplier and customer, as well as on the increased individuality of the performance for customers. Fig. 12 shows a systematic of business types.

The care and protection of business relationships, aimed at positively influencing the **repurchase behavior** of customers, takes the center stage of marketing in the supplier industry.[48] Customers are usually manufacturers of finished products that process the supplied goods and services into their own products. Thus the supplier industry is mainly characterized by organizations of suppliers who group together, into buyer associations, to buy or sell with economies of scale.

This encourages the development of long-term business relations between suppliers and organizational customers characterized by **customized performances**. Quite often, suppliers and customers jointly develop new product technologies that are specially produced by the supplier. The customized performances of suppliers in the automobile industry are a good example. This also means, however, that suppliers and customers are tied together for the duration of the product life cycle.

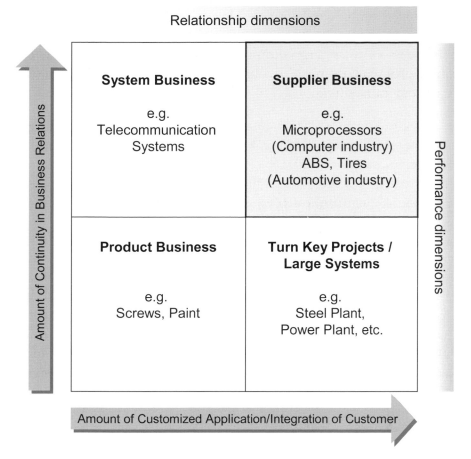

Fig. 12. Systematic of business types

Usually, OEMs exert strong market power over businesses in the supply industry. Due to intense competition in this arena, it is usually the OEMs that can enforce their own conditions over those of the component manufacturers. To break the OEM market power is one of the major opportunities offered by implementing an Ingredient Branding strategy for suppliers.

Procurement Process/Industrial Buying Process

The industrial buying process is of significant importance in the supply industry; it can therefore also influence the Ingredient

Branding strategy of a supplier. Before establishing an Ingredient Branding strategy, it is essential for component manufacturers to analyze its customers' procurement process. It is especially important to check whether the reputation and image of the final product brand can be positively used to support a supplier's own marketing activities in the context of InBranding.

Before an **end product manufacturer** (OEM) can become an ideal business partner for a potential InBrand, there are several obstacles that have to be overcome in the industrial buying process by the component manufacturer. Extensive decision making processes form the basis of procurement in the supply industry. The majority of these decisions are rational decisions based on much more criteria (e.g. price, features/functionality, service) than in the consumer goods area.[49]

In contrast to consumer markets where products or services are demanded directly by end consumers, the industrial buying process is characterized by multiplicity. Any industrial buying decision is a complex process. Due to the complexity, an organizational purchase usually involves inputs from many different departments in the organization. People from different disciplines, at various levels in an organization, contribute their expertise to assure the selection of the best solution for the organization.[50] Because so many different individuals use such a wide-range of aspects in the decision-making process, the duration can be extended significantly.

Buying Center

As mentioned above, the buying process of business customers differs in many ways from the buying patterns of private consumers. The main reason for this difference can be found in the multiplicity of the procurement process, which is characterized by a **collective decision**.[51] Depending on the respective buying situation, there are several participants involved in the purchasing decision, forming the so-called **buying center**.[52] Its size and composition varies greatly depending on the complexity of the respective need that has to be satisfied.[53]

A buying center is usually composed of several participants who decide on which materials, components, or parts to buy. Such a buying center can include up to 20 representatives from different levels and departments (e.g. finance, production, users, purchasing, engineering, external consultants, management etc.) within an organization.[54] The buying center is the relevant target group for any marketing efforts of the supplier.

In practice, though, due to cost and time reasons, it may be extremely difficult for a component manufacturer to direct focused marketing efforts at all of the different representatives of such a buying center. Therefore, most marketing activities and efforts are directed at merely one or two people. Usually, deciders, buyers, and users are the most important targets within a buying center.[55]

The **decider** tends to be someone in an executive position who makes the final decision for a product or a supplier. **Buyers** are formally authorized to pre-select suppliers and arrange the purchase terms before the actual purchase and to negotiate the final contract after the decision has been made.[56] The **user** is the person inside the company that will directly use the purchased products. The influence of the user on the buying decision depends on their sector of activity as well as the corporate culture. The more qualified the user, the more weight is given to his/her opinion. The experiences of these three targets are usually decisive in the success or failure of the purchased products.[57]

Successful implementation of Ingredient Branding not only depends on the right execution of the InBranding strategy, but also on the current conditions of the industry or company. In order to determine the strategy, it is necessary to first analyze certain market conditions to help predict the outcome. Therefore, it is very important to have a clear picture of the current situation in your particular industry.

This does not mean that conditions could change, as we have seen illustrated by the examples given. For many years, the automotive industry was very reluctant allow any component brands to get near their customers minds. However, today you find **Bose sound systems**, **Brembo** brakes or **Recaro** seats in many automobiles.

The electronic industry is very different from the car industry. Many components help to enhance the product performance for the end user. The power situation has changed even in this industry. Corporate suppliers are driving the innovation and pricing conditions. Other industries have their distinct conditions for InBranding. Clothing and consumer electronic industries have been particularly successful in this respect, as well as chemical and food industries.

If you begin to analyze the role of established brands in the industries mentioned, you can determine the dominant position of the product performance for the customer. Domination is seen in certain industries by the applications and ingredient suppliers, or by the product functionality, such as the laminates in the cloth industry or the microprocessors in the computer industry. You can find a similar situation in the soft drink industry where sweetness determines the product favorability. NutraSweet was very dominant for many years until a generic alternative became available.

There are also industries in which components and their suppliers do not play a key role. This could easily change however as component suppliers begin to understand ways in which they can bring their brands into the minds of customers. There are more options out there, even when you "own the market" like the **Almond Board of California** who owns 75% of the world's total production of almonds. The almonds are grown in Northern California in the San Joaquin and Sacramento valley, where, not so long ago, the Almond Board started a campaign: **'Almonds are in'**. They did not understand the potential for customer loyalty as the customers started asking for **"California Almonds"**, and therefore did not develop an Ingredient Branding strategy.

Competition Intensity

The competitive intensity is another influential factor. Considering these situations in the earliest of our Ingredient Branding concept, it could help to not waste efforts and investments if, in a particular industry, competition is fierce and price-cutting dominates over innovation and quality improvement. In such a situation, an Ingredient Branding strategy would be a risky undertaking. To cut through multiple layers of the value chain and fight off lower prices can be a difficult endeavor. If component suppliers operate in a market environment, however, with less competition triggered by a limited number of suppliers and a large number of OEMs, then the situation may be more suitable for implementing an Ingredient Branding strategy. The competitive conditions for InBranding are shown in Fig. 13.

The main condition for application of successful InBranding is the possibility to differentiate the component for the final product. When the end user also recognizes this, and its perceived value is high, then the chances are high.

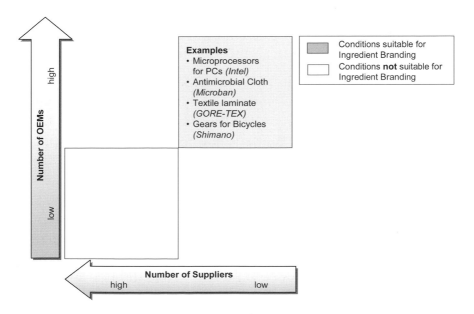

Fig. 13. Competitive conditions for InBranding

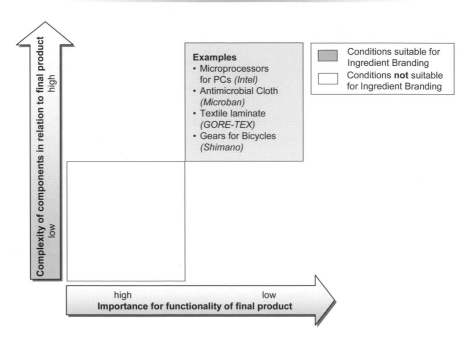

Fig. 14. Suitability array for InBranding

Another pre-condition is component complexity in relation to the final product. If this is high and the importance of the functionality to the final product is high, Ingredient Branding has a strong starting position. The suitability array for InBranding is shown in Fig. 14.

By analyzing the majority of Ingredient Brand strategy formulation, it can be seen that at the origination of the concept only a few competitors were present. First mover advantages were capitalized mostly on low markets and applications. Increased customer sophistication and knowledge of the product features is the ultimate facilitator of InBranding efforts. Understanding this is preeminent for any further action.

In established markets and existing product categories, other aspects are also important. Researchers have found that efforts on the part of the component supplier for the OEM are an important stimulator to the success of InBranding. In contrast with low brand value of the final product, this could lead to high customer appreciation. Using an example from industrial end users, like construction companies or building contractors, Chinese construction equipment, powered by **Perkins Engines**, or **Bosch Rexroth Hydraulics** equipment, could boost the success of the OEM.

Similar situations can be found where a secondary market exists, like in the automotive industry with their "aftermarkets". Customers replace components when they are worn out or for better performance with product supplies that have superior quality or better features. An example of this is the **Recaro** seats in cars (see Fig. 15).

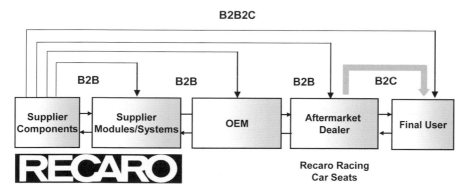

Fig. 15. From aftermarket selling to InBranding

As mentioned previously, the situation in an industry and its competitive environment are influential factors on the amount of influence a particular company has at a certain point in time. They have to understand the environment and the given product constellation. With a deep understanding, and with the help of product and Branding innovation, the situation can be changed.

InBranding is not beyond reproach. It can create complicated partnerships in which the balance of power could change over time, resulting in tension-filled relationships between partners. For example, in the automotive industry there are only a few companies that have managed to keep their brands mentally and visibly present for end customers, or their brand visible in the automobile.

In Europe, examples of this include, **VDO** with fittings, **Bosch** with electronic parts, **Blaupunkt** and **Becker** with car radios and **Recaro** with car seats. Quite often, these suppliers provide many other components that are part of a finished automobile, yet they are not able to make them visible to the end customers. In addition, there are numerous other suppliers in the automobile industry who are not able to accomplish what the aforementioned examples have achieved due to their lack of positioning power in the industry.

As system and module suppliers rise to the challenge and grasp technological advancements and promote leadership through innovation, they are increasing their position of power in their industry. This is being increasingly perceived by car drivers due to extensive investments in marketing communications. Car drivers are beginning to demand specific Ingredient Brands at the retail level. As a result, the influence of systems and modules to the image of the end product car is growing steadily with the OEM bearing the financial burden of this. Suppliers are challenged in terms of brand strategy and end customer contact.

InBranding offers a way to inform consumers about the additional benefits they are receiving from superior component brands and prime offerings. In one of our preliminary analysis in 2004, we found that end customers are indeed supporting this notion: Every third car buyer makes his decision based on the origin of parts and components.[58] The right component brand names translate into guarantees of safety, comfort and ideal cost/performance ration.

It took five years for Intel to first achieve results from its InBranding strategy and ten years to reach market supremacy. Intel showed the world that InBranding could make a difference. They understood their position as a component supplier for electronic components in the computer industry and used the opportunities in the market to become known by the public. By creating market awareness at the end user, Intel increased their market power versus OEMs and **established an outstanding market position.** They created chances for competitive differentiation and established entry barriers for competitors. Over the years, this strategy increased customer loyalty and created the necessary demand-pull, resulting in establishing themselves as irreplaceable. For their partner, Intel created a positive image of the OEM brands and achieved the price-/volume premium, particularly for the tech-savvy segments, in the early product life cycle stage. One can see here the pull-creation having had its full effect. As a result of their efforts, Intel has achieved the creation of brand equity comparable to the level of consumer goods.[59]

2.4   Benefits and Risks

Despite the risks, the 'Intel Inside' campaign proves that InBranding can be an excellent strategy to help suppliers:[60]

- Capitalize on the positive image of end products

- Increase awareness among end users

- Establish entry barriers in their sector

- Increase customer loyalty

- Establish a price premium for their product and

- Increase their brand equity.

Establishing brand value is the result of a time-consuming learning process. Competitors may need years in order to catch-up and create their own brand image.

It is also important to consider the asymmetry of this process: a brand image can be destroyed rather quickly. A good example for this is the "Elk test". When the **Mercedes-Benz** small model A-class car rolled over during a test at market introduction, it needed a long time to become re-established. Similarly, when Olestra with the brand name **Olean** came under fire for potentially causing gastro-intestinal problems, Pringles, a product-brand that used **Olean** (fat replacement), also suffered. Additional risks associated with In-Branding include:[61]

- Vulnerability of the Ingredient Brand to negative publicity involving the host brand

- Possibility of loss of host brands' customer base to the Ingredient Brand partner

- Lack of sustainable competitive advantage of host brand if there is no exclusive agreement between partners

- Host brand may copy the Ingredient Brand and ultimately become a competitor

The initial perceived quality of and attitude toward the partner brands might have implications on the outcome of an Ingredient Branding strategy, as well as on the selection of Ingredient Brands by host brand managers.

Despite these factors, there are still many opportunities for ingredient suppliers. Recent years have shown that particularly in the food industry, where soy based products and sugar replacement (Xylit, Splenda, etc.) products have made their way to the market. There are also the well-being and care product categories which have ingredients playing a bigger role in the mind of the customers: **Nanotex**, **Ingeo**, **CoroWise**, **Z-trim**, **Amicor**, etc.) Many of these companies are small or medium-sized and they are looking for ways to differentiate. Ingredient Branding is their chance. They will have the opportunity to:

- Become known to the public

- Create chances for competitive differentiation

- Establish entry barriers for competitors

- Increase customer loyalty

- Establish pressure on demand

- Establish protection from interchangeability

- Create a positive image for the OEM brand

- Achieve a price/volume premiums

- Pull-creation

- Increase their market power versus the OEMs

These are all very good reasons, but there are also major risks involved for the suppliers of ingredients, when they start putting their names on the final product. The biggest risks for the suppliers are:

- Increased dependency on quality problems of the OEM

- High cost and management time

- Increased need for quality assurance

- Become visible targets for competitive attacks

- Can be affected by the negative image of the OEM

- Heavy resistance from industrial customers

So the stakes are high for the supplier to initiate Ingredient Branding, but after cutting through the multi-layer value chain, the benefits are high as well.

The possible pull-effect can change a whole industry, as we have seen with microcomputers. Even in the automotive industry, specialty suppliers like **Brembo** (brakes) or **ZF** (gear boxes) are investing heavily to get recognized. **Texas Instruments** invested in its **DLP** In-Brand in the NASCAR series and hoped to create the pull. This may not have been the most recommended course of action as current developments have shown. However, these component suppliers cannot do it alone. They need the cooperation of the OEM or other participants in the value chain. This could be, for example, VAR (Value Added Reseller), which uses components and delivers specific systems or product modules to the market. Another example is **Kohler Industrial Division**, which sells auxiliary power units to their large customers. **Kohler** purchases all diesel engine products from **Cummins Engines**; they can also get this power supply unit with a **Deutz** engine. The OEM or VAR creates a variety of benefits, such as:

- Enforce a positive image

- Differentiate from other competitors

- Lower marketing costs

- Increased product value

However, all this has a price. There are increased risks and conflict potentials. In many cases, it is a question of judgment and understanding of future prospects.

When Dr. Dieter Zetsche from the former **DaimlerChrysler AG** was in charge of **Chrysler**, he avoided any dilution of the Chrysler brand. After his departure and after the split off from the merger, **Chrysler's** high-performance models like 200 CSR T8 were factory fitted with Brembo braking systems. Land Rover and many other car manufacturers followed this example and made Brembo one of the most respected brake manufacturers in the world. Now its other rivals, such as Bosch, are forced to improve their end user reputation as well.

An interesting example of this is **Torsen Inc**. For a company with a huge Ingredient Brand potential, it missed the mark largely due to their changing ownership. Toyota trucks are only putting the Torsen brand sticker on their off-road vehicles. **Torsen** supplies to most of the other off-road cars, like **Audi**, with the name **Quattro** or **Syncro** at **VW (today 4Motion)**. They even supply to the **GM Hummer, Mazda, Ford, Lexus BMW** and many others, but with no brand recognition.

Summary

- **Establishing brands in a B2B environment is different** from Branding to the general public. The role and the mechanism of an industrial brand strategy have to be more focused than those pursued and implemented in consumer markets.

- Using Ingredient Brands as a **brand extension** concept for host brands is only one way of using the power of Ingredient Brands.

- Ingredient Branding concepts from the supplier side (InBrands) provide a new way to make the component brand relevant for the final user.

- The final user will accept InBrands when their functional features provide them with additional benefits for the usage and enjoyment of the final product.

- In recent years Branding efforts have increased and created large amounts of InBrands in different industries (see Chapter 5 & Appendix).

- The Intel Inside campaign created visibility for the Ingredient Branding concept, but for many companies it was difficult to copy this success.

- Brand cooperation can be accomplished in many ways of co-Branding; Ingredient Branding is just one form of them.

- Consumer brand companies can also create their own **self-Ingredient Brands** to communicate their advanced component offerings in the final stage (**reverse Ingredient Branding**).

- The understanding of the **push- and pull** principle is important to create the foundation for an InBrand.

- The InBranding framework can provide a conceptual basis for developing and implementation but it **requires the understanding of a multi-level Branding concept** for consumer products.

- **Consumer brands** (e.g. Northstar and Cadillac, Quattro and Audi) can also use InBrands to enhance their brand recognition with a combination of the **push- and pull principle.**

Understanding both the B2B and the B2C market environment is necessary to conceptualize an **Ingredient Branding strategy,** and the use of secondary markets (e.g. aftermarket for automobiles) is one way to get consumers attention for the component supplier.

Notes

[1] Kotler and Keller (2008); Kotler, P.; Kotler, P., and Pfoertsch, W. *B2B brand management: Building successful business brands.* Heidelberg, New York, 2006.

[2] Norris, D.G. „Ingredient branding: A strategy option with multiple beneficiaries." *Journal of Consumer Marketing* 9 (1992): 19–31.

3 Bartlett, C.A., Ghoshal, S., and Birkinshaw, J.M. *Transnational management: Text, cases, and readings in cross-border management.* 4th ed. Boston, 2004; Trinquecoste, J.F. „Pour une clarification théorique du lien marketing-stratégie." *Recherche et Applications en Marketing* 14 (1999): 59–80.

4 Kapferer, J.N. *Reinventing the brand. Can top brands survive the new market realities?* London, 2001.

5 Rooney, J.A. „Branding: A trend for today and tomorrow." *Journal of Product and Brand Management* 4 (1995): 48–55.

6 Norris, D.G. „Ingredient branding: A strategy option with multiple beneficiaries." *Journal of Consumer Marketing* 9 (1992): 19–31.

7 Hillyer, C., and Tikoo, S. „Effect of co-branding on consumer product evaluations." *Advances in Consumer Research* 22 (1995).

8 Havenstein, (2004); McCarthy, M.S., and Norris, D.G. „Improving competitive position using branded ingredients." *Journal of Product & Brand Management* 8 (1999): 267–285.

9 Desai and Keller (2002).

10 Kleinaltenkamp, M. „Ingredient branding: Markenpolitik im Business-to-Business-Geschäft." In *Erfolgsfaktor Marke,* edited by R. Köhler, W. Majer, and H. Wiezorek. Munich, 2001.

11 Dover, J. „Adding value through the „intel inside" brand." In *Customer value: Moving forward – back to basics,* edited by B. Donath, 1997.

12 Pfoertsch, W., and Schmid, M. *B2B-Markenmanagement: Konzepte – Methoden – Fallbeispiele.* Munich, 2005.

13 Kotler, P., and Keller, K.L. *Marketing Management.* 13th ed. New York, 2008.

14 Kleinaltenkamp (2001).

15 Kotler, Keller (2008).

16 Haller, T. „Ingredient branding" *Textil Zeitung,* August 16, 2001, pp. 21ff.

17 George, R. *When the parts become greater than the whole: Fueling growth through ingredient branding,* 2002.

18 Simon, H., and Sebastian, K. -H. „Ingredient Branding: Reift ein neuer Markentypus?" *Absatzwirtschaft* 45 (1995): 42–48.

[19] Bugdahl, Volker (1996): Ingredient Branding – eine Markenstrategie für mehrere Nutznießer, in: Markenartikel, Vol. 3/1996, p. 111.

[20] Baumgarth, Carsten (1998): Ingredient Branding – Begriff, State of the Art & empirical data, Working Paper, Department of Marketing University of Siegen, Siegen, p. 10.

[21] Bugdahl, V. „Ingredient branding: eine Markenstrategie für mehrere Nutznießer." *Markenartikel* 58 (1996): 110–113.

[22] Simonin, B.L., and Ruth, J.A. „Is a company known by the company it keeps?: Spill-over effects of brand alliances on consumer brand attitudes." *Journal of Marketing Research* 35 (1998): 30–42.

[23] Janiszewski, C., and Osselaer, S.M.J. van. „A connectionist model of brand-quality associations." *Journal of Marketing Research* 37 (2000): 5–20.

[24] Keller, K.L. „Conceptualizing, measuring, and managing customer-based brand equity." *Journal of Marketing* 57 (1993): 1–23.

[25] Desai and Keller (2002).

[26] Co-branding Agreement, Infineon Technologies Munich, 2002.

[27] Kleinaltenkamp (2001): p. 267.

[28] Bruhn, M. *Marketing, bases for study and practice.* Wiesbaden, 2004.

[29] www.brandchannel.com/education_glossary.asp#C.

[30] Ludwig, W.F. „Branding erobert auch die Investitionsgüterindustrie." *Markenartikel* (2000): 16–25.

[31] Ludwig, W.F. „Ingredient branding: Markenpolitik im Business-to-Business-Geschäft." In *Erfolgsfaktor Marke,* edited by R. Koehler, W. Majer, and H. Wiezorek. Munich, 2001, p. 275.

[32] Baumgarth, C. „Ingredient branding: Markenkonzept und Kommunikationsumsetzung." Working paper, 1999.

[33] Kleinaltenkamp (2001): p. 263; Pepels, W. *Handbuch moderne Marketingpraxis.* Düsseldorf, 1993, p. 100.

[34] Kleinaltenkamp (2001): p. 263f.

[35] Luger, A.E., and Pflaum, D. *Marketing: Strategie und Realisierung.* Munich, 1996, p. 187.

36 Pfoertsch, W, and Mueller, J. Die Marke in der Marke – Bedeutung und Macht es Ingredient Braning, Springer Verlag Heidelberg, 2006.

37 Worm, S., and Durme, J. van. „An empirical study of the consequences of co-branding on perceptions of the ingredient brand." Proceedings EMAC 2006 Conference.

38 Norris, D.G. „Ingredient branding: A strategy option with multiple beneficiaries." *Journal of Consumer Marketing* 9 (1992): 19–31.

39 Desai and Keller (2002); Hillyer, C., and Tikoo, S. „Effect of co-branding on consumer product evaluations." *Advances in Consumer Research* 22 (1995).

40 Aaker, D.A. „The power of the branded differentiator." *MIT Sloan Management Review* 45 (2003): 83–87.

41 Baumgarth (2001).

42 If you want more information or purchase clothing from these vendors, you can order online http://www.murphyandnye.com/.

43 Kleinaltenkamp (2001): p. 261.

44 Homburg, C., and Krohmer, H. *Marketingmanagement.* Wiesbaden, 2003, p. 882.

45 Backhaus, K., and Voeth, M. *Industriegütermarketing.* 8th ed. Munich, 2007, p. 669.

46 Kleinaltenkamp (2001): p. 261.

47 Homburg, C., and Krohmer, H. *Marketingmanagement.* Wiesbaden, 2003, p. 882.

48 Backhaus (2007): p. 674.

49 Koppelmann, U. *Produktmarketing: Entscheidungsgrundlage für Produktmanager.* Stuttgart, 1989, p. 41.

50 Vitale, Robert P.; Giglierano, Joseph J. (2002): Business to Business Marketing. Analysis and Practice in a Dynamic Environment, p. 61.

51 Meffert, Heribert (2000): Marketing. Grundlagen marktorientierter Unternehmensführung. 9th edition. Wiesbaden: p. 139.

52 Webster, Frederick E.; Wind, Yoram (1972): Organizational Buying Behavior, pp. 33–37.

[53] Malaval, Philippe (2001): Strategy and Management of Industrial Brands. Business to Business Products and Services, p. 23.

[54] Vitale, R.P., and Giglierano, J.J. *Business to business marketing: Analysis and practice in a dynamic environment,* 2002, p. 62.

[55] Luger, A.E., and Pflaum, D. *Marketing: Strategie und Realisierung.* Munich, 1996,p. 251f.

[56] Pepels, W. *Handbuch moderne Marketingpraxis.* Düsseldorf, 1993.

[57] Meffert, H. *Marketing: Grundlagen marktorientierter Unternehmensführung.* 9th ed. Wiesbaden, 2000.

[58] Pfoertsch, W. Ingredient Branding für Automobilzulieferer, Marketing Management Bulgaria (2004).

[59] In 2006, Intel achieved USD 30,9 billion brand value in 2007 according to Interbrand Top Global Brands, Newsweek, 31 July 2007.

[60] Rao, A.R., Qu, L., and Ruekert, R.W. „Signaling unobservable product quality through a brand ally." *Journal of Marketing Research* 36 (1999): 258–268.

[61] Leuthesser, L., Kohli, C., and Suri, R. „2+2=5?: A framework for using co-branding to leverage a brand." *Journal of Brand Management* 11 (2003).

CHAPTER 3

Intel Inside – The Ingredient Branding Success Story

In 2008, more than sixty years after the invention of transistors, the fundamental component used to build computer chips, Intel is the leading provider of the 'brains' for the personal computers (PC). Intel, the B2B component provider, revolutionized the electronic industry and the marketing concepts of components. In January 2006, thirty-seven years after the introduction of the Intel Inside logo, Intel changed its approach again—Intel wanted to become a final product company and aimed to reach 100 billion USD in 2020 (with 40 billion USD revenues in 2007).

This strategy shift and re-Branding was developed by the new Chief Executive Officer (CEO) Paul S. Otellini and was then formally announced on January 3, 2006. Andrew S. Grow, founder of Intel, approved this radical shift of the company focus and the change to a master Branding approach. Moving away from the concentration on microprocessors that power personal computers, Intel extended its focus to final products, including consumer electronics, wireless communications, telecommunications, automations, and healthcare. Rather than just concentrating on computer chips, Intel creates all kinds of chips, as well as software, and then meld them together into what Eric Kin called "platforms". The idea is to power innovations from the living room to the emergency room.[1]

They would provide not only the silicon for the telecom switchboards, but also supply: single board computers, platforms, both

P. Kotler and W. Pfoertsch, *Ingredient Branding: Making the Invisible Visible*,   55
DOI 10.1007/978-3-642-04214-0_3, © Springer-Verlag Berlin Heidelberg 2010

classic and switches, including all the accessories. Intel would provide all the necessary products and tools that a telecommunication
company needs in order to make the job easier. They did not plan to
take their current customers' business away, but add so much value
that one day, they could.

For this kind of product offering, Intel also needed another Branding strategy. The famous Intel logo, with "dropped-e" had to go
and the Intel Inside concept had to change. Until then, not too many
people had noticed that the sticker on their new PC or laptop does
not show the Intel Inside anymore. Currently it shows their new
logo and names the product with Inside™. Intel had been driving to
this fundamental shift in its approach to the market for a while. It
began with the development of the Intel Centrino® mobile technology platform. The company reorganized itself around the platform
model in 2005, and is now focused on four key market segment opportunities: mobile, digital home, enterprise, and health.[2]

The original Intel Inside program was launched in 1991. The program was the first time a PC component manufacturer successfully
communicated directly to computer buyers. The Intel Inside Program is still one of the world's largest co-operative marketing programs, supported by thousands of PC makers who are licensed to

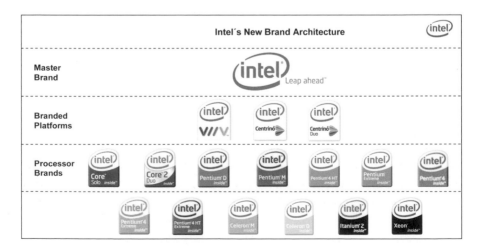

Fig. 16. Intel's new brand architecture

use the Intel Inside logo. The Intel brand is one of the top ten known-brands in the world, in a class with Coke®, Disney® and McDonalds®, according to various rankings.³ The new brand architecture has three layers (see Fig.16) today.

In addition, Intel is the world leader in silicon innovation. After three engineers founded it in 1968, the company began to develop technology for silicon-based memory chips and soon revolutionized the electronics industry. An opportunity to make history came in 1981 when IBM selected the Intel 8088 chip for the IBM PC, placing Intel at the top of the list as a chipmaker for microcomputers.⁴ Since the dawn of the personal computer in the late 1970s, computer vendors and software publishers have mainly driven marketing. During that time, the rapid technical advances of Intel processors played a central role in transforming the PC from a basic production and business management tool in the 1980s, into rich, new, information, entertainment, and education tool, along with being a well-used business tool.

The processor drove the rapid increase in performance, which, in turn, helped systems run more smoothly, quickly and reliably. But Intel relied on its PC vendor customers to convey this message, but these PC vendors were OEMs. Thus, Intel had little brand identification among users who knew no more about the processor or the company that built it than they did about the company that built the engine in their cars. In fact, computer users were generally unaware of which advanced processors were available or of the continually improving cost performance that was being delivered by "Moore's Law".⁵ Intel believed people needed to know more about the processor and the company behind it.

Intel marketing manager, Dennis Carter, formed a small group and, for the first time, launched a program aimed at marketing a microprocessor, the 386SK, to the Information Technology (IT) managers who purchased PCs for business. Early in 1989, Carter convinced CEO Grove to let him undertake a marketing experiment. According to Carter, Grove told him, "Here's $5 million. Spend a tenth of that, and if you prove your thesis, you can spend the rest."⁶

Carter and a team of three others, including Ann Lewnes, who were in the corporate communications group, began by conducting some market research. The research confirmed Carter's suspicions: most computer buyers believed that the 286 was capable of doing everything they needed it to do; they therefore felt no need to upgrade to the 386 processor. In addition, the research revealed that many computer buyers were concerned that the software they used with their 286s would not be compatible with the 386 chip.

In order to try and change these perceptions, Carter's team decided to try a low-cost experiment using billboard advertising in a single market. They began by covering billboards in Denver with a large 286 enclosed in a circle. They then splashed a big, graffiti-style, red "X" over the numbers. After a few weeks, they added a large 386 enclosed in a circle. The 386 sat alongside the crossed-out 286, and the billboards promoted the fact that the 386 was now the same price as the 286 but with many more advantages. A PR campaign accompanied the promotion. Although many commuters undoubtedly scratched their heads over what Intel dubbed the "Red X" campaign, CIOs (Chief Information Officer) and IT managers apparently got the message; sales of the 386 processor began to pick up in Denver almost immediately. Subsequent market research revealed that customers had indeed changed their buying plans as a result of the limited six-week campaign. The logos of the 286 X campaign and the Intel "dropped-e" are shown in Fig. 17.

Based on the success of the experiment, Carter, who eventually became Intel's head of marketing, took what was left of the $5 million

Fig. 17. Intel 286 X campaign and the Intel "dropped-e" logo

and extended the campaign to ten cities. At the time, there was significant skepticism among Intel managers about the idea of Intel marketing directly to consumers. Some were concerned about the mixed message associated with "Red-X'ing" Intel's most popular product; others were wary of the "graffiti" look of the Red X. But as Carter recalled, "Luckily, our Red X campaign was successful – not only in Denver, but in the other cities as well. By the time our test was completed, we'd created a bit of excitement in the company because it had worked."

IT decision makers learned about the new 386SX and converted to it rapidly. Several challenges quickly emerged, however, like legal issues. In the late 1980s, Intel assumed its 386 and 486 processors were protected trademarks and that no other company could use them. When the courts ruled that they were not trademarks, it opened the door for rivals to use them at will. The time was ripe for a new marketing program.

In order to correctly communicate the benefits of new processors to PC buyers, it became important that Intel transfer any brand equity from the ambiguous and unprotected processor numbers to the company itself, while raising awareness of its name. Intel invested heavily in developing cutting edge technology and in assuring performance and reliability. A stronger brand was needed to communicate this to consumers, separating Intel from the pack. Clearly, marketing directly to the end user was a novel idea for a semiconductor company. Although the company was widely recognized among computer manufacturers, the brand had little name recognition amongst end users, despite the fact that Intel microprocessors were the "brains" inside their PCs. The media raised questions as to whether a pure technology company could play in the same league with Procter and Gamble, General Motors and McDonalds. Even to many within the company, the program seemed like a stretch.

A second issue was that the processor, although a key component of personal computers, was only a component. To effectively market this component to the PC buyer, it was important to work with the computer manufacturers. After all, the processor was buried deep inside the computer and, despite its significance; it was hard to tell which processor the PC contained before it was purchased. Carter and his team studied successful consumer marketing techniques and examined tactics used by well-known companies supplying a component or ingredient of a finished product, like NutraSweet™, Teflon™ and Dolby™. They also embarked on a variety of marketing experiments and soon started to envision ways in which a branded ingredient program would play out in the computer industry.

The key to this strategy was gaining consumer's confidence in Intel as a brand and demonstrating the value of buying a microprocessor from the industry's leader and the pioneer of the microprocessor. Upon the suggestion of its advertising agency, Dahlin Smith and White, Intel adopted a new tag line for their advertising: "Intel. The computer inside." Using this to position the important role of the processor and, at the same time, associating Intel with "safety", "leading technology" and "reliability", the company's following, as well as consumers' confidence, would hopefully soar. That would create a new "pull" for Intel-based PCs. The final tagline was "Intel Inside".

The important role of the microprocessor was communicated, but to be truly effective, the ingredient status needed to be dealt with as well. In 1991, Carter launched the Intel Inside co-op marketing program. The heart of the program was an incentive-based cooperative advertising program. Intel would create a co-op fund where it would take a percentage of the purchase price of processors and put it in a pool for advertising funds. Available to all computer manufacturers, it offered to share, cooperatively, the advertising costs for PC print ads that included the Intel logo. The benefits were clear. Adding the Intel logo not only made the OEM's advertising dollar stretch farther, but it also conveyed an assurance that their systems were powered by the latest technology. The program launched in July 1991. By the end of that year, 300 PC OEMs had signed on to support the program. It was a resounding success.

After the OEM program was underway, Intel started a global print advertising campaign to explain the logo to consumers. In early

1992, Intel debuted its first TV advertising stressing speed, power and affordability made by George Lucas' Industrial Light Magic. It used state-of-the-art special effects to take viewers on a sweeping trip through the innards of the personal computer before hovering over the campaign's raison d'être – the then new Intel i486™ processor. The corporate advertising account at Intel was estimated at $14.8 million in 1991 billings for DSW.[7] Intel had begun working with DSW in 1990. Previously, Intel had worked with Chiat Day Mojo of San Francisco for nine years, followed by nine months of searching for a replacement ad firm. At the time of the switch, the Intel account was valued at approximately $10 million.

In March 1996, Intel announced it was consolidating the company's $100 million worldwide advertising business under one agency, Paris-based Euro RSCG,[8] which had recently acquired a majority interest in DSW.[9] Euro RSCG was to provide global account management and consumer advertising counsel. Tokyo-based Dentsu would continue as Intel's Japanese agency with an account estimated at $30 million,[10] and Euro RSCG would take over the account in Europe and Latin America. Euro RSCG subsidiary Ball Partnership Ltd. in Hong Kong would continue as Intel's Asia Pacific agency. Ann Lewnes, Intel director of worldwide advertising, explained:

> "DSW has been a strong force in our Branding efforts and we are pleased to be able to maintain that creative energy. Publicis has also been an excellent agency for us in Europe. But the globalization of our business requires that we seek international reach and we now have the opportunity to develop a unified international strategy."[11]

Television was especially effective in communicating the Intel Inside program messages to the consumer. Along with colorful TV advertisements, Intel added a distinctive and memorable three-second animated jingle (known as a signature ID audio visual logo), displaying the logo and playing a five-tone melody. Starting in 1995, the now-familiar tone helped cement a positive Intel image in the minds of millions of consumers.

The marketing investments were beginning to pay-off in terms of consumer mind-share, aided by the high-profile launches of the Pentium® Pro (1994) microprocessors. The advertising results were stunning. Dennis Carter commented:

> "I believe that there has been a lot more (industry wide) advertising because of the Intel Inside program than there would have been otherwise. That has helped to create more PC demand. If you believe that advertising works, then more people are getting educated about the benefits of the PC because of the Intel Inside program."

Intel allocated heavy resources to brand building. In early 1993, the company launched a sports line and a back-to-school clothing line, featuring geometric patterns that resembled microprocessor chip layouts with the slogan "Intel Outside." It was believed that during the second quarter of 1994, Intel was spending over $15 million on advertising for the Pentium microprocessor. The "Intel Inside" campaign was thought to have cost in excess of $300 million after only three years. For Pentium alone, Intel had budgeted $150 million in merchandising support, triple the level allocated to any previous product. It was thought that approximately half of the ad budget was paid for the TV commercials in Europe and the U.S.[12]

By the late 1990s, the program was widely regarded as a success. Intel's innovative marketing helped broaden awareness of the PC, fuelling consumer demand while prices continued to plunge. This paved the way for the PC to become more commonplace in the home, emerging as a business, entertainment and education tool. Intel became a lightening rod for this electronics revolution. When Intel's "Bunny People"™ characters danced their way across the TV screen during a break of the 1997 Super Bowl, according to Advertising Age, "They became nothing less than the whimsical icons of a go-go PC industry". After six years, and almost two decades in the PC business, Intel had attained a place in public consciousness as a world-class player. Its brand was known worldwide, and its name was synonymous with the computer industry.

While the Intel Inside Program continues to evolve, it will remain true to its heritage of promoting: "technology leadership", "quality" and "reliability". These features were as important to online users and high-end server buyers today as they were to the desktop computer buyer in the 1990s. As a result of the Intel Inside campaign, awareness of the company's chip increased from approximately 22% of home PC buyers in 1992, to more than 80% two years later.[13]

In 1994, Branding rights were being defined along the supply chain instead of between direct competitors. Compaq, the largest PC manufacturer and a major Intel customer, objected to the cost of Intel chips, claiming it should receive a discount because it was such a large customer, and declined to affix the "Intel Inside" logo to its machines. To keep prices competitively low, Compaq began to use less expensive chips made by Intel rivals. The rift between Compaq and Intel went public as Compaq CEO Eckhard Pfeiffer complained Intel was deliberately trying to undermine Compaq with its ad campaign, asserting the Ingredient Brand took precedence over the product brand.[14]

However, by 2002, the Intel Inside initiative had become one of the world's largest cooperative marketing programs with over 1,000 PC makers using the logo (a total of 2,700 computer makers licensed).[15] Intel and other companies had spent over $4 billion on advertising since the slogan was launched in 1991, and the Intel brand had been ranked many times as one of the top 10 best-known brands in the world.[16]

This successful approach has reached the final step in the ingredient development (see Figure 4 in Chapter 2). Intel has entered the Fiesco-Effect with full force. After HP acquired Compaq, there was no bigger Windows-based PC manufacturer in the market using the Intel brand.

At the start of the InBranding development, Intel competed with IBM, Hitachi, Motorola and Siemens, and, with the help of the OEM, became known (step 1). With the Intel Inside campaign, they achieved recognition. The breakthrough was made possible as a result of the

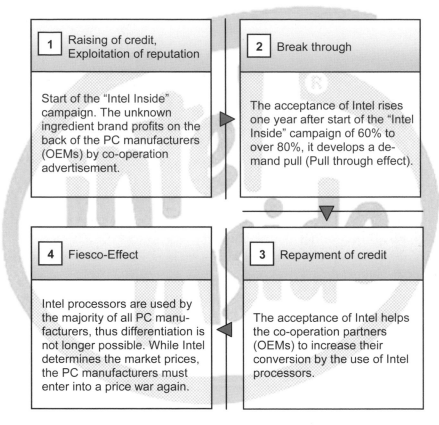

Fig. 18. Stages of the Ingredient Brand development

outstanding results of the "Intel Inside" cooperative marketing approach. Over the next several years, Intel "repaid" the credit they had received (stage 3) from their OEM as shown in Fig. 18.

On June 6, 2005, Steve Jobs officially announced at the Apple Developer Conference in San Francisco that Apple would switch from IBM PowerPC to an Intel processor. They first transitioned the low-end machines and, by mid-2007, all Macs were powered by Intel. This was the final blow to the competition and the differentiation possibilities: the Fiesco-Effect had taken place and the Intel Branding strategy had to change. Fig. 19 visualizes this by showing the Intel processor unit market share by segment. The management team came up with an answer.

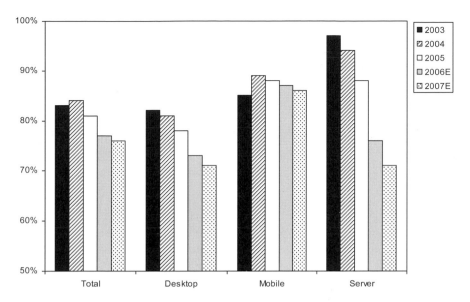

Fig. 19. Intel processor unit market share by segment

Intel shifted its marketing paradigm. It was inspired by a new CEO Paul S. Otellini and the CMO (Chief Marketing Officer) he recruited from Samsung Group, Eric B. Kim.[17] Intel jumped ahead into the world of becoming a master brand with its new slogan "Leap ahead". Like other great technology brands such as Sony, Nokia, Samsung and Motorola, Intel has come to realize that technology is of little use on its own. If you own a marketplace all that counts is what users get out of it. Applications are shifting and every year, hundreds of millions of people discover the digital world for the first time: these technology products have to be communicated in a much simpler and clearer way about what technology can do for the customer.

The "Intel Inside" Branding succeeded in getting people to view technology as reliable and trustworthy, but never really made a strong enough emotional connection to place Intel into people's hearts, as opposed to just in their minds. As Kim says, "This evolution will allow Intel to be better recognized for our contributions, establish a stronger emotional connection with our audiences and strengthen our overall position in the marketplace". The new master brand concept for Intel aimed at developing a relationship with the end user. Kim stated at the launch, "Helping people's lives to improve, and not just about making silicon".

This approach has enormous implications for Intel's business direction and strategy. Since 2006, more than 2,000 external managers, mainly with marketing backgrounds, have been hired, and most of the 98,000 employees got new jobs by creating new business units for each market. Instead of only focusing on the personal computer market, Intel entered and expanded several new markets, including consumer electronics, wireless communication, healthcare and others. Intel also intends to enter the entertainment market using consumer electronics such as DVD's, game consoles and cell phones. Other markets are also on the checklist, and strategic alliances with Apple, Nokia, Samsung, Google and Research in Motion are on the move.

Intel will still be an "ingredient" brand for its product brands, but will change the line-up of product brands to replace the Pentium range, which is to be phased out. The Pentium range was introduced to make life easier – a consumer brand shorthand for understanding what various products did. The new products are, first and foremost, improved microprocessors, as well as complete chipsets and boards, followed by blade servers and then complete products. This would mean that Intel would be supporting its clients and finally eating up their markets. This will not be an easy road to success. In 2006, Intel had to invest heavily while their sales and EBIT fell to 17.61% (2006). In 2007, however, they gained ground again and prospects for the future became bright. Table 2 shows Intel's key financial figures.

To signify the entire change in business and brand direction, Intel has changed its logo with the dropped "e" and replaced it with a "swoop" around the Intel name. It has also removed the famous "Intel Inside" tagline, replacing it with "Leap ahead" as shown in Fig. 20. The need to educate consumers globally about all these changes, including what the tagline means to the end user, does not come cheap, and the investment in the re-Branding and organizational change will be large. It must be remembered however, that it

Table 2. Intel's key financial figures 2008

Three Years Ended December 27, 2008 (In Millions, Except Per Share Amounts)	2008	2007	2006
Net revenue	37,586	$ 38,334	$ 35,382
Cost of sales	16,742	18,430	17,164
Gross margin	20,844	19,940	18,218
Research & development	5,722	5,755	5,873
Marketing, general and administrative	5,458	5,417	6,138
Restructuring and asset impairment charges	710	516	555
Operating expenses	11,890	11,688	12,566
Operating income	8,954	8,216	5,652
Gains (losses) on equity method investments, net	(1,380)	3	2
Gains (losses) on other equity investments, net	(376)	154	212
Interest and other, net	488	793	1,202
Income before taxes	7,686	9,166	7,068
Provisions for taxes	2,394	2,190	2,024
Net income	5,292	$ 6,976	$ 5,044
Basic earnings per common share	0.93	$ 1.20	$ 0.87

is less important how much a company spends on Branding, but rather how wisely it is spent.

In recent years, Intel has lost ground in Interbrand global brand scoring. It moved from the fifth position in 2000 to seventh in 2008 and lost 4% of its brand value ($30.9 billion). The long-term goal was to increase the value, but the big question for the future is whether the move away from the Ingredient Branding strategy to a master brand strategy will bring the expected results and whether the existing customers are willing to see that happen without interference?

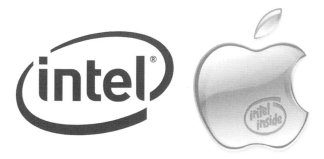

Fig. 20. New Intel logo and fabricated Intel logo inside Apple

Even with a marketing blitz and advertising spending of more than $2.6 billion budgeted over the next three years, many things can go wrong. Execution is the key for Intel, as with any brand management success.

With the shift to more marketing efforts within the company, the chances are very good; the current CEO Otellini is the first non-engineer to run the company and with a CMO in place, the chances are high that Intel will even hire a Chief Brand Officer (CBO). Yet, it is a huge task, especially for a company that has never had much success outside the computer industry. Companies that have been good at transforming themselves such as Nissan (formerly Datsun), Apple or Texas Instruments, typically need a crisis to precipitate change. However, a great leader can sometimes achieve this without a crisis.

Summary

- Intel's Ingredient Branding strategy started as a humble exercise.

- Market research and instant sales success inspired the company to enlarge the program.

- Convincing the company internally was as important as being successful in the market.

- Spending marketing communication dollars was considered as investment into the market.

- Marketing experiments and continuous adjustments improved the marketing communication concept.

- The introduction of cooperative marketing program propelled the investment to new heights and established closer relationships within the value chain.

- Environmental change was recognized, accepted, and marketing concepts were adapted.

- The implementation of the Ingredient Branding concept resulted in an unprecedented business success and changed the industry structure.

- Continuous change is needed, even when there is a proven concept; new thinking needs new minds, as recognized by the Intel leadership.

Notes

[1] Inside Intel – Paul Otellini's plan will send the chipmaker into uncharted territory. And founder Andy Grove applauds the shift, Business Week Cover Story January 9, 2006.

[2] Intel launches new logo and brand renewal. Digital Trends, December 30, 2005.

[3] See the Intel website: Intel Inside Program, Anthology of a Brand Campaign, www.intel.com.

[4] Babson College Case Studies, Building Important Brands: Intel, Nov. 2002.

[5] Industry guiding principle, named after Intel's co-founder and Chairman Emeritus Gordon Moore, that states that the number of transistors on a microprocessor roughly doubles every 18 months to two years.

[6] Moon, Y. „Inside intel inside." Harvard Business School case No. 11, 2002.

[7] Lang, N. „Wild things." *Marketing Computers,* May 1, 1992.

[8] Euro RSCG Worldwide moved its headquarters to New York in 1997. In 1996, Euro RSCG was the No. 7 largest global advertising agency. By 2002, they had become No. 5.

[9] At this time Intel accounted for an estimated 80% of DSW billings.

[10] Johnson, B., and Crumley, B. *Euro RSCG acquires global role at intel,* March 18, 1996 *Advertising Age* (March 18, 1996).

[11] www.intel.com/pressroom/archive/releases/rscgre.htm.

[12] See PC Week, June 6, 1994, TV ads in the U.S. had been particularly effective on the two programs Northern Exposure and Star Trek.

[13] Morris, B. „The brand's the thing." *Fortune Magazine,* March 4, 1996.

14 Mitchell, A. „Get ready for a brand new battle." *Marketing Week,* September 25, 1994.

15 www.intel.com/pressroom/intel_inside.htm.

16 By 2002, PCs were to be found in approximately 60% of U.S. households, 49% in Western Europe, and 38% in Asia Pacific, according to an Intel press release of July 1, 2002, „Intel Celebrates the Industry's 1 Billionth PC."

17 Temporal, P. „Case study: Intel corporation's re-branding." 2009, http://www.temporalbrand.com/publications/articles-260806.shtml.

CHAPTER 4

Implementation of InBranding Within a Company

Building a distinctive product offering can be challenging in many industries. Proliferation, commoditization and other factors contribute to diminishing margins, and other threats exist to the development of a lasting and valuable brand. One opportunity to counter this is through Ingredient Branding, the emphasis of a recognizable ingredient in your products or services, or the promotion of your products or services as a component in a third party's products or services. In a recently published summary article, Harvard Business School professor John Quelch outlined the four conditions for Ingredient Branding[1]:

1. The ingredient is highly differentiated, usually supported by patent protection, and so adds an aura of quality to the overall product.

2. The ingredient is central to the functional performance of the final product.

3. The final products are not well branded themselves, either because the category is relatively new, because customers buy infrequently or because there is low perceived differentiation among the options.

4. The final products are complex, assembled from components supplied by multiple firms who may sell the "ingredients" separately in an aftermarket.

P. Kotler and W. Pfoertsch, *Ingredient Branding: Making the Invisible Visible*,
DOI 10.1007/978-3-642-04214-0_4, © Springer-Verlag Berlin Heidelberg 2010

This conditions can lead to establish credibility to an otherwise unknown brand. Although Ingredient Branding has become increasingly popular, it is important that suppliers thoroughly examine InBranding and co-Branding options to ensure it is the right strategy before moving ahead. More and more industries are taking up this concept, such as textile producers, food and cosmetics companies like **3M, DuPont and Bayer**.

Even countries are using enhanced brand perception via country of origin promotion. Most of the time when a brand is involved in the Ingredient Branding cooperation they meet various power levels and they are exposed to the customers directly. The fit between the partners and the brand essence of both brands have to make sense to the customer. Unlike most temporary co-Branding arrangements, Ingredient Branding is a relationship in a precise context. In this relationship, suppliers and final product companies have only certain choices. If the ingredient supplier has the opportunity to go direct to the market, the company can take this as their first choice.

We would like to mention here the Aloe Corporation, the largest supplier of Aloe Vera products. The company was founded in 1988 and they marketed their products directly. In 2007, they saw another option for business, selling to food companies using their ingredients, but they did not opt for an Ingredient Branding program. They considered the investment into the marketplace as too big to

Fig. 21. Ingredient Branding options for Cable & Wireless

handle for their company. Cable and Wireless, a telecom company, did not followed the same conceptual thinking and designed a marketing communication program, where various options for endorsement with their brand logos could be chosen by their industrial customers to show performance to the final customer. They could have chosen: powered by, networked by, hosted by Cable and Wireless as shown in Fig. 21.

4.1 Significance of the Brand Concept

"We are living in the attention economy now. If there is attention around your ingredient or your brand, you will make money."[2] With this statement, or rather, the idea behind this statement, nutritional supplements specialist, Shane Starling, sets out the basic tenets and objectives of InBranding, or any other kind of Branding for that matter, in clear and simple terms. His premise is that success for a supplier, as well as for an end product, depends primarily on the attention its brand is able to attract. Increased **brand attention** should not be viewed as the *only* success factor for a product though. Especially for suppliers, increased brand presence in the attention of all their clients (OEMs and private end consumers) offers an opportunity for differentiating themselves from competitors and their products. Until recently, focus on customers was directed solely at the next, i.e. adjacent or neighboring level in the market, or in other words, with customers operating solely in the B2B sector.

It is now virtually impossible, however, to achieve any level of product differentiation solely through improvements to products and innovations, or through additional forms of service support, faster and more reliable deliveries or even through lower prices. The market power of customer demand for upstream products (meaning demand by the end consumer that goes beyond the immediate OEM to the suppliers of the OEM, or "upstream") has led to a situation where – by virtue of their detailed specifications – many **supplied products** scarcely differ at all from one another in terms of performance characteristics, scope and quality. Branding is an opportunity which offers supplier companies, with the help of a

House of Brands concept a way to achieve enduring differentiation for themselves and for their products.

Before going into the **brand-based concept** of Ingredient Branding, it is first necessary to clarify the importance and function a brand has in a company's deliberations about their sales policy, and what value it ultimately represents for the company.

To this end, some of the world's largest manufacturers have demonstrated that the value of their brand(s) constitutes often more than 50% of the market capitalization of the corporation. This clearly illustrates that the brand is a key to success in the value creation process of any company.[3]

Creation and Function of a Brand

According to Linxweiler[4], the creation of a brand is a task primarily assigned to the marketing department and the leadership in a company.

Since this is where all market-oriented, internal company production activities reside, the primary objective of any marketing department is to *convert a product into a brand*. To achieve this, companies avail themselves of the full gamut of **marketing policy instruments**. At the end of the day, a brand is the culmination of the entire range of marketing activities, from product and range decision to pricing, distribution and communication policies.

Why is it necessary to create a brand out of a product? In order to answer this, a brand can be viewed as a kind of translation cipher, which, with the help of a unique brand name or symbol, reflects the performance characteristics and the quality of a product. Strong brands provide a USP (unique selling proposition) for customers which distinguishes their product from other manufactured equivalents, and which imbue it with a distinct and unique position on a market.[5] Table 3 provides an overview of additional functions a brand serves.

Table 3. Functions of a brand

Function	Description
Distinguishing function	A brand differentiates one company's goods and services from those of other companies.
Guarantee and confidence function	A brand guarantees the quality of a product, associated with progress in terms of technology and research.
Quality function	A brand guarantees that a given product possesses identical or superior properties to another comparable product from a different company.
Identification, promotional and origin function	A brand enables a product to be identified and recognised.
Orientation function	A brand makes it easier to sort offers and to reach a purchase decision.
Transparency and insurance function	Since a brand can be monitored carefully, it can also act as an instrument for consumer protection.

The distinguishing function of a brand is differentiation of one company's goods and services from those of other companies, as well as positioning the company in the market. Trust and quality functions assure the customers purchasing decision. Identification, orientation, transparency and insurance functions give guidance for the customer in the various product phases.

The Brand as a Transporter of Values

With InBranding, individual functions of the brand satisfy the same purpose for the product being marketed to OEMs, as brands do for consumer goods. In particular, the identification, promotion and origin-specific aspects of a brand's functions ensure that various **upstream products and supplied components** are built into the brand of the end product. This forms the basis for successful Ingredient Branding. Without Branding of the components, any House of Brands (i.e. multiple brands) marketing approach involving Ingredient Branding will fail to deliver any real impact, because it cannot establish the emotional connection with the customer.

Once an InBrand has achieved initial success on the market, other functions begin to add to this success, e.g. the trust function and the quality function, as well as the marketing policy and associated activities conducted by an upstream product manufacturer. As a consequence, as mentioned before, these functions can be viewed as a form of translation cipher with which the brand name itself is able to make a positive statement, in terms of buyer perception, about the performance capabilities and quality of a product. Because the consumer has trust in the product without requiring extensive testing, or understanding all benefits of the product, down to the last detail, the brand becomes the **'transporter'** of all the values of a product.

Typical factors which determine the value of a brand include recognition, image and the relevance of a product to the end consumer, as well as the level of competitive differentiation. Particularly in the case of supplier companies whose products were previously only sought after by the supplier market, the brand image of a product now becomes the decisive criterion in determining the success of any Ingredient Branding strategy.[6]

Development of Brand Value

If you take a closer look at the development of value in familiar brands, you will see that their success did not occur from one day to the next. Instead, the growth of brand value is the result of an intensive and time-consuming **learning process**, one that is associated with a substantial investment of time and money for the company concerned. Nevertheless, it constitutes a decisive competitive advantage which competitors can only catch up after a considerable amount of effort. Once a brand has established itself successfully on the market, 'attackers' need an extensive amount of time to develop correspondingly strong brand images for their own products. Also, it is important not to lose sight of the fact that a brand – despite its long **development period** and its success – can be destroyed very rapidly through unfortunate incidents, e.g., major incidents in the chemicals industry or pollutants in foodstuffs.

To eliminate errors of this nature, and their ramifications for the brand, it is particularly important to retain a long-term view of the success of any brand strategy. This aspect applies to brand development in consumer goods as well as in industrial goods sectors. It follows from this that the Ingredient Branding process is one that requires a great deal of patience and endurance before the desired level of success is ultimately achieved.[7]

4.2   Brand Conception with Ingredient Branding

The brand concept of Ingredient Branding does not differ in any significantly distinguishable manner from the brand concept associated with a conventional consumer or end product. While it is true to say that the products involved are directed at different segments of the market. The **sales policy measures** and activities of both have the private end consumer as their primary target group, because, as mentioned previously, Ingredient Branding is only able to generate a demand pull through a direct appeal to the end consumer – the primary objective of any House of Brands marketing activity.

Even in cases where the end product manufacturer constitutes the direct customer for a supplier company, the intention behind employing Ingredient Branding and the resultant demand pull is to achieve a growing preference on the part of the private end consumer for certain supplier components. In turn the manufacturing customer of the upstream product indirectly is than compelled to install components from a defined ingredient manufacturer into that company's products.

Although the conception of brand in the supplier and consumer goods sector does not differ greatly in any key respect, with Ingredient Branding it is first necessary to define a strategic orientation for the brand in terms of its **breadth of expertise** and its vertical **depth of expertise**.[8] In contrast to the brand development of consumer goods, it should be noted that, for InBrands, most supplied brands have been present for an extended period on the B2B market, before the advent of House of Brands marketing imbued them with a new approach to their previous sales policy. With Ingredient

Branding, it is therefore not absolutely essential for an existing product to develop an entirely new brand from the bottom up. Instead, the focus should be on adapting the brand or product to a new strategic direction within the context of the Ingredient Branding process. As pointed out several times in this book, part of this new strategic direction, is targeting the end consumer as well as the next step OEM in the value chain.

For the purpose of conceptual structuring, Baumgarth devised a matrix for Ingredient Branding conception which subdivides the brand conception element of Ingredient Branding into three levels: the target level, the strategy level and the marketing policy tools required to implement that strategy as shown in Fig. 22.

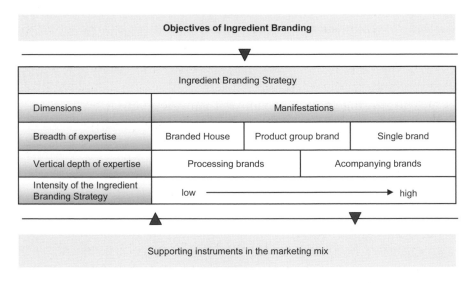

Fig. 22. Ingredient Branding conception

These include the various instruments of the 'marketing mix' (product policy, price policy, communication policy and distribution policy), among which the **communication policy** in Ingredient Branding constitutes the most important marketing instrument because the primary interest of an ingredient manufacturer is to create a demand pull through more intensive efforts in communication.

The Objectives of InBranding

These target levels form the 'roof' of any brand conception, though strategy and other supporting marketing instruments are directed primarily towards the process of **formulating objectives**. Through the use of InBranding, supplier companies' goal is to lead their products out of the previous **anonymity inherent in supplied components**. Through an increase in brand awareness, a level of competitive differentiation is created which will lead to maximization of profits or an increase in the market share of the product or component being marketed.

The general objectives of a brand strategy within the context of Ingredient Branding includes such aspects as the creation of preferences among the target group, improved customer **brand loyalty** (customer loyalty) and increase the potential for sales penetration. The creation of leverage in terms of **price policy** (price premium) can challenge the market in various ways. These objectives are, however, all subordinate to the actual main objective (that of maximizing profits and increasing market share) and can, depending on company and product, be assigned greater or lesser levels of priority.

4.3   Strategy Options

Once the various objectives of InBranding have been formulated and quantified by the ingredient manufacturer, an implementation strategy needs to be devised. Initially, this involves defining the level of intensity and the precise scope required for the Ingredient Branding strategy. This process takes into consideration the breadth of expertise as well as the vertical depth of expertise inherent in the supplied brand.

Breadth of Expertise

In any analysis of individual Ingredient Brands, it is clear that these brands tend not to relate exclusively to a single product. A brand can encompass several products which possess very diverse characteristics. This tendency is most apparent in the automotive and computer sectors. Here, all supplied components (e.g. ABS (Anti Block Systems), ESP (Electronic Stabilization System)braking systems, rain sensors) manufactured by Bosch for the automotive industry bear the brand name of the company, though they diverge substantially from each other in terms of properties. The situation in the computer sector is similar. Here, most manufacturers use the name of their company (Hewlett-Packard, Sony, Samsung) as a brand for their products – whether it be for a computer, a printer or a monitor.

Once a company has formulated the objectives for its InBranding strategy, the next step is to define the **breadth of expertise** of that brand. This stipulates the precise scope and performance characteristics which a brand should encompass. Depending on this breadth of expertise, brands can be sub-divided into individual brands, product group brands and/or family brands, branded house and multiple brands (the 'House of Brands' concept). Table 4 provides an overview of the respective **brand strategies**.

Individual brands are most commonly found in the consumer goods industry. This is where most companies tend to conceal their identity with familiar names: the company of Ferrero is concealed with the brand names of Nutella, Duplo, Giotto and Raffaelo while Procter &

Table 4. Brand strategies

Brand Strategy	Description
Individual brand strategy (Single Brands)	Every product from a company is offered under its own brand name. The name of the provider usually remains hidden from the consumer.
Branded House strategy (Branded House)	All products and services provided by a company are grouped together under the company brand.
Product group brand strategy (Product Brands)	Uniform brand designation enabling several related products to be marketed under a single brand name. The individual products benefit here from the image of the entire brand family.
Multiple brand strategy (House of Brands)	Different brands (individual brands) are offered within the same product range and/or in similar market segments in parallel fashion.
Hybrid brand strategy (Hybrid Brands)	A combination of the Single Brand and Branded House strategies

Gamble is the company behind the brands of Mr. Clean, Head and Shoulders, and Pampers. There are also a few examples of this in the B2B sector, such as YTONG, made by Xella International GmbH, a company whose product range also includes multipor, fermacell, aestuver, silka, etc.. Another example would be DuPont, a company with strong product brands such as Teflon (coatings), Vespel (seals), Corian (surfaces), BAX System (foodstuff inspection), etc.

When it comes to **branded house** strategies, all the products and services of a single company are grouped together under the company brand. Examples of this include automotive manufacturers (Porsche, BMW, VW), most companies from the computer and software sector (Dell, SAP, Hewlett-Packard, IBM, Microsoft) as well as companies in the mechanical engineering sector. In AZO from Osterburken, Germany (www.azo.de), a medium-size company which manufactures automatic delivery systems for various industries, the branded house concept has been constructed in a very clear and distinctive manner:

- AZO Food for bakery goods, cereals, spices, etc.

- AZO Vital for pharmaceuticals, dairy products, confectionery, etc.

- AZO Chemie [Chemicals] for hygiene, cosmetics, colors, paints, etc.

- AZO Poly for plastics processing, compounding, etc.

Product group brands, on the other hand, are frequently encountered in application areas such as the magnet technology manufactured by Kendrion B.V. (www.kendrion.com): magnet technologies for automotive applications are marketed under the name Binder (www.binder-magnete.de), while magnet technology for industrial applications is marketed under the name of Thoma (www.thoma-magnettechnik.de).

Multiple brands are most commonly found in highly saturated markets. Companies use them to pursue the objective of achieving added value by offering different brands within similar market segments. For example, we would like to cite OSCAR WEIL GmbH from the German town of Lahr, who uses the product brand name of RAKSO steel wool for the industrial sector while at the same marketing the brand name of *abrazo*, said to be the "most popular cleaning pad in the home". In the consumer goods sector, it is popular to employ different brands in the washing products and cigarette markets.[9] By using this approach, companies operating an advanced form of brand management, and who have grown through acquisition, gain an interesting brand instrument.

Filtrox AG based in St. Gallen, Switzerland, sells filtration products and complete solutions for various industrial applications through its subsidiaries in various European markets, and has adopted a House of Brands strategy for doing so. The company has deliberately chosen not to adopt a uniform brand across its markets, preferring instead to introduce different brands for specialist customers in various different markets. These brands are being retained deliberately. The objective of the Filtrox brand strategy is to be represented in each market with at least one **'premium brand'** and one **'challenger brand'**. The **House of Brands** strategy permits vertical differentiation within markets as well as horizontal differentiation by price segment. Another example is Atlas Copco, which, in the compressor market, one of its core sectors, it has incorporated the Chinese low-cost brand of LIUTECH in its product range, which they finally acquired.

In order to establish which brand strategy can best achieve the objectives of InBranding for a particular company, it is first necessary to take a closer look at the opportunities and threats facing each individual brand strategy. On the one hand, an **individual brand strategy** makes it possible to focus consistently on a given target group and to achieve specific profiling for the brand. On the other hand, through the process of sharing a marketing budget across many individual brands, there is an increased risk of reducing the probability of achieving a high-level of recognition for those individual brands.

The **branded house strategy** has the advantage of grouping all products made by one company under a single brand (company brand), thus enabling every single product to benefit from the general level of public awareness of the branded house. This means that all products share the cost of Branding on a joint basis. Moreover, the brand is not tied to the life cycle of a single product, and the introduction of new products is promoted through the branded house goodwill effect. However, there are a few threats that may offset the opportunities inherent. For example, it is almost impossible to achieve clear profiling of production goods within the context of a branded house strategy, or focus on individual target groups. Furthermore, "cannibalization effects" can occur if the branded house also fields goods eminently suited to act as substitutes.

With the **product brand strategy**, a situation exists similar to that of the branded house strategy in terms of opportunities and threats. However, in this case, profiling of products is easier to achieve because, in contrast to the branded house strategy, products can be grouped together in different groups. Of all these brand strategies, the ones least suited to Ingredient Branding are the **House of Brands strategy** and **the hybrid brand strategy**. When these are employed, companies primarily hope to achieve better penetration of heavily saturated markets. If you take a closer look at the supplier markets, you see that the number of potential customers in a given market segment is relatively modest, which means that market saturation can occur fairly easily. As a consequence, it becomes necessary for a supplier to **differentiate** his products from those of other providers in order to increase market share and to circumvent the potential threat of substitutes eroding sales of his own products.[10]

Frequently, **hybrid** structures arise in the context of corporate takeovers and are really only conceived of as transitional forms. At IWKA Group, the intention is to combine the flexibility, creativity and speed of company units with an SME ethos, together with the synergies, volume effects and capital power of a medium-sized corporate group structure; and to leave individual brands to exist alongside one another. This enables the company to respond rapidly in dynamic markets and, at the same time, to remain close to its customers around the world. An overview about the various brand strategies is given in Table 4.

It is not possible to issue a general statement about which is the 'correct' brand strategy to adopt for InBranding because this choice is derived first and foremost from the formulation of objectives within the brand conception, which can vary widely depending on sector, company and product. It is possible, however, to observe that most In-Brands are structured across the board on a branded house strategy. Examples are Intel, NutraSweet, Shimano, Dolby and Tetra Pak.

One reason why a great number of ingredient manufacturers decide in favor of the branded house strategy might be that companies, prior to implementing their InBranding strategy, have already incorporated their product brand within their **Corporate Identity (CI) concept**. As a result, any individual brand strategy for a supplier component will entail a relatively high commitment in terms of finance and time for the upstream product manufacturer, given that pricing and product policy play a leading role within the B2B sector.

In contrast, the branded house concept offers an additional advantage: the introduction of new products with the benefit of existing brand value. This means that the branded house approach also performs the function of a **quality emblem**, enabling a product to enjoy the trust of end customers even before they have been informed in detail of its **performance characteristics**.

In American literature about brands, potential brand strategies tend to be presented in the form of a brand relationship spectrum. On the one hand distinctions are drawn through sub-division of product brands into what are referred to as sub brands and endorsed brands. On the other hand, a much greater degree of differentiation is demonstrated in the superordinate categories. Furthermore, it is accepted that a multitude of mixed forms can arise, and these are designated as hybrid brands[11].

Vertical Depth of Expertise

In contrast to breadth of expertise, which provides information about the scope and capabilities of a brand, **vertical depth of expertise** characterizes the range of the brand within a multi-level or 'branded house' approach to marketing. Baumgarth distinguishes this clearly in his matrix between "accompanying brands" and "processing brands". The term "accompanying brands" is applied to the brands of production goods which continue to be applied and used on downstream manufactured products. This means that they are used throughout all levels of the value chain and are ultimately communicated to the end consumer. With "processing brands", the brand of each production item is only applied directly to one market level, or to the adjacent level within that market. In this case, no Branding of that specific component occurs on the final product.[12]

The vertical depth of expertise, therefore, defines the intensity of an Ingredient Branding strategy. It should be noted here that most companies, when implementing their Ingredient Branding strategy, position their brands in terms of their vertical depth of expertise as "accompanying brands", aiming to achieve a high level of 'intensity'. This is necessary because it is the only way of achieving the desired level of demand pull or 'pull effect' with the end consumer. Even though the financial cost of **comprehensive Branding**, all the way from supplied components through to the end product, may constitute a threat to supplier companies. In the SME sector, it is brand awareness and the level of demand from private end consumers that, at the end of the day, will determine the success or failure of an Ingredient Branding strategy.

4.4   Communication Policy

To achieve the objectives of an Ingredient Branding strategy, various sales policy measures need to be taken. First and foremost, these include the standard instruments of the marketing mix (product, price, communication and distribution policy). In the previous chapter, we explained the form that the various marketing mix activities need to take to best suit the strategy for Ingredient Branding, as well as which instruments most effectively support the objectives of branded house marketing. Whereas, in the past, **product**

and price policy reigned supreme in terms of strategy among B2B products, the focus of Ingredient Branding activities is directed primarily at the communication policy. With the assistance of the right policy, the product brand is communicated across all levels of the market to the end consumer in order to create preferences and demand for the in-house product. The standard instruments of **communication policy** mainly include:[13]

1. **Advertising:** This includes, but is not limited to, advertisements in trade and public-domain magazines, commercials on radio and television and billboard posters.

2. **Personal presentation:** Direct presentation of a product to one or several interested parties (e.g. sales presentations and trade fairs).

3. **Sales promotion/special campaign:** This takes the form of short-term buying incentives to boost sales revenues such as presentation of goods on shelves in a retail outlet, special discounts and special advertising campaigns.

4. **Public relations:** Image and the company's engagement in society.

Though the primary focus, the communication policy within the InBranding approach should not be allowed to eclipse the other instruments available in the marketing mix. The only way of achieving optimum communications success for a brand is through the careful orchestration of all these various instruments.

Implications for the Communication Policy

The communication policy as a sales instrument has to contend with a few problems within the context of Ingredient Branding. It is, for example, entirely possible for a brand to be incorrectly identified by the customer at subsequent levels in the market, because comprehensively applied and unique Branding of a component may not be apparent to that customer. What is required here, by means of labels, attachments or stickers, is to draw attention to the fact that **a further processing product or end product** incorporates a defined InBrand.

A further problem is posed by the credibility of the assured benefits of the brand. This is primarily due to the fact that the InBrand only constitutes a limited share of the end product, and that it is only through the interaction of all components that the overall benefits of an end product can be clearly identified. This might create an impression in the mind of the consumer that, despite the high value InBrand, other components and the individual production processes might diminish the performance and quality of the end product, thereby falsifying the actual benefits.

To counteract this, companies are called upon to communicate the benefits of their products as directly to the **end consumer** and to enter into a close relationship or link with strong end product brands. For example, NutraSweet distributed packs of chewing gum sweetened with NutraSweet to millions of households throughout the USA to present the benefits of its product directly to consumers. Intel, during the initial stages of its Ingredient Branding strategy, focused strongly on co-advertising with strong PC brands such as IBM or Compaq. By bundling these brands, Intel was able to demonstrably raise the credibility and the perceived benefits of its InBrand exercise, as well as that of the end product.

Vertically integrated communication constitutes another problem area, one with which an ingredient manufacturer is confronted in the context of his communication policy. The end product manufacturer may communicate divergent information or different benefits about the InBrand to those of the production goods manufacturer within the context of his **multi-level marketing or branded house strategy**. To prevent this from occurring, the ingredient manufacturer has the option of linking the end product to a system of promotional cost contributions which better enables that manufacturer to influence and/or exert management control over **communication contents**.[14] This is explained in greater detail in the next chapter, using the example of Intel Corporation.

Building Customer Loyalty Through Contributions Towards Promotional Costs

As explained previously, the "Intel Inside" campaign run by the microprocessor manufacturer Intel Corporation is one of the most successful and most familiar examples of Ingredient Branding in the world. One of the cornerstones of this success was the differentiated system of **contributions towards promotional costs** which it developed internally. This approach has enabled Intel to influence the communication of its brand, through the end product manufacturer, thereby ensuring that Intel and the OEMs (Sony, Hewlett-Packard and Dell) were communicating the same contents about the brand and/or the product to the end consumer, i.e. were "singing the same tune". The cornerstone of this system of contributions to promotional costs is formed by the material inducement for OEMs to participate in the "Intel Inside" campaign. Quite simply, the PC manufacturers received what became known as "Intel Inside Dollars" whenever they incorporated the "Intel Inside" logo in their communication and brand policy actions.[15] The actual level of these

Table 5. Determinants for the level of contributions towards promotional costs from Intel

Determinants	Description
Purchased volume of microprocessors	The purchased volume is the most important factor in determining the level of contributions towards promotional costs. The greater the number of microprocessors ordered, the greater the number of 'Intel Inside Dollars' the PC manufacturers receive.
Generation/type of microprocessors	Here, it is the generation and/or type of processor which the OEM offers in the context of PC advertising which determines the level of contribution towards promotional costs. To support the market launch of new types of processor, new Intel processors tend as a general rule to be awarded more 'Intel Inside Dollars'.
Type of OEM promotional vehicle	The type of promotional vehicle which the PC manufacturer communicates about a product and about the Intel processor it contains within the context of cooperation-based advertising also has a bearing on the level of the Intel contributions to promotional costs.

contributions towards OEM promotional costs and their level of dependency is illustrated in Table 5.

With this system, Intel was able to ensure that the vertical communication of its brand was recognized clearly and across the board by the end consumer.

The system that Intel has established and its continuously improving paid off dearly. How much of the effects can be contributed to the Branding efforts is hard to determine from the outside. Since Intel is very rigorous about their performance measurements and they are continuing their investment in the consumer recognition, we can assume that the impact is considerable. This and many other cases prove that Branding is an effective tool for generating profits and shareholder wealth for companies that are active in a business-to-business environment. Other factors such as innovation and manufacturing efficiency – or the lack of these – can also create or destroy shareholder wealth.

Lars Ohnemus from the Copenhagen Business School together with Per Jenster from CEIBS[16] proved on an examination of almost 1,700 companies (listed either on the United States or European stock exchanges) that Branding is a determining factor in the companies' success. Their study revealed that the crucial relationship could be described as a W-shaped curve with five distinctive phases, depending on the strategic Branding position of the company: **Aspiration,**

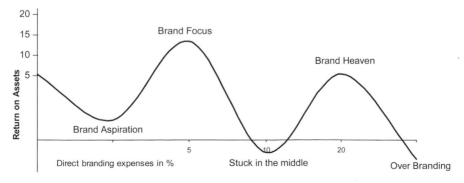

Fig. 23. Simplified W function

brand focus, stuck in the middle, brand heaven phase, and **over Branding** (see Fig. 23). Intel is currently in the brand heaven, but had been in two valleys during their brand development. These findings give us an insight to determine current positions and possible development scopes.

This study also showed that Branding used strategically generally yield a return to their shareholders (5%-7% higher). It is therefore vital that key executives, including the board of directors, systematically assess and monitor the strategic Branding position of their company and how their Branding investments are performing against key competitors. Investing in a brand is part of the strategic development. Strong brands with market clout can be leveraged to higher price premium or they can be leveraged to sales increase, the operational management has to determine which way to go under which circumstances. It is very difficult to move in both directions. Depending on their strategic priorities and investment capabilities companies can move to either market share increase or cash flow generation. These alternatives have to be carefully evaluated before putting into practice.

Summary

- Ingredient Branding is a strong way to overcome brand proliferation.

- The implementation of Ingredient Branding follows the same principles as regular brand management, except the main focus is on creating the demand-pull.

- Conscious efforts are needed to use a brand as transporter of values.

- Various brand strategies are possible, but many InBrands start as single brands and move mostly to product group brand strategies.

- Marketing communication is an integral part of the InBranding marketing mix. Since we operate in a multi-level communication concept, various participants have to be integrated.

- Contributions towards promotional costs to partners in the distribution chain are a well-established concept that could lead to customer loyalty improvement if applied properly.

Notes

[1] Quelch, J. „„Blank" inside: Branding ingredients." *Harvard Business School Working Knowledge,* October 10, 2007.

[2] Starling, S. „Branding: The vital ingredient for marketing success." June, 2002.

[3] Keller, K.L., ed. *Strategic brand management: Building, measuring, and managing brand equity.* Upper Saddle River, NJ, 1998; Linxweiler, R. *BrandScoreCard: Ein neues Instrument erfolgreicher Markenführung.* Gruß-Umstadt, 2001, p. 4.

[4] Linxweiler, R. *BrandScoreCard: Ein neues Instrument erfolgreicher Markenführung.* Gruß-Umstadt, 2001, p. 31.

[5] Diller, H. „Preis- und Distributionspolitik starker Marken vor dem Hintergrund fortschreitender Handelskonzentration." In *Erfolgsfaktor Marke,* edited by R. Köhler, W. Majer, and H. Wiezorek. Munich, 2001, p. 118.

[6] Simon, H., and Sebastian, K. -H. „Ingredient Branding: Reift ein neuer Markentypus?" *Absatzwirtschaft* 45 (1995): 42–48.

[7] Ditto.

[8] Baumgarth, C. „Ingredient branding: Markenkonzept und Kommunikationsumsetzung." Working paper, 1999.

[9] Bruhn, M. „Die zunehmende Bedeutung von Dienstleistungsmarken." In *Erfolgsfaktor Marke,* edited by R. Köhler, W. Majer, and H. Wiezorek. München, 2001, p. 149.

[10] Baumgarth (1998), p. 36ff.

[11] Aaker, D.A., and Joachimsthaler, E. *Brand leadership.* New York, 2002, p. 105.

[12] Baumgarth, C. „Ingredient branding: Markenpolitik für Produktionsgüter." In *Tagungsband zur 1. Kunststoff-Marketing-Tagung,* edited by H. Breuer and D.E. Willich, 1998, p. 42.

[13] Kotler, P., Andersen, G., Wong, V., and Saunders, J. *Principles of marketing*. 4th ed. London, 2004, p. 668.

[14] Baumgarth, C. „Ingredient branding: Markenkonzept und Kommunikationsumsetzung." Working paper, 1999, p. 13f.

[15] Schmaeh, M., and Erdmeier, P. „Sechs Jahre „Intel Inside"." *Absatzwirtschaft* (1997): 122–129, p. 124.

[16] Ohnemus, L., and Jenster, P. „Corporate brand thrust and financial performance: An examination of strategic brand investments." *International Studies of Management and Organization* 37 (2007): 84–107.

CHAPTER 5

Success Stories of Ingredient Branding

After the **Intel Corporation** applied the Ingredient Branding concept and launched such a success, many other component manufacturers in the computer industry jumped on the bandwagon. They started to revise their strategy and initiated to communicate their product offerings and performance differences to **end consumers**. These included brands like AMD, MSI, ATI and nVidia (CPU, main board and graphic cards manufacturers). These companies have succeeded in securing partnership agreements with PC manufacturers to have their logos shown on the computers. They also convinced the retailers and final users that their component is superior and makes a difference for them. It should be pointed out, though, that there are limits to the number of brand labels that can be featured on a computer. Currently, the main logos that appear on the PC are the processor, graphic card and operating system software since these are perceived as having the greatest impact on either the computer's performance (processor, graphic card) or its quality in terms of user friendliness or security (operating system software).

Positioning, differentiation and business growth can be achieved by making strategic decisions based on principles. The principles discovered for successful InBrands are similar to the concepts revealed by Renee A. Mauborgne and W. Chan Kim in their "blue ocean strategy[1]". They demonstrate that successful business is not either low-cost providers or niche-players. Instead, "blue ocean" thinking proposes finding value in other ways that defy conventional wis-

P. Kotler and W. Pfoertsch, *Ingredient Branding: Making the Invisible Visible*, 93
DOI 10.1007/978-3-642-04214-0_5, © Springer-Verlag Berlin Heidelberg 2010

dom and segmentation. Ingredient Branding is one way that creates new market space by changing the rules of the game.

As the business waters become increasingly choppy, owners and management teams would be well advised to frame strategic vision through a sharply focused lens such as "blue ocean strategy". However, blue oceans are largely uncharted waters. The dominant focus of strategic thinking has been on competition-based red ocean strategies. Intel showed how rewarding it could be. If you look around, you will notice other brands who jumped in to create uncontested market space such as Dolby, Realtek, Lycra, Gore-Tex, Teflon, Nomex, Nanotex, Schott Ceran, Zeiss and Shimano, just to mention a few from the long list in the appendix of this book.

Over the period of time, every industry develops a set practice: who your customers are, who your competitors are, which market is yours, etc. However, more than defining, these practices are limiting. The rigid wall defining the market thwarts growth, and the entry of more and more players' kick-starts cutting throats, and coloring the competitive water red. InBranding can shatter the conventional business wisdoms and redefine the reach of the brand. The end result can give a brand a huge untapped market, free of bloody competition. Therefore, it is necessary to develop a sustainable edge that even the giants of the red waters will find hard to surpass. For that, we need to understand the characteristics of the industries and the strategic options for the brand. Other great business schools authors have already explored this options and come up with astonishing results. Unfortunately, their analysis was conducted a few years ago and did not consider the Branding impact in their equation. In the 1980s, when Tom Peters and Bob Waterman analyzed corporations around the world and then published "In Search Of Excellence"[2], they were focusing on understanding customer's need and delivering consistent and lean products. Jim Collins in "Build to Last"[3] followed the same footsteps ten years later and enhanced his analysis for "Good to Great"[4] to answer why some companies make the leap and others don't. He examined companies and drew exceptional conclusions. His analysis also applies to Ingredient Branding companies, but he did not put the Branding dimensions in his selection criteria. Today we know that brand management[5] is an additional instrument for success.

Using a Strategy Canvas to Identify Innovative InBranding Opportunities

We would like to use Chan Kim and Renee Mauborgne's technique for visualizing competitive differentiation and innovation opportunities with the so-called "Strategy Canvas". It is both a diagnostic tool to show you what your current competitive situation looks like as well as a planning tool for identifying untapped innovation opportunities. The Strategy Canvas condenses a significant amount of information in a very compact format. The horizontal axis contains a list of factors that the industry competes on and invests in, as well as potential areas where customer value could be created. The vertical axis indicates the degree to which each competitor invests in each factor. To create the Strategy Canvas, you simply plot points for the current performance of your company and all competitors, and then "connect the dots" to create a series of lines that represents the "value curve" for each company. The Strategy Canvas offers several advantages to innovators:

1. It enables you to quickly see areas were your strategy and those of your competitors converge (where everyone is following the same orthodoxy or set of assumptions on how business is done).

2. It shows areas of divergence, where your company's strategy differs significantly from that of your competitors.

3. It also helps you to see "white space" opportunities for innovation and competitive differentiation.

The Strategy Canvas also reveals if your company has taken a scattershot approach to creating customer value. If your company's line on the Strategy Canvas looks like a zigzag, with high values in some areas and low values in other areas, it indicates that you and your strategic planning team needs to address that issue. The well-known example is Southwest Airline (see Fig. 24).

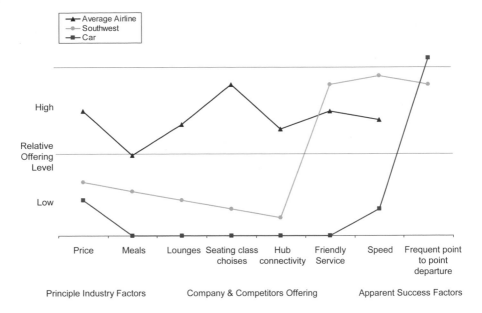

Fig. 24. Strategy canvas of Southwest Airlines

This example clearly shows how Southwest Airlines, by focusing on only three factors – friendly service, speed and frequent departures – has succeeded in differentiating itself from other airlines and competing forms of transportation (i.e., via car).

We think this is a powerful planning tool that is also very easy to use which needs to identify:

- Principle factors in the industry and current state of play.

- The company and competitors' offerings.

- The "apparent" success factors in product, service, perception and success factors in product, service, perception and delivery.

For a selection of industries, we have developed a Strategy Canvas and highlighted the strategic options under these conditions for successful Ingredient Branding, and we will now discuss the extent to which the Ingredient Branding strategy is an appropriate and viable approach for businesses such as suppliers to automotive, textile, glass and sweetener industries. This chapter provides a brief summary of current developments in each of the industries and indicates what opportunities Ingredient Branding can provide.

5.1   Automotive Components

The automotive industry is one of the world's leading sectors and plays a key role in the global and national economies. In 2007, for example, the total turnover of the automotive industry was around €350 billion. This contributes about 6% to total manufacturing employment and 7% to total manufacturing output and around 10% of the country's GDP. With the 2008/2009 financial crisis and fall out of the automotive industry, the situation changed considerable[6]. Global competition manifested in falling manufacturer margins, overcapacities and continually increased pressure to consolidate. This has forced most automotive manufacturers to implement cost-saving measures.[7] The sobering effects that result from focus on shareholder value, growing customer expectations and the rapid introduction of new technologies across all sectors of industry represent additional challenges to which OEMs need to respond.

Not only automotive manufacturers but also suppliers have to battle in tougher market conditions, as the cost and performance pressures faced by OEMs are passed on directly to their suppliers. As a result, global competition, new technologies, a new pattern of consumer behavior and deregulation are increasingly demanding structural changes in the automotive industry to adapt to changing market realities.

The Auto 2010, a study conducted by Accenture found that the following changes could drive structural upheaval in the automotive industry:[8]

- **New competition:** Suppliers from other industries such as telecommunications, financial services and entertainment will appear as future competitors in the automotive industry alongside parts suppliers, manufacturers and dealers.

- **Service as a new requirement for manufacturers:** The high **fixed cost burden** faced by automotive manufacturers will increasingly result in the development, production, integration and assembly of vehicles being outsourced to specialists both inside and outside the industry. This will signal the transition from a sales- and product-driven corporate strategy (push strategy) to a focus on customer needs and services (pull strategy).

- **Technology expertise and production from suppliers:** The current economic situation is forcing automotive manufacturers to implement draconian cost-cutting measures, which they are passing directly on to their suppliers. This may result in manufacturers outsourcing activities such as research and development, production and assembly and transferring responsibility for product innovations and vehicle performance to suppliers. Fig. 25 shows how the share of value-added in the main modules of a vehicle could be outsourced in favor of supplier companies, as revealed in a study by Mercer Management Consulting[9].

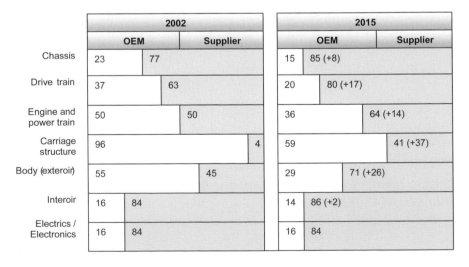

	2002				2015			
	OEM		**Supplier**		**OEM**		**Supplier**	
Chassis	23	77			15	85 (+8)		
Drive train	37		63		20		80 (+17)	
Engine and power train	50		50		36		64 (+14)	
Carriage structure	96			4	59		41 (+37)	
Body (exterior)	55		45		29		71 (+26)	
Interoir	16	84			14	86 (+2)		
Electrics / Electronics	16	84			16	84		

Fig. 25. Main modules – trends in share of value-added, OEMs and suppliers (as %)

- **The Internet as an "enabler":** The Internet enables greater market transparency[10] and is becoming increasingly more important in the handling of B2B processes and the sale of vehicles.

Fig. 25 compares the share of value-added of OEMs and suppliers in 2002 and 2015 (estimated).

In the next chapter we will look more closely at how these **structural market changes** have a positive effect on the success of Ingredient Branding for suppliers and what factors can have a decisive influence on them.

Brands as a Success Factor

A study by Prof. Sattler carried out in 1999 revealed that the value of a brand as an immaterial asset makes up as much as 56% of the total value of a company. His more recent analyses confirm the importance of this phenomenon[11]. The results of this study clearly underline the **importance of Branding** as a key factor in the success of the business. This finding particularly affects the automotive industry because a higher brand value gives the company a higher profile and greater acceptance, allowing the use of price premiums and more sales, a larger share of the market and long-term customer loyalty.

However, the current economic situation and the growing interchangeability of technology, makes it ever more difficult for automotive manufacturers and their brands to differentiate their vehicles. Cars and other vehicles are too similar in terms of their technical features and quality. In addition, brand image has lost a certain amount of importance as a factor in purchasing decisions due to the **strained economic situation**. The factors now at the forefront of people's minds are aspects like value for money.

Now automotive brands are offering comparable performance features and quality and therefore losing the power of differentiation. Therefore, manufacturers are forced to make strategic changes to their brand policy and brand management. Ralf Kalmbach, Managing Director and automotive expert at Mercer Management Consulting, states that we will witness a clear trend from product orientation to customer orientation where **brand differentiation** is no longer based on technical differences but the total customer experience – including service (e.g. in the workshop) or other services (such as finance) offered by the manufacturer. These structural changes will be underpinned by altered sales and service structures. Hence the new Group Exemption Regulation in Europe allows independent multi-brand dealers to sell different automotive brands under the same roof. This will remove even more brand differentiation. It is primarily the suppliers to the brands who stand to benefit from these changes to the industry structure.

Market Power of OEMs

Globalization has changed the structure of the automotive industry enormously and given OEMs increasing power on the market. This is particularly evident in the growing cost pressure being experienced by automotive manufacturers, which are passed on to their suppliers. Many OEMs are cutting down on the number of suppliers they use and demanding, for instance, that they give up their original production sites and relocate to "supplier parks".

In these areas, a large number of suppliers are situated in a star pattern around the manufacturer, simplifying the OEM's processes greatly. Additionally, more and more corporate activities like **research and development** (R&D) are being outsourced to supplier companies. Therefore the entire supply industry is not only being forced towards growing consolidation as a result of increased cost pressure, Supplier companies are in fact facing a policy decision: to position themselves as a tier one supplier with high cost levels (where system integrators assemble components and handle delivery) or to submit to the cost pressure and operate as a tier two supplier (parts and components manufacturer) in order to appraise the business risk.

Ingredient Branding: A New Opportunity for Automotive Suppliers

The Ingredient Branding strategy is one way of reinforcing a company's long-term position in relation to OEMs and competitors. Note that although supplier companies may be responsible for up to 75% of the finished product, the consumer is scarcely aware of the contribution of the supplier to the production of the vehicle. Small wonder, then, that of the world's 15 biggest supplier companies (in terms of sales), only the **Bosch** brand is familiar to the majority of vehicle buyers. Brands like **Valeo** and **ZF Friedrichshafen** are largely unknown despite the fact that their products make a crucial contribution to the performance of the vehicle. Supplier components are permanently at risk of being substituted due to their brand anonymity. It follows that it must be in the interests of the supplier to enhance the status and profile of its brand. To date, however, **marketing policy measures** and activities on the part of suppliers have been limited to product and pricing policies to back up their sales policy. The most important step that they can take now to reinforce their brand value is to give the communication policy greater weight in the marketing mix. Only when consumers are aware of the brand and its benefits, a long-term **pull effect** will occur which can help to counter the substitutability of the products.

The advantages for the supplier primarily result from the multiple brand policy, which triggers rising consumer demand for particular component brands in the vehicle due to the pull effect. The pull effect increases the pressure on the manufacturer only to source certain components from a particular supplier. This growing consumer interest allows the supplier company not only to introduce a **price premium** but also to reduce the risk of being substituted as a result of structural changes on the market. Thus, Ingredient Branding underpins the corporate goals of a sustainable growth strategy

From the 25 Ingredient Brands we identified in this industry (see complete list in the appendix) most of them are from the USA, the country where the new marketing concept originated. The European component suppliers have recently started to apply the ingredient concept. So far, only a few have stated that they use the concept, despite the fact that many do, but most of them are actually not aware of the principles of the concept. There is one self-ingredient brand named Northstar from General Motors, where it is shown to customers that high performance engines can make a Cadillac into a "ferocious driving tool"[12]. In most cases the application started in late stages of the life cycle particularly during growth and maturity phase. The companies are very careful in their communication to the end user and try to avoid any conflicts with the large OEM partners. The power and brand awareness of the automotive OEM is very large and conflicts could create frictions with the OEM clients of the ingredient provider. In many cases the final brand owners sponsor the research and development work. But with complexity of components in relation to final product, which have high importance for functionality of final products, various concepts of InBrands have been successfully launched. The support of downstream companies is very low, but with the increased value added in the value chain the component position becomes more prominent

Fig. 26. Examples of automotive suppliers InBrands

and the brand strength for components could become very strong, e.g. with **Recaro** seats or **Brembo** brakes. The up-rising companies with the new Ingredient Branding concepts are normally midsize companies and their communication budget is limited, but some of them have shown success in terms of profit and growth in recent years. Examples of automotive supplier InBrands are given in Fig. 26.

There still remain a number of risks by applying an Ingredient Branding concept, which supplier companies need to take into account. The implementation requires high financial and time commitments. There is a need for end customer communication – something that many SMEs cannot invest without a certain degree of uncertainty. The clear allocation of responsibility for product defects poses another problem. If an individual defect occurs, well-known **supplier brands** run a much higher risk of being frozen out of future contracts by a large number of OEMs in order to avoid potential damage to the image of their automotive brand. Added to this is the fact that product defects or quality issues with the vehicle itself, for which the supplier is not responsible, can have a negative effect on the supplier's own brand image.

The automotive manufacturer, on the other hand, may benefit from an increase in brand value. OEMs can profit from the positive **image of supplier brands** and thus differentiate themselves from other manufacturers. Additionally, incorporating strong supplier brands can give the customer a positive image of the vehicle even at the launch stage for new models or special editions without entailing a significant increase in marketing costs. Table 6 shows the Top 15 automotive suppliers worldwide in terms of sales.

Manufacturers, like suppliers, face certain risks in this respect. For OEMs there is a risk that the image of their vehicle will be negatively influenced by product defects or quality issues in supplier components. But the automotive manufacturers' biggest concern is the proverbial brand inflation surrounding the vehicle.

The structure and performance of a vehicle depends on too many different and important supplier components, all of which are candi-

Table 6. Top 15 automotive suppliers worldwide in terms of sales

Ranking	Company	Sales in 2008 (in millions of US$)
1	Bosch	39 006
2	Denso	33 213
3	Magna Steyr	26 067
4	Bridgestone	23 356
5	Michelin	22 664
6	Delphi Automotive Systems	22 024
7	Aisin Seiki	21 982
8	Johnson Controls	21 887
9	Continental	21 078
10	Goodyear	19 664
11	Faurecia	17 359
12	Lear	15 995
13	Siemens (VDO + Osram)	15 184
14	ZF Group	14 915
15	ThyssenKrupp	14 893

dates for Ingredient Branding. This could result in a weakening or watering down of the manufacturer's own brand.

Fig. 27 shows how **brand inflation** might look in a car. We therefore need to ask ourselves the question: given the high number of different components, can consumers actually focus on any given supplier brand when choosing which car to buy? What priorities would they attach to the individual components when making their choice?

In an explorative study[13] carried out at the **Pforzheim University** in 2004, 83 people's familiarity with the major automotive suppliers was tested. 90% of the respondents were familiar with Bosch and 66% with Continental and Recaro. The least known brands were Delphi (21%) and TRW (12%). Male respondents were more familiar with all suppliers than females. It was striking, however, that the difference in familiarity between men and women was greatest for

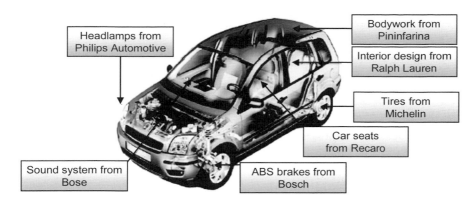

Fig. 27. Car powered by Ingredient Branding

Recaro and **Hella**. The difference for each of these companies was over 30%.

The key finding of this study was the willingness to spend more money on a car with components from a particular manufacturer. In response to the question "Would you be prepared to spend more on a car with components from a particular manufacturer?" 48% of respondents answered "Yes". There are of course variations within different customer segments. Amongst price-conscious consumers the willingness to spend more is at 42%; this rises to 59% for individuals with a high level of affinity. The consumer familiarity with automotive suppliers by gender is shown in Fig. 28.

Empirical findings such as these serve to confirm the approach of the world's largest automotive supplier Robert Bosch GmbH, which can rest assured that its investments in end customer marketing communication do indeed bear fruit. In 2005 Bosch celebrated 10 years of **ESP**.

Now that the company has succeeded in registering the acronym **ESP** as a trademark it can implement very specific and targeted marketing communication. As an example, Video clips are being broadcasted on Chinese television and POS activities are being implemented in Germany. Promotional campaigns are being run in the US for other products such as the **Common Rail** fuel injection system.

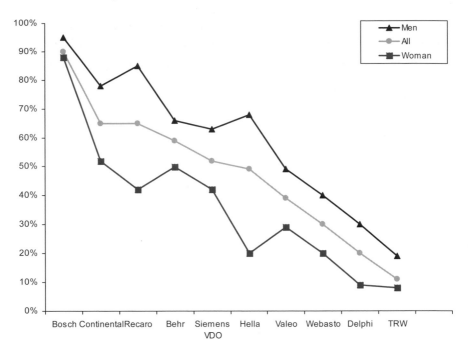

Fig. 28. Consumer familiarity with automotive suppliers

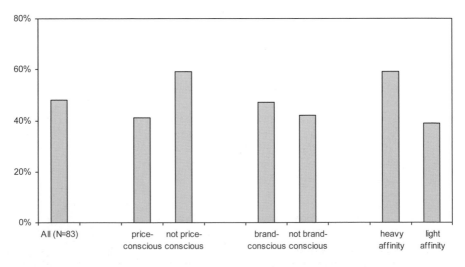

Fig. 29. Willingness to pay more for Ingredient Brands in a vehicle

The opportunities for Ingredient Branding are primarily linked to development-intensive components where close cooperation is required between supplier and OEM. Of course many components require this level of cooperation, but the same limitation we have seen before applies here: the more visible, tangible, noticeable and appealing the supplier's product is and the greater the choice as **special equipment** for the end customer, the more favorable the prospects for ingredient marketing and/or Ingredient Branding.[14]

Fig. 29 shows the willingness to pay more for Ingredient Brands in a vehicle by consumer's consciousness of price and brand as well as consumer affinity.

Bose – Better Sound Through Research

An example of the Ingredient Branding concept, which speaks for itself, is the Bose product strategy with the question, "How do you incorporate a concert hall in a car?" Bose collaborates with leading car manufacturers to develop customized, premier quality sound systems.

Bose sound systems are specifically designed to suit each individual car model and installed in the factory. Countless measurements are

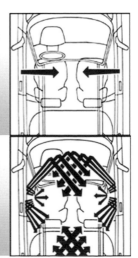

Conventional stereo sound:
The interior acoustics
are not taken into account.
Less sound distribution is compensated
for by turning up the volume.

The legendary Bose surround sound:
The sound system is optimally
adapted to the individual acoustics of the interior,
creating an unequalled music experience.

Fig. 30. The Bose "concert hall"[15]

made before the components are optimally positioned and the electronics fine-tuned to deliver balanced stereo sound. The Bose "concert hall" in a car is displayed in Fig. 30.

Bose has a unique profile in the Strategy Canvas. It distinguishes itself through high innovativeness and service offerings. But they also foster the importance of the brand and initiate the pull effect by end user communication.

With the help of other product offerings they also initiate customer experience possibilities, so that they are well known by the educated user and can distinguish themselves from the other car audio system suppliers (see Fig. 31).

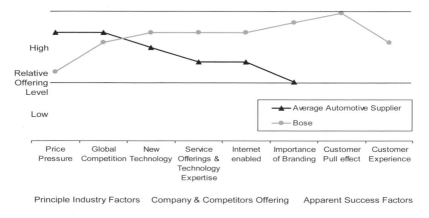

Fig. 31. Strategy canvas of Bose as automotive supplier

Brembo Car Brake Specialists

Together with its unique know-how in the manufacturing of braking systems for high performance vehicles, Brembo is able to guarantee top quality standards and the most advanced technology knowledge, making it a world market leader in its sector. Brembo is the natural choice for use in the most sophisticated sports vehicles and high-class sedan cars. Its skill ensures an unsurpassable performance level in the best cars produced in Europe, the USA and Japan today. It is distinguished by its vertical integration of the production process, embracing all the work phased and making the company the ideal partner for those who seek "state of the art" brake discs. Brembo use its own foundries in the industrial process, whereby bringing a thorough knowledge synergy in the optimization of the production cycle. The research and development phase is flanked by the testing phase, with static comfort test, on-the-road tests and dynamic tests on the test benches, finally arriving at the definition of the product and its successive marketing. Astonishingly, Brembo is not mentioning Ingredient Branding in any of their statement, despite the fact that they are applying the concept.

In early 2009 Brembo brakes were chosen for the first time by Hyundai as the standard equipment for the 2.0 L and 3.8 L engines of the new Genesis Coupe (Track version). Many other sports and high-end cars are equipped with Brembo brakes, the Ferrari F1 supplier. Brembo's performance brakes are a highly sought after product for car enthusiasts. Brembo equips many cars with its brakes like:

Alfa Romeo 159, Alfa Romeo Brera, Audi A8, Audi Pikes Peak, Aston Martin V8 Vantage, Land Rover Range Rover, Dodge Charger SRT – 8, Cadillac CTS – V, Ford Nuova Mustang V. Cobra, Nissan Z350 Roadster, Mercedes McLaren SLR, Mercedes Cl Class, Dodge Viper, Ford Shelby GT500 and many more.

Brembo was founded in 1961, and a few years later Brembo began manufacturing the first Italian brake discs for the aftermarket. Until then, discs had been imported from Great Britain. They started with 28 employees including the four founding partners. At present, **Brembo employs nearly 6000 people**, over 9% of these are engineers and product specialists working in research and development. The company currently operates in three continents with production plants in 11 countries; their commercial sites are also based in Sweden, France, and USA, while they sell their products in 70 countries in the world.

Unlike other brake manufactures the company is in continuous contact with customers. They started the communication through their offering of aftermarket products for racing enthusiasts and retrofit cars. The participation in racing, particularly in Formula1 created attention from many people. Now Brembo even "equips" cars and motorbikes of the most popular videogames with its brakes. The wide car fleet of these videogames shows how Brembo is held as a benchmark for tuning fans, which compete on different tracks. An example of Brembo products is shown in Fig. 32.

Fig. 32. Brembo products example

Brembo is one of the rare applications in cars where the logo and the unique red color are visible; the customers appreciate that very much. In 2008, for the third year, Brembo was the preferred brake system producer according to a survey carried out from the specialty magazine "Auto Motor und Sport". The enormous growth rate in the last 20 years really demonstrates the success of their marketing concepts. They clearly use all aspects of Ingredient Branding, but they do not use the term in their official statements.

It is also important to maintain a distinction between **B2B marketing** (e.g. training initiatives) and **B2C marketing**, which penetrates right through to the OEM's end customers. B2C marketing measures may still pose a significant challenge to suppliers, but they are becoming increasingly essential. The example of Bosch demonstrates how suppliers can still address their end customers even if the necessary conditions for a "supplier inside" are not in place. On all accounts, a supplier brand can be furthered by a well-executed **corporate identity**, effective brand communication and targeted cooperation between supplier and manufacturer.

5.2   Branding of Fibers in the Textile Industry

The textile industry would be virtually unimaginable without Ingredient Branding. Textile products occupy a crucial position in all aspects of life. Therefore, we generally attach a great deal of importance to their quality, focusing on aspects such as gentleness to the skin, durability and functionality. Manufacturers who operate an Ingredient Branding strategy address these consumer expectations by making clear at the actual point of purchase that they are behind the **key product components**. The USA has the most Ingredient Brands and the most sophisticated management teams. Almost 80% of all fiber InBrands comes from the States and the appropriate companies admit that they use this concept. Since the number of OEMs is huge and there are multiple applications, there is no need to hide or disguise what the component suppliers are doing. So far none of the OEM has started to develop their Self-Ingredient Brand.

Most of the Ingredient Brands started out with the invention of the product, early in their life cycle, but since many are now already twenty and more years in the market, they are reaching maturity stages and still use the InBranding concept. They are successful, even though or particularly because they have changed their owners (e.g. Lycra). Their communication to the final user is strongly supported by all kinds of media usage and their marketing communication budget is pretty high. Of course the functionality of the ingredient must be very high to create a base for differentiation, and the industry is continuously developing new innovative fibers. The down-stream companies do not support the component supplier's efforts in big ways, since many more steps in the value chain are needed to deliver the final product. A highly fragmented, often regionalized consumer market does not allow the OEM to support the InBrands heavily. Some actually do not need it due to their high brand recognition resulting in high profitability and enormous growth rates. One of the conceptual issues of this InBrands is the risk to run into the Fiesco trap. For example, Gore-Tex limits its InBranding partners and preserves exclusivity for the sake of not growing so fast, but have a secure partnership base. Other challenges may

Fig. 33. Selection of fiber InBrands
(All rights reserved by the logo owners)

emerge as we experience more maturity in the market. In Fig. 33 we show the logos of a few InBrands, most of them are well known around the globe.

One of these companies is Trevira, which established its company name as a brand and has been presenting its ingredients to the end consumer as quality features ever since the company was founded in 1956. Initially a division of Hoechst AG, Trevira spun off in 1998, and now belongs to Reliance Industries, India. Trevira is one of Europe's most important manufacturers of **polyester fibers**, with production sites in Germany, Belgium and Denmark and customers from the textile industry all over the world. Its core activities, however, are still in Europe. Trevira's product range comprises fibers for a wide range of applications. This includes high-quality clothing, sportswear, windproof and weatherproof clothing, flame-resistant household textiles, curtains, fleece materials and bedding.

The Trevira brand started life as a linguistic error and in truth this happened long before 1956, the year it was first used as a brand of polyester fiber. "Trevira" had already made its entry into the trademark register in 1932. This was at the hands of Adolf Kaempf,

works-manager of what was then an artificial silk factory in Bobingen, near Augsburg. Professor Paul Schlack who was himself
works-manager from 1946–1947, recalls: "Kaempf wanted to take
the trademark from the Latin name of the city of Augsburg, but actually this was not Augusta Treverorum, as he thought, (which is
Trier), but Augusta Vindelicorum. "While the mistake was cleared
up, the trademark stuck its use changing with the times. Sometimes
it was not used at all, until at the start of fifties." Schlack claimed it
for the factory in Bobingen for the process of approving "second-
hand goods". Ultimately it provided the name for the new polyester
fiber from Hoechst in 1956.

At the end of 1954 Bobingen factory, which had belonged to Hoechst
since 1952, started production of staple fibers in polyester, then the
last innovation in the still young man-made fiber market. For the
production launch on the German market, Hoechst initially distributed the new fiber in conjunction with Vereinigte Glanzstoffabriken
(later ENKA), under the Diolen trademark. The start of 1956 saw
the addition of continuous thread (filament yearns), initially under
the Trevira name. First production of the new fiber in 1956
amounted to just 5,000 tons, which was to become over a million
tons worldwide by the time the restructuring came about in 1996.
The Hoechst polyester division expanded the takeover of textures
Ernst Michalke and Kaj Neckelmann in Denmark (today Trevira
Neckelmann). In 1987 the American Celanese was added and after
reunification the man-made fiber combined Guben.

Following the fiber crisis at the end of the seventies the business
gradually changed from commodities to increasingly specialized
functional fibers and yarns. These included microfilaments for light
fabrics and fleece materials, low-pill fibers for outer and corporate
wear, elastic yarns, special types for non-woven and technical applications for the automotive industry and for hygiene products.
They came in small quantities rather than in mass production, but
they were high-value, essential and tailor-made.

All of the logos for the individual product brands have the same design. They are distinguished from other sub-brands solely by the ad-

dition of a name in the color associated with the particular sub-brand. The Trevira brand is omnipresent, ensuring that the end consumer always recognizes it no matter which end product they are buying. In order to get permission to use the logos for advertising purposes, Trevira's customers, yarn and fabric manufacturers are required to sign a **brand agreement**. For example, before approval can be issued for the sub-brand Trevira CS, fibers used for flame retardant materials, a material sample must be provided and subjected to a fire test. The material must be made of 100% flame-resistant Trevira. Applications to use other brands also require material samples to be tested, and a material must contain a specified minimum quantity of Trevira branded polyester before it can carry the brand name.

Assuming that the material passes the test, permission to use the brand is issued for a maximum of five years. The fabric manufacturer is then entitled to use the brand to label its textiles and also to use the company's advertising material. For each brand, Trevira provides display material, brochures, stickers, various product tags and customized sewn-on labels showing the material composition and care symbols. The fabric manufacturer can also pass on permission to its customers (e.g. clothing manufacturers or fabric wholesalers). These companies are also required to sign a brand agreement with Trevira, after which they are entitled to use the brand and the associated advertising material to promote their products.

One key benefit of Trevira's brand strategy is the advantage for the processing company, who can use the Trevira ingredients to distinguish their textiles from competing products and avoid being seen as identical or interchangeable. As previously mentioned, consumers value familiar brands as components of a textile product and will give preference to these brands over **no-name products**, particularly when it comes to clothing. In view of these consumer preferences, manufacturers of end products such as sportswear, bedding, soft furnishings, curtains etc. prefer to use branded ingredients in their fabrics.

Trevira takes advantage of the demand for high-quality, functional fabrics and fibers, and because this demand exists throughout

Europe, it is widely recognized. By employing a strategy of continuous cultivation of the brand and its sub-brands, Trevira has created a mark of quality that gives consumers confidence and also emotionalizes the products by highlighting the positive characteristics of the brands and the company itself.

In terms of print advertising, Trevira primarily focuses on its direct customers – yarn and textile manufacturers. Stylish, contemporary advertisements in European trade journals advertise the various sub-brands, drawing the attention of processing companies to the key advantages of the individual products. End consumers, traders and converters are only addressed directly in print through print advertisements produced jointly with Trevira's customers.

In line with the **multi-level marketing** concept, Trevira aims to offer its partners first-rate support throughout the textile value-added chain. For example, it provides an online database where users can find the addresses of all companies that process and utilize Trevira products, using various search criteria.[16] To help sales advisors, the company also provides the marketing material mentioned above such as brand brochures, certificates and expert reports on the fabric's tendency to repel dirt, ecological properties etc., as well as prepared sales arguments.

Trevira makes full use of the pull effect. The company's goal is to cultivate its brand image and make it recognizable and emotionally charged so that consumers will always ask for it, creating a **pull effect** with a strong incentive for retailers to stock products made with Trevira fibers. If these articles are found on the retailer's shop floor, end customers will also learn about the advantages and benefits of the high-tech fibers through the retailer and customers sales advisors, increasing demand yet further.

Textiles containing Trevira are labeled in different ways to attract the attention of (potential) customers. **Fabric manufacturers and converters** who have their own website often include a reference to their partnership with Trevira in addition to their own patterns and models. Interior design stores, for example, often display the Trevira logo conspicuously on swatches of upholstery fabric or samples of curtain material. In mail order catalogues the brand features beside clothing and curtains – sometimes in the shape of the logo, sometimes with the name simply being stated as one of the raw materials (e.g. 100% Trevira).

Trevira's direct communication with end customers is limited almost exclusively to shared advertisements. The aim is to develop the end customer's awareness of the brand through continual exposure to it in brochures, swatches in retail stores, mail order catalogues and so on. Customer sales advisors are given the very best support with targeted sales aids. The task of addressing customers and **communicating the advantages** of Trevira high-tech fibers therefore belongs almost exclusively to sales advisors, whose job it is to increase the demand for the products.

The reason for this is that Trevira is the first link in a very long value-added chain.[17] Firstly, the Trevira fibers are spun into yarn, and then woven by a weaving company, then printed by a printing company and then converted or stitched if necessary by textile manufacturers before they are finally presented to the end consumer on the shop floor. In the context of a pull strategy, communicating with all the downstream stages of production is highly complex. It may be assumed that Trevira perceives the processing and selling stages of the chain as being the most important target for its advertising and communication, and therefore concentrates on these rather than on promotional efforts aimed at end customers. For the time being, at least, if Trevira were to adopt the general trend towards all-embracing Ingredient Branding, this situation would change, resulting in more intensive **communication** with the **end consumer**.

Ingredient Branding at Sympatex

Sympatex® Technologies specializes in high-tech components for functional clothing and accessories. The company develops products that combine various qualities and functions in many different ways.

Therefore it does not offer just one Sympatex product but eight, catering for individual protection and comfort. Sympatex guarantees breathability in all its products. Its individually designed products are also windproof and waterproof and offer other qualities such as heat reflection and the removal of moisture from the garment.

The German company Sympatex Technologies GmbH was founded in 1980. Back then, no one would have guessed that Sympatex would become an established branded product with numerous applications, especially since, in the early 1980s, the synthetic fiber industry was experiencing only modest sales growth

Initially, Sympatex opted to concentrate on a product that had already been developed: a polymer made of Copolyetherester, which, as once hoped, would provide a more environmentally friendly alternative to cellophane wrapping in the food industry. But Sympatex carried out extensive research into the waterproof and windproof polymer and came up with the innovative idea of producing a membrane with a non-porous structure.

A **membrane** is the same weight as a standard letter (80 grams) and is one hundredth of a millimeter thick. The next stage was to produce a laminate, i.e. a composite of membrane and carrier material, since the membrane was difficult to convert on its own. The decision to manufacture only the membrane in-house but not the laminate proved to be the right one, since it allowed the company to use the knowledge of several specialist firms and work collaboratively with them.

The first company to make the laminate was Ploucquet. Sympatex now belongs to the Ploucquet group of companies. The research department there evidently recognized the additional benefits of this type of product for the clothing industry, and the first Sympatex jacket was developed in collaboration with the textile technology department. In 1986 the company achieved its major breakthrough with this everyday wearable jacket. Since then, the Sympatex brand has been a synonym in Europe for functional clothing systems and accessories.

Meanwhile, the marketing concept was being developed. To create the right parameters for Ingredient Branding, the brand had to be presented and identified on the end product. The company began by choosing the "Sympatex" name and designing the blue triangle, an image that – with continuing minor changes – has continued to represent function in clothing to the present day[18]. This form of Branding makes the brand familiar and highly recognizable. It becomes associated with quality, so when the triangle is displayed on a jacket it justifies the higher price asked by the manufacturer.

The concept was based on the idea of a **pool of brands**, the basis on which the company steered all marketing activities surrounding the trademark. These activities were largely financed by revenue from the membrane. The company was now in a position to launch its own brand image. Traders responded positively to the concept, recognizing the advantages of the new product and presenting it to end consumers as a **quality product** that would pay for itself. So everyone involved was able to benefit from the successful marketing concept. The fame and image of the Sympatex brand soared, which in turn served to increase differentiation from the competition.

The company operates a range of business development programs. In addition to brand marketing and public relations the company offers a wide range of effective, high-quality decorative materials such as product-specific information packages, Sympatex light boxes, functional shoe models etc., to help its partners sell products and communicate a uniform image. Using the slogan "The brand that makes other brands strong", Sympatex organizes national point-of-sale campaigns in partnership with retailers and offers **retailer and sales advisor training**. The company maintains an extensive, integrated public image from the point of sale to trade fairs and print advertising Adverts aimed at specific target audiences are featured in specialist publications like Brigitte, Runner's World and Outdoor Magazine, conveying the Sympatex message: "2004 sees Sympatex back on the hottest pages – building sustained success for itself and its partners". Promotional campaigns run all year in well-known department stores like **Macy's, Sears, Galleria, etc.** Table 7 shows the brand value of Sympatex.

Table 7. Brand value of Sympatex

Sympatex	Brand value
Market Share Shoes Jackets	24.0% 45.0%
Familiarity (graded)	67.7%
Satisfaction	98.0%
Ownership	27.0%

Sympatex issues licenses to material converters. This has two advantages: firstly, licensing allows the partner to participate in the marketing program and benefit from joint advertising. Secondly, it binds the material converter to comply with stringent processing guidelines and therefore guarantee the product quality associated with the Sympatex triangle. This is an essential aspect of successful Ingredient Branding. This **quality assurance system**, which applies to all product stages, is therefore one of the most highly developed in the European textile market. It gives the end consumer a guarantee of consistently high quality, and it works: within a short space of time Sympatex has created a brand with a recognition rating of around 70%.

The **role model** for membrane clothing in Europe carries a great deal of responsibility on its shoulders, because a brand has to deliver quality to its customers and licensees. For this reason, Sympatex monitors its products at every stage of production. To do this the manufacturer uses a wide range of tests: spray tests, abrasion tests, simulated walking and pressure tests. The products are also tested in rain machines (the Enhanced Dynamic Garment Rain Test) and are required to pass skin model tests. Even on the shop floor, random samples of the products are purchased and tested for the required quality. This is the only way to ensure consistent quality and value, which are indispensable requirements of this particular marketing strategy.

Active marketing and **consumer-oriented innovation management** are at the heart of the Sympatex Technologies philosophy, and they are what make the company so successful. Customers associate Sympatex with high quality and they have trust into the brand. Because of this, they actively seek out functional clothing featuring this brand (the pull effect). In contrast to the branded ingredient clothing, "second-choice" clothing, without branded components, is rejected. Retailers sell garments with the 'blue triangle' even without a great deal of persuasive selling, and at a higher price than they would get for a comparable no-name product "Sympatex stands for continuity, quality and the constant search for improvement[19]

The Gore-Tex Component Brand

A fierce competitor of Sympatex is Gore-Tex. W. L. Gore & Associates, Inc was founded in 1958 by Wilbert L. (Bill) and Genevieve Gore. Their son Bob Gore, a chemical engineer, also joined the company, which today has become a global market leader in the application of fluoropolymers.[20]

By stretching polytetrafluoroethylene (PTFE), Bob Gore discovered a fluoropolymer, a very solid, micro porous material with a whole range of new properties. Today, this material is marketed all over the world under the trade name Gore-Tex and thousands of new products have been developed on the basis of this very material. Today the company manufactures in the US, Scotland, Germany and Japan. Various products have been developed under the Gore-Tex brand name. Gore-Tex is used in:

- Medical implants in vascular and heart surgery, dental surgery, oral and maxillofacial surgery, orthopedic surgery and neurosurgery
- Flour polymer fibers, e.g. packaging yarns, fibers, dental floss

- Industrial membrane technology, e.g. industrial filtration, micro-filtration, ventilation

- Advanced dielectric materials for electronics

- Functional textiles

In 1969, W. L. Gore & Associates launched a product that revolutionized the textile industry and created a whole new market segment, the outdoor clothing segment: the Gore-Tex membrane. The membrane's key feature is its pores, which are 20,000 times smaller than a drop of water but 700 times larger than a molecule of water vapor. This makes Gore-Tex laminates – where the Gore-Tex membrane is laminated with textile components (the outer fabric and sometimes the lining) – permanently waterproof as well as windproof but also extremely breathable.

The Gore-Tex membrane has undergone continual development and many new applications have since been discovered. Even today, it is still the keystone of the success of functional clothing. The market model adopted by W. L. Gore & Associates is that of Ingredient Branding[21], although the company actually accomplishes a lot more on the market than a classic Ingredient Brand.

It was a long road to the company's current leading position in the textile and clothing industry. The Gores first founded the company in Newark, Delaware. Bill Gore had previously been working as a chemical engineer at DuPont where he was developing a concept to improve the conductivity of electric cables for the incipient computer industry. When this project came to an end he decided to realize his vision of product and corporate culture in his own company.

Working from the basic conviction that people can work most creatively in a team with equal rights, Gore invented the lattice organization. This model consists of small units with flat hierarchies where commitment, self-responsibility and direct communication between associates lead to success. The model is based on four guiding principles:[22]

Freedom: Every associate has the freedom to grow his or her own skills.

Commitment: A voluntary commitment, as opposed to following orders from a "superior".

Fairness: Every individual endeavors to be fair in all his or her actions.

Waterline: An analogy. You can only make a hole in the boat (the company) below the waterline (e.g. take a critical decision or action that could affect the success, reputation or financial survival of the company) by agreement with the people in the boat (the people involved, the experts).

The company's business activities are still based on the processing of PTFE. Both this year and last year, the company was named for the eighth time as one of the 100 best companies to work for by Forbes magazine in the US – today it ranks second. In Britain, Gore was voted best company for the second time by the Sunday Times (having come in second in 2005) and it came in amongst the top ten in both the Financial Times competition and Germany's Capital competition for best employer.

The introduction of the "guaranteed to keep you dry" promise in 1989 was the most important turnaround in the business model. [23]. Up till then Gore was primarily engaged in selling its intermediate product, the "functional textile", but as of this point the company took on direct responsibility vis-à-vis the end consumer for the functionality of Gore-Tex products in the finished garment or shoe.[24]

The change in business model came about at a time when the European textile industry was experiencing an economic slump. There was falling purchasing power on the market. Declining sales and growing cost pressure, resulting in minimal profit margins or even losses, prompted a relocation of production to Eastern Europe and job cuts in the textile industry in Western Europe.

Gore's introduction of a comprehensive consumer guarantee triggered a fundamental change in the relationship between upstream and downstream production. Gore issues licenses to partner manufacturers and only allows material to be converted at certified production facilities. Throughout the value-added chain the company concentrates on the quality of the component as a functional textile and on ensuring that the consumer is aware of its capabilities. This includes developing specific design and production methods for clothing and shoes that make the product promise reality. In addition, comprehensive testing techniques are applied at all stages of the value-added chain.

One decisive factor in the success of the Gore-Tex guarantee was the fact that consumers can see the materials on the shop floor and identify the Gore-Tex brand on the end product. This was accomplished using a brand label: the black and gold diamond and the word Gore-Tex. With the colored hang tag with its professional-looking design and the word displayed on the end product; consumers could recognize a Gore-Tex garment immediately. Everyone involved (the converter, the retailer, the consumer) benefits from the Ingredient Branding strategy. The components that go into the production of the functional material are also part of this strategy. The company maintains a very close partnership with its raw material suppliers in a bid to improve the characteristics of the raw materials and therefore continuously optimize the Gore-Tex laminate.

Expert design also plays an essential role. The company works with designers and fashion design schools around the world to create new trends and introduce innovations to the market.

In the late 1990s, for example, ARC'TERYX developed an innovative product design for mountain sports clothing based on Gore-Tex functional materials. The minimalist and functional design created fresh impetus for growth in the industry and triggered a new wave of innovation in mountaineering. Fig. 34 shows how the Gore-Tex membrane works.

The Gore-Tex membrane is breathable because the pores are 700 times larger than a molecule of water vapour, making it easy for the vapour to escape.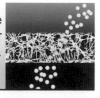

The Gore-Tex membrane is waterproof because the pores are 20 000 times smaller than water droplets, preventing water from penetrating the material.

Gore-Tex membrane is windproof because the complex structure of the stretched membrane stops the wind from getting through.

Fig. 34. How the Gore-Tex membrane works[25]

The Gore-Tex fabric system is supported by a wide network. Gore-Tex products are available around the world in many different variants. The materials are used in clothing, footwear, gloves and mittens for mountaineering, hiking, skiing, motorcycling, water sports, golf and also everyday wear. This diversification results in relatively broad distribution and close links with retailers, while stopping short of an actual business relationship. The company's broad presence allows it to advertise Gore-Tex products at the point of sale using promotional material and presentations (display windows, test displays, shop-in-shop solutions etc.) The media and sports professionals are also part of the network, helping to raise the profile of the Gore-Tex brand even more.

W. L. Gore & Associates was founded on the principle that every associate is entitled to develop and grow. The figures bear witness to the success of the innovative technology company: In 2004/2005 Gore generated a turnover of around US$1.8 billion and employed 7,300 people at 45 sites around the world. In Germany the company employs more than 1,100 people at three sites covering four corporate divisions.

These divisions are:

- **Electronic Products,** special cables and cable assemblies for specific applications, e.g. aerospace
- **Medical Products,** e.g. vascular replacement for minimally invasive treatment
- **Fabrics,** branded functional textiles for sportswear, leisure-wear, work wear and protective clothing
- **Industrial Products,** e.g. for the membranes in fuel cell technology, and special fibers and fabrics for architectural applications

A brand profile study by Stern magazine in 2004 revealed that of the 800 brands from 19 different industries surveyed,[26] Gore-Tex had the strongest emotional bond after Nokia. Small wonder, then, that the majority of leading clothing manufacturers now use Gore-Tex in their product ranges.

The key features of the Gore-Tex brand are:

- Commands a price premium, which also has the effect of enhancing the perceived quality of the end product,
- Reduces the complexity of the end product by focusing on the Ingredient Brands, thus increasing differentiation,
- Simplifies the purchase decision because of the trust created by Ingredient Branding,
- Reduces advertising costs through the use of joint activities.

In a world where consumers are overwhelmed by different products, people like being able to place their trust in a familiar brand with which they already have a positive experience. This creates loyalty to the Ingredient Brand, which in turn is transferred to the end products of other manufacturers and other types of products. Thus, for example, end consumers who are happy with their Gore-Tex gloves may well opt for a product containing Gore-Tex when it comes to buying walking shoes.[27] Another advantage is the fact that the products are widely available. In Europe alone, more than 24,000 retailers' stock products made with Gore-Tex. There are estimated to be over 100 million Gore-Tex products currently in use around the world.

Innovation is of tremendous importance to the long-term success of the brand. Since the mid-1990s the company has launched at least one new product per season, including new products for its other brands, Windstopper® fabrics and Airvantage® adjustable insulation. The brand's high profile and technological sophistication give it a very specific position on the market. The integrated communication process and the way the brand is anchored in the value-added chain are crucial elements: they ensure that consumers ask for innovations while the media writes about them. Fig. 35 shows a selection of brands owned by W. L. Gore & Associates.

Fig. 35. Selection of brands owned by W. L. Gore & Associates

One key aspect of the brand's success is the fact that the company collaborates with its partners in the value-added chain to create a direct pull effect on the part of consumers. This pull effect strategically differentiates the brand from the competition and maneuvers it into a premium position on the market. Permanent innovation and a solid anchoring of the value-added chain keep this process going. In 2003, the company documented this complex process, which has long been a global one. As far as advertising is concerned, Gore-Tex collaborates with the likes of rucksack manufacturer **Deuter** and **Giant**, a manufacturer in the cycling sector. For **sales promotion** purposes,

Gore-Tex maintains partnerships with glove manufacturers.[28] The company also uses TV advertising and its most **famous Gore-Tex advertisement** was broadcast in the 1990s:

> A young couple is traveling through the Australian out-back in their 4x4 when they come across a kangaroo on the road. The driver only just manages to brake in time to avoid hitting the animal. He gets out and consider-ately drapes his Gore-Tex jacket over the distressed animal. His partner finds this hilarious and starts taking photos of the scene. Then she asks him to take a picture of her with the kangaroo. As she hands him the camera, the kangaroo bounces off with the jacket – with the car keys still in the pocket. The couple can only watch as the animal disappears from sight.

This memorable ad made a lasting impression on its audience and played a key part in popularizing Gore-Tex. Gore-Tex acts in accordance with its motto, "We test inside our labs and outside in your world"'. Moreover, the company sponsors various kinds of sports.

The current strength of the Gore-Tex brand is the result of the "brand in a brand" concept. It has now reached stage 2 (breakthrough), which means that customers will specifically look for[29] Gore-Tex clothing or shoes and only attach secondary importance to the name of the actual manufacturer. What began as anonymous components have now become a "brand personality". Gore now has an obliga-tion to maintain the excellent quality of its Ingredient Brand. There-fore, direct contact with end consumers is given high priority. This has resulted repeatedly in new waves of innovation and growth in the textile industry over the past 25 years.

Today, the functional clothing market is a successful, growing seg-ment in an industry that is fighting declining sales and margins on virtually every front. The Gore-Tex brand has raised the company value to a level it would not have achieved as a pure B2B company, a value estimated by external sources to amount to nine figures in

US dollars. In our estimation, this positive trend has medium- to long-term prospects. Other Ingredient Brand suppliers must take all possible stages to avoid a "Fiesco-Effect".[30]

Ingredient Brands of Invista

Before moving on from InBranding fiber, we would like to direct your attention to the company Invista, the brand owner of several brands of which the most famous are Lycra and Stainmaster (formerly owned by DuPont). The company and the brands have been owned by Koch Industries since 2004. They are the largest privately owned company with more than $90 billion.

In early 2008, the leading fiber producer Invista, introduced a new global campaign for its flagship Lycra fiber brand, entitled "Some Clothes Love You Back™." Fig. 36 shows InBrands of the textile fiber company Invista.

Fig. 36. InBrands of the textile fiber company Invista

The launch of this new campaign marks the culmination of a year long process for Invista and London based advertising agency, Fallon. A single trade and consumer campaign has been developed to build on the unique understanding the Lycra brand fiber has of how consumers want their clothes to move, look and feel. The campaign was featured across an extensive range of media around the world, as well as online.

In Ingredient Branding fashion, the new campaign builds on consumer insights collated by Think-tank research, which demonstrated that consumer understanding of Lycra fiber as a trusted brand with a strong emotional connection to consumers led to its preference by more than 60% of consumers polled over plain "stretch" options and recognized by 90% of consumers globally.

The Lycra fiber brand campaign differentiates Lycra fiber through particular emphasis on the way clothes make a woman look and feel. Consumer testing of the campaign across four continents has shown that campaign taps into a strong consumer love for their favorite clothes and the way that those clothes make them feel.

The campaign also wants to demonstrate that Lycra fiber remains a fiber of choice among leading names within the fashion and textile industry. **Zac Posen**, denim brands, **True Religion, JBrand**, and lingerie icons **La Perla and Chantell**, are all featured in the initial images for the "Some Clothes Love You Back" campaign.

Lycra, continuing in its role as one of the driving forces behind the development of the fashion industry, the **Lycra** brand was a focus in **Invista's** joint promotion in China with Dragon TV, sponsoring the Chinese pop talent TV show; **"Lycra My Hero"**. The **Lycra** brand has come to mean much more to the Chinese consumer than a mere textile Ingredient Brand that makes clothing comfortable. It has come to symbolize fashion, innovation, and creativity, driving entire new fashion movements in the market. As part of **Invista's** long-term strategy in promoting the **Lycra** brand, the company sponsors innovative, highly rated television programs that introduce the latest fashion trends and promote a modern lifestyle to the

Chinese people. All these marketing campaigns impress on the customer the **Lycra** brand and arouse incentives to buy clothes made of **Lycra** and clothes with a small triangle tag hanging inside, printed with the **Lycra** logo. This pull effect greatly motivated sales of those clothes made of Lycra and more customers preferred to buy Lycra to other "real brands" of clothes. Lycra's InBranding strategy and pull marketing communication brings both great return to Lycra and its partners.

The strategy canvas of Lycra shows clearly the difference of the value offerings and the apparent success factors.

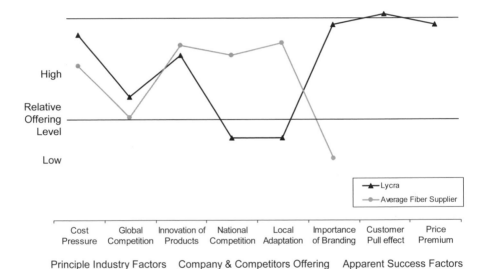

Fig. 37. Strategy canvas in the fiber industry with Lycra

How an Ingredient Brand Can Strengthen Market Position

The examples of fiber InBrands showed clearly the benefits of the application of the Ingredient Branding concept in an overcrowded market. They capitalized on a unique differentiation effort to break away from competitors. Other companies in similar sectors could follow the example of the mentioned successful fiber companies and implement an Ingredient Branding strategy to get into a better market position. Examples are Turkish cotton and textile companies that could achieve a competitive advantage over cheaper Asian textiles by branding their high quality products.[31]

5.3 Glass as an Essential Component

Human beings began manufacturing glass around 3,500 BC. The key ingredients of glass – sand, potash and lime – have not changed over the millennia.[32] Glass is generally an inorganic product of fusion that solidifies without crystallizing. Chemist Gustav Tammann defined it more simply as a super cooled solidified liquid.[33] The unique characteristics of different types of glass are achieved by adding pigments and pacifiers and through the use of different production and finishing techniques, making it one of the most versatile materials known.[34]

Because there are many hundred different types of glass, and thousands of glass formulas, it is by no means easy to categorize glass into groups. The most common typology of glass relates to its chemical composition. Glass can also be categorized according to its purpose or form.[35]

To simplify matters, and to avoid excessive chemical or scientific references, the authors will distinguish the different types of glass according to the traditional divisions in the glass industry: flat glass, flat glass finishing and processing, container glass, recycled and special glass, crystal and table glassware and mineral fibers. The crystal and table glassware sector of the glass industry is of little interest in this context as it consists almost exclusively of end products (for table and kitchen use) and not industrial goods.

The world gross production value of the glass industry was $82 billion in 2006, and had the following product groups (see Fig. 38). Just three companies: NSG Group, with the Pilkington brand from Great Britain, **Ashai** (Japan) and **Saint-Habain** (France) are dominating the industry. These conglomerates supply about 60% of the world glass demand. Over the last 20 years, the industry was growing faster than the GDP and is expected to grow over 4% per year for the next decade. Glass is a **fascinating material**, particularly since it is so versatile and can be used in numerous different applications. The significant potential for innovation in the use of glass is due not only to its chemical composition but also to a large extent the development of new areas of application. No longer simply a cheap commodity, glass has come to form the basis of the cutting-edge technologies of our time, including photonics, nanotechnology and bionics.[36]

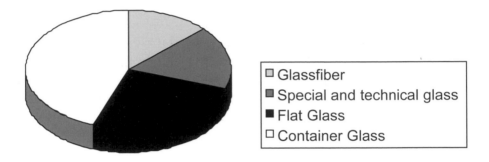

□ Glassfiber
■ Special and technical glass
■ Flat Glass
□ Container Glass

Fig. 38. World glass gross production 2006: $82.6 billion

Structure of an Ingredient Brand in the Glass Industry

The key requirement for a successful Ingredient Branding strategy is that the components must be an essential part of the end product and therefore have a positive impact on the success and/or perceived quality of the end product. Only when they are visible or tangible in some way to the end consumer, or when they are imbued with an essential importance by multi-level marketing, it does make sense to implement an Ingredient Branding strategy.[37] This means that the buyer must be able to experience a real or subjective added value through the use of additional Branding.

Another requirement is high **potential for innovation** or a comparative competitive advantage on the part of Ingredient Brands. In addition, it is virtually impossible to implement an Ingredient Branding strategy without the collaboration of downstream stages in the selling process and the market. The end product manufacturer must agree to a collaborative push-pull strategy and must be willing to mark the end product clearly and meaningfully with the Ingredient Brand and inform end customers about the associated product benefits.

We will restrict ourselves to examining the following sectors, which are the most important with almost three quarters of the glass industry production: flat glass (production, finishing and processing of flat glass) and container glass. A more comprehensive analysis covering all areas of the industry in sufficient detail would far exceed the scope of this book. The almost unlimited possibilities in terms of product design and the **areas of application** in other sectors of industry, particularly in the case of recycled and special glass, make it impossible to offer any general statements on the applicability of Ingredient Branding strategies.

Flat Glass

In this sector, it is possible to proceed with the assumption that the glass or glass product represents a fundamental part of the end product (e.g. furniture glass, safety glass, insulating glass, solar glass, heat-insulating glass, and mirror glass). As mentioned above, glass generally offers very high **potential for innovation**. The industry is constantly looking for new and improved material compositions, particularly for safety glass, insulating glass and solar glass. Some of the world's leading manufacturers have succeeded in developing a new self-cleaning glass. This unlikely-sounding achievement is the result of intensive research combined with the powers of nature. Other examples include anti-theft glass for vehicles and electro chrome glass that regulates the transparency of car windscreens electronically.

However, there are many manufacturers in the flat glass industry who produce absolutely identical, interchangeable products. In these cases, careful thought would have to be given to the question of whether an Ingredient Branding strategy (aimed directly at the end customer without any involvement of the end product manufacturer), in other words a **processing brand strategy**, would be worth the investment. Flat glass suppliers in India, for example, have been engaged in an aggressive brand war for the past two years. The main companies operating in the industry there are Modiguard, Saint Gobain and Asahi. Their argument is similar to that in the consumer goods industry: if the products are essentially the same, the only way to raise your product above the rest is through Branding and image. The communication channels and design elements used by the companies to differentiate their products are discussed in more detail in the chapter on "Building Brand Appeal" in the publication on B2B brand management[38].

Container Glass Industry

If we point out the successful Ingredient Brand **Tetra Pak** as a model for Ingredient Branding in the packaging industry, we might be tempted to believe that it must be possible to implement this type of strategy in the container glass industry, too. Glass packaging is often a key **component of a product** and the potential for innovation, particularly in terms of form, design and color, is relatively high. For many drinks manufacturers, however, glass packaging is already part of their brand personality. This is illustrated by the fact that many branded products in the food, drink and cosmetics industry are recognized solely by their glass packaging (e.g. **Coca-Cola, Chanel No.5 perfume).**

In the authors' view, the possibility of implementing Ingredient Branding in the container glass industry can therefore be largely ruled out. In order to establish a successful Ingredient Brand, the packaging manufacturer would have to take on responsibility for the part that constituted the **potential for differentiation**. The drinks manufacturer, however, would not benefit from any added value and would therefore have no incentive to participate in an Ingredient Brand. In the authors' view the classic product of the container glass industry, the standardized glass bottle, does not offer the required potential for differentiation. The product is interchangeable with any other and does not offer added value.

In the context of an Ingredient Branding strategy, manufacturers can choose from three basic alternatives: a single brand strategy, a product group strategy and a branded house strategy. In addition to these pure forms it is also possible to combine these concepts, particularly for the purposes of Ingredient Branding. The following fig. 39 shows the design requirements operated by Schott AG for Ingredient Brands. The Schott company brand is associated with the relevant **product brand**.

Fig. 39. Packaging design for Ingredient Brands at Schott

The circle represents the "O" from the name "Schott". For components without an individual brand the company simply uses the slogan "Powered by Schott" (see Fig. 39). Only very few product brands from the industrial goods industry and the glass industry are familiar to the general public. Ceran® from Schott is one of the few exceptions. We will elaborate on this in a case study in the next chapter. It is noticeable that the choices of name and brand design are dominated by a factual, objective approach. [39] Many brand names reflect the key characteristics of the particular glass product (heat-resistant, fireproof etc.): Pyrex® from Corning, Pyran® from Schott, and Saint Gobain from Glass Pyroswiss®.

In contrast to Schott Ceran, the other brands are marketing their products directly to the final consumer as a separate brand or even license the brand to other companies. Pyrex from Corning sold off its consumer products division in 1998 as World Kitchen but retained the Pyrex brand name, licensing it to World Kitchen and other companies that produce Pyrex-branded cookware (e.g. Newell Rubbermaid's Newell Cookware Europe). The brand in Europe, the Middle East and Africa is currently owned by ARC International who acquired the European business in early 2006 from Newell Rubbermaid who in turn had acquired it from Corning in the 1990s.

Carefully selected images and emotions can trigger a sympathetic response. Even in the glass industry, where manufacturers assail their customers with a flood of chemical data, specifications and characteristics, they are able to effectively differentiate themselves and trigger **"key experiences"** in the customer. This emotionalization can, of course, be extrapolated to Ingredient Brands. The flat glass manufacturer Modiguard for example, ran a campaign using analogies from the animal kingdom and the natural world and successfully created an emotional link to its activities, which could hardly have been generated using the company's general or specific competencies as a selling point.[40]

Saint Gobain glass is another example from the Indian flat glass market that used a TV advertising campaign focusing on the "clarity" of glass. The campaign advertises Saint Gobain glass in a purely emotional way without going into detail on the characteristics of the glass.

In this difficult B2B environment, Branding is the norm and the final product manufacturers are selling the products with their retail brand. Only a few companies are sticking it out, we identified six brands (see Fig. 40: Examples of glass industry InBrands).

On of them is the Schott AG in Mainz, Germany. They follow the general industry pattern but in a few instances they were able to apply the Ingredient Branding concept and reach reasonable success. As already mentioned Schott Ceran is the brand, which reaches the customers and creates the demand-pull. In Chapter 6 we will describe the brands history and approach in detail in a case study. Another example is Swarovski Elements with its InBrand Crystallized, which we will discuss in the following section in detail.

The brands are not particularly concentrated in one country, but Europe seems to be the center of gravity for the companies in this industry, working out innovative marketing concepts. None of these companies adapted a self-ingredient brand concept. Since the glass industry has been around for many thousands of years, none of the companies started in an early stage of a product life cycle. Rather, they started in the maturity phase and added innovations. The added product functions and the complexity of components in relation to partners are not very high, so supplier companies in the glass industry do not get much support from their down-stream partners. The industry relies on them and their degree of value added is growing. They not only provide the raw products but also product modules. In the meantime, they have built up brand strength that overshadows the OEM brands due to their size and strength and the fragmentation of the industry. The maturity of the industry gives stability to the business but does not create huge growth rates. Therefore, successful Branding concepts can create good returns. With the digitalization of the camera industry the optical lenses producer identified a new field of application for their glass lenses. Since they did not have the capability to compete in this field, they licensed and branded their products in these cameras, camcorders, etc. Samples are shown in Fig. 40.

Fig. 40. Examples of glass industry InBrands

CRYSTALLIZED™ – Swarovski Elements

Swarovski, established more than 114 years ago, is the world's leading manufacturer and supplier of cut crystal. The company saga began in 1895, when founder Daniel Swarovski invented a **revolutionary machine,** which made it possible to industrially cut crystal to a superior level of perfection and precision than achieved before by traditional manual methods. Three years later, he founded the *Swarovski Company* in Wattens, Austria, which has remained fully independent ever since. The company is currently run by the fourth and fifth generation descendants of founder Daniel Swarovski. In 2008, 23.900 people worldwide contributed to a consolidated group turnover of € 2.52 billion.

Swarovski is a globally recognized brand that has made innovation, trend research, creative products and product perfection its hallmarks. These are all perpetuated elements of the philosophy of the company's founder, Daniel Swarovski. His motto "to constantly improve what is good" and vision to "use crystal to bring joy to man" still form the core philosophy that drives the company today. *Swarovski* stands for **exacting workmanship, quality and creativity** all over the world.

Their product range comprises almost everything related to cut crystal: Crystal components as well as crystal objects, crystal jewelry, and crystal accessories. With the brands *Swarovski* (jewelry, accessories, watches, crystal objects), CRYSTALLIZED™ – *Swarovski Elements* (cut crystal elements), ENLIGHTENED™ – *Swarovski Elements* (genuine or synthetic gemstones), *Tyrolit* (grinding, cutting, sawing, drilling and dressing tools and machines), *Swareflex* (reflectors for road safety), and *Swarovski Optik* (high-quality precision optical equipment) the company has also obtained leading market positions in related areas.

Swarovski covers both consumer and business customers with one brand. The corporate division of crystal components is one of the major B2B areas. *Swarovski* supplies crystal components and semi-finished products to the fashion, accessories, jewelry, interior design, and lighting industries. With a collection of more than 100,000 stones and a wide range of pre-fabricates, it is a competent partner for businesses that use cut crystal in their products.

In 2006, the company introduced "CRYSTALLIZED™ – *Swarovski Elements*" as the product brand for Swarovski's loose cut crystal elements. This was the first time that the department of crystal components directed any marketing activity directly at the end user. The company thus created the label "Made with CRYSTALLIZED™- *Swarovski Elements*" in response to the demand for a visible proof of quality, authenticity and integrity. The label clearly represents a guarantee of the highest quality and perfection in the manufacture of loose cut crystal elements.

In the **complex** shopping **environment** of today consumers are confronted with a variety of choices where strong brands can provide clear direction of what they stand for. Brands therefore can give consumers the important assurance that they have made the right decision. Since the label "Made with CRYSTALLIZED™ – *Swarovski Elements*" is a symbol of quality and prestige for both *Swarovski's* business partners and for its consumers, it makes CRYSTALLIZED™ products even more attractive and provides further arguments for the added value. Furthermore, the traditional and approved core competencies of *Swarovski* – innovation and diversity, product and service quality – are emphasized which further differentiates the brand from its competition.

Due to of the limited physical Branding possibilities, the company decided to go its own way and designed special tags. Depending on the end product of fashion items, jewelry, accessories, and home decor the label can be a high-class silver metal tag, an off-white colored paper tag or sticker that testifies the authenticity of the crystals. The "Made with CRYSTALLIZED™ – *Swarovski Elements*" label is the customer's assurance that only CRYSTALLIZED™ – *Swarovski Elements* have been used in the production of the end product. To officially certify this assurance, each label carries a specific number certified by *Swarovski*.

The Ingredient Brand was launched with a global advertising campaign in 2006. Print ads in key fashion magazines such as *ELLE, Vogue, InStyle, MarieClaire and Cosmopolitan,* as well as promotional material, posters, and postcards displayed in stores were used to promote the new InBrand.

In 1995, *Swarovski* celebrated its 100th anniversary. For this occasion the company commissioned the renowned artist Andre Heller to create Crystal Worlds – a sensual journey through the fascinating world of crystal in an artistic installation adjacent to the company headquarters in Wattens, Austria. With Crystal Worlds, *Swarovski* created a continually evolving exhibition that also hosts special cultural events from time to time. With more than 8 million visitors it has even become one of Austria's most popular tourist attractions. The exhibition is promoted by its own website (www.swarovski.com/kristallwelten).

Some people falsely construe that the only or main purpose of a company website with an online database is to act as some kind of online catalog. Wrong! A website can be a means to communicate your brand. A study conducted by *Accenture* dealing with preferences of online buying decisions in B2B revealed some surprising key findings. According to their report a familiar, reputable brand is the single most important factor to online buyers followed closely by service, price, and variety. Moreover, 80 percent of B2B customers regarded prices as less important.

In the **virtual world,** there is no physical product to touch or feel, no familiar bricks-and-mortar emporium to patronize, and too many comparable sites from competitors to differentiate from. Size may not matter in this respect anymore, since every small or medium sized company can afford to rent space on a server and create a professional website. Online Branding efforts therefore need to be different from traditional approaches. Online Branding capitalizes on the two major advantages that the Internet offers for individuals and corporations:

- **Information:** Instant distribution of the most current information available.

- **Simplicity:** Possibility of business transactions to take place at any time, in any place.

Seamless business processes and accurate information are the prerequisites for any online business. If you want to enhance the brand experience, the various elements of the brand impressions have to function at all times. In principle, we have a one-to-one brand experience opportunity with every online interaction. This could either be executed in a standardized way and millions of visitors to your website could get the same impression or it could be customized, and it should!

The *Wall Street Journal* does this for its subscribers. The user can choose what he or she wants to see on its entry page. The content and the services can be selected and the feeling of the *Wall Street Journal* brand is part of the client's every day experience. Similar online success can be seen at *eBay*.

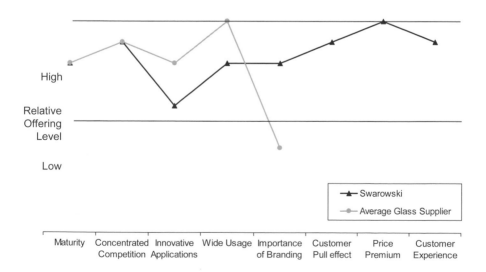

Fig. 41. Strategy canvas of Swarovski in the glass industry

From a strategic point of view Swarovski shows comparable strength to most of his competitors but adds apparent success factors mainly through its Branding efforts, and position itself clearly apart from the rest of the industry players (see Fig. 41).

5.4   Food Industry Example

In the past 10 years, the food industry has created a great base for differentiation particularly with its dietary supplement. The **food industry** is a complex, global collective of diverse businesses that together supply much of the food consumed by the world population. As consumers grow increasingly removed from food production, the role of product creation, advertising, publicity becomes the primary vehicles for information about food. With processed food as the dominant category, marketers have almost infinite possibilities in product creation. Due to the magnitude of suppliers there is a big struggle to make them visible for the consumer. We have identified a number of companies and brands who have

Fig. 42. Selected food and dietary supplement InBrands

(All rights reserved by the logo owners)

left the conventional way of just serving the next customer of the value chain but also market their offerings to the final user, the physical consumer of the product. Fig. 42 shows selected food and dietary supplement InBrands.

One of the classic cases of Ingredient Branding is that of NutraSweet Property Holdings Inc. They develop the InBrand NutraSweet and made it a household name around the world.

NutraSweet sweetener was discovered in 1965 by researcher James Schlatter at G. D. Searle and Company. In 1985 the firm was taken over by Monsanto before being sold to J. W. Childs Equity Partners II L. P. in 2000. **Childs Associates** had experience in the food, drink and food ingredients industry which it shares with NutraSweet through a management partnership. NutraSweet now operates as an independent company with a worldwide reputation. The firm's headquarters, including administration and production, are located in Chicago, Michigan in the USA. CEO Lawrence S. Benjamin has led the company since October 2002. In 1981 NutraSweet innovated the sweetener industry with the launch of "NutraSweet brand aspartame".[41] NutraSweet is the company's brand name for the synthetically manufactured sweetener **aspartame** and is found in more than 5000 products. It is currently sold in over 100 countries, reaching 250 million consumers worldwide.

Aspartame is what is known as a sugar substitute (E 951). It is 200 times sweeter than conventional sugar and contains only 4 calories per gram. The human body breaks it down like a protein. Because it does not raise the blood sugar level and does not contain a lot of calories, it is popular with diabetics and people watching their weight. The authentic sugar flavor also gives it advantages over products like saccharin and cyclamate. Aspartame is not heat-stable; it breaks down at temperatures in excess of 200°C and is therefore unsuitable for baking and cooking.

People who suffer from **phenylketonuria** cannot metabolize phenylalanine properly. The US Food and Drug Administration (FDA) therefore requires all foods and drinks containing this substance to be labeled "Contains phenylalanine"'[42]. The sweetener NutraSweet is most commonly found in the food industry but is also used in the manufacture of pharmaceutical products such as SCITEC NUTRITION Anabolic Whey[43]. There are primarily sugar-free foods, drinks and "diet" products that are sweetened with NutraSweet[44].

Example: Coca-Cola and NutraSweet

The success story of Coke Light® started in 1982 with the market launch of NutraSweet aspartame. It was the first low-calorie, "diet" version of a soft drink to be successfully established on the market. Today it is found in several different varieties (e.g. Diet Coke with Lemon and a caffeine-free version).

In the first four years, global consumption of sweeteners increased by 73% per year. On the US market alone the annual increase was 119 %. Japan followed in second place with 68%, while the European market grew somewhat more slowly at 9% per year.

By 1986 the market for sweeteners had established itself to the extent that no more explosive growth would follow in subsequent years. Nonetheless, for the period 1986 to 1991 statisticians calculated retrospectively an annual increase of 12% on the global market, 9% for the USA, 15% for Japan and 27% for the European market.

After NutraSweet was launched on the US market in 1981 and on the international market one year later, the **NutraSweet** brand enjoyed rapid growth. The food industry was extremely successful at conveying the "fat-free, low-calorie, suitable for diabetics and much sweeter than sugar" message to consumers. As a result, consumers began paying more attention to the **ingredients** listed on the packaging of sweet products, other foods and drinks. This had the effect that a growing number of customers discovered the benefits for themselves and began buying more "diet" products. NutraSweet aspartame became a byword for low-calorie food with no loss of flavor.

The company enjoyed enormous success with its strategy of expanding after the first year and conquering the world market. Europe and Japan soon caught up and started bringing more and more diet products on to the market. Attention-grabbing labels like "0% fat", "40% less calories" and "suitable for diabetics" were used to attract the attention of diabetics and other target groups.

Another success secret of NutraSweet was the decision to concentrate early on a single **main target group:** soft drinks manufacturers. The Coca-Cola company is the market leader for soft drinks and in addition to hugely successful brands like **Coca-Cola, Fanta, Sprite, Mezzomix, Nestea, Powerade, Qooo, Kinley, Bonaqua,** etc., it also produces a number of diet variants – **Diet Coke, Diet Coke with Lemon** and so on. It is the world's most famous company and in recent years has never been out of the world top 3 in terms of brand value. In obedience to the pull principle, the success of Coca-Cola as a manufacturer has a knock-on effect on the sweetener supplier NutraSweet[45], without the brand name being explicitly stated on the end product.

It may be possible to further extend the potential of **NutraSweet** by adopting new approaches in communication policy. For example, NutraSweet could opt to enter into a brand partnership with chewing gum manufacturer **Wrigleys**[46]. One conceivable approach might be to identify specific target groups (such as secondary school pupils or dentists) and distribute free samples of a new sugar-free chewing gum sweetened with NutraSweet that actually cares for the teeth. An approach of this nature could enable NutraSweet to expand its main areas of business and, most importantly, **reinforce** the **NutraSweet** brand itself.

The global market for producers of sweeteners is limited to just a small number of companies. One of the best-known manufacturers on the European market is **Canderel**. Unlike NutraSweet, this company markets its own dietary products (e.g. diet chocolate) and is not solely an ingredient supplier[47]. On a world level, NutraSweet now controls around three quarters of the sweetener industry[48].

In the USA, chemists have introduced a new sweetener to the market. The product, which is called Splenda, has no strong aftertaste.

Only half the equivalent volume of sugar needs to be used. Splenda contains no calories, because it passes through the digestive system without being absorbed.

This sweetener has now become the **highest-selling product** and the only one to be made from sugar. The product is manufactured by McNeil Nutritionals, a part of the Johnson & Johnson group. The company pursues a classic Ingredient Branding strategy and sells the product at a premium price. In the USA the new sweetener costs five times as much as sugar; in Great Britain the price is even higher. The product has not yet arrived in Germany, although it could well "sweeten" the lives of people with lactose intolerance. Splenda is manufactured using a chemical substance which was first discovered in 1976 and which has long been well tested.

Numerous syrup manufacturers are already using this sugar substitute, while the manufacturers of soft drinks and caffeinated drinks are increasingly discovering the benefits of the new product. According to figures from Datamonitor, in 2004 Splenda was used in over 1,436 new products in comparison with 573 in 2003 and only 35 in 1999[49].

In summer 2005, Coca-Cola and Pepsi became embroiled in a bitter contest in the USA for the ever-growing market for low-sugar drinks. Pepsi introduced Pepsi ONE® and Coca-Cola launched Zero®. According to information from the company, the new variety of Coke, partially sweetened with Splenda, will be the group's seventh addition to the diet range. The world's biggest soft drinks manufacturer states that this new product is primarily intended for the US market. This is an area where Coca-Cola recently suffered a downturn in sales. The company now plans to win back its leading position with the help of the Ingredient Branding strategy of the **sweetener** Splenda (see Fig. 43): an approach we would interpret as Inverse Ingredient Branding.

Compared with other suppliers in the food industry the examples display a clear differentiation strategy compared with many other food ingredient providers. The industry is very diverse but also

Fig. 43. Can of Diet Coke with Splenda sweetener

very competitive and is becoming more centralized. There are also big concerns about profitability and one question is why companies such as corn sweetener are able to remain profitable, and other companies, such as flour milling have not been as profitable. Most of the companies with Ingredient Brands could escape and position themselves as asset for the consumer choice.

In this highly competitive industry, where the power shifts more and more to the large concentrated retail chains, the role of the single brands gets increasingly overshadowed by the retailer's own cloud or his own brands. Through many mergers & acquisitions these large organizations have bought or integrated many well-known consumer products in their own portfolio. Fig. 44 shows strategy canvas of selected InBrands in the food and dietary supplement industry.

In our list of Ingredient Brands we have identified 22 offerings, but we are sure that we could not identify all of them due to regional and national conditions and the rapid innovation rate. Some of

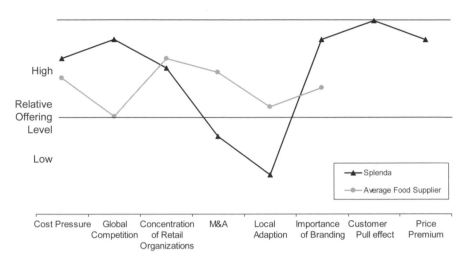

Fig. 44. Strategy canvas of selected InBrands in the food and dietary supplement industry

these brands use explicit the InBranding concepts. More than 60% of the companies do all the important aspects of InBranding but do not publicly announce its Ingredient Branding strategy. In addition we could not identify self-ingredient brands from the OEMs.

The Wild Blueberry Association of North America and Canada (WBANA Canada) use the Ingredient Branding approach to clearly differentiate their offerings from the ordinary, cultivated berries. For advanced food product designers, wild or low bush blueberries, offer many advantages over their cultivated cousins. Smaller and more compact, with a more intense flavor, they freeze extraordinarily well and perform beautifully in a wide range of applications. Wild blueberries also have more total antioxidant capacity than cultivated blueberries, and generally more beneficial antioxidant and phenolic compounds – making them a winning choice for blueberry products.

With its extraordinary offering, Wild Blueberries creates a real advantage for their users based on the following criteria:

Extraordinary Taste – A unique mixture of sweet and tangy wild blueberry varieties produces a delicious burst of flavor that can't be duplicated with other berry ingredients. This means wild blueberry products will have a remarkable, memorable taste that end customers love.

Special Size – Naturally smaller and more compact, Wild Blueberries deliver more berries per pound–up to three times more berries than cultivated, high bush blueberries. End products will show more of the juicy blueberries consumers are looking for, with more wild blueberry taste in every bite.

Superior Performance – Wild blueberries add flavor while maintaining their taste, texture, shape and color throughout a variety of manufacturing processes. In fact, individually quick-frozen (IQF) Wild Blueberries maintain their quality for up to two years and can be used frozen in food preparation for easy handing. Available year-round in a variety of forms and sizes, Wild Blueberries always perform beautifully.

Marketable Mystique – By nature, Wild Blueberries have a "wild mystique" all their own. One of only three berries native to North America; they have an appealing "wild imagery" that powerfully distinguishes wild blueberry products from all others. Adding to that their status as health heroes will result in a proven way to bring added value and excitement to a product line.

With its benefits the WBANA approached first manufacturers, bakeries, food service. As a result with their reputation as a healthful ingredient spreading around the world, Wild Blueberries are turning up everywhere, in products of all kinds. From cereals and muffin mixes to jams and jellies, from teas and juices to yogurt, smoothies and ice cream, wild blueberry is an ingredient that adds taste, color and extra-healthy appeal.

When Ingredient Brands are initiated, they are heavily communicated to the end user. For making the ingredient supplier successful in the food industry the added function product is of superior importance, because the consumer has to be convinced about the functional benefits that could come from many final product offerings. This industry structure with a big number of OEMs is complemented by only a few ingredient suppliers. They cannot expect lots of support from their downstream partners and therefore have to invest heavily in the marketing communication to create the pull effect. Some of this InBranding companies have the financial strength others do not, and therefore we differentiate development paths and success of this ingredient suppliers.

Summarizing the results of this industry analysis of Ingredient Brands, we would like to acknowledge that there are variations within the industries, but the achieved benefits demonstrate that InBranding is a great way to differentiate and to maintain the competitive advantage. Ingredient Branding has demonstrated to be one way to enter blue oceans and to leave the other suppliers behind without competing with them head to head. In the next chapter we will give more detailed explanations in a selection of case studies, which can assist the reader to develop a more thorough understanding of Ingredient Branding.

Summary

- By using the Strategy Canvas, the advantages of Ingredient Brands can be demonstrated in the following areas: principle industry factors, companies and competitors offerings and apparent success factors.

- Possible advantages and disadvantages for InBranding concepts have been demonstrated in the illustrated industries.

- Even when industries are strongly commoditized, differentiation concepts could be developed and successfully implemented.

- The selected industries are only in areas where advanced marketing innovations through Branding can create competitive advantage in an industry.

Notes

[1] Mauborgne, R.A., and Kim, W.C. „Blue ocean strategy: How to create uncontested market space and make the competition irrelevant." 2004.

[2] Peters, T., and Waterman, R.H., jr. *In search of excellence.* New York, 1982.

[3] Collins, J., and Porras, J.I. *Built to last. Successful habits of visionary companies.* New York, 1994.

[4] Collins, J. *Good to great. Why some companies make the leap ... and others don't.* New York, 2001.

[5] Kotler, P., and Pfoertsch, W. *B2B brand management: Building successful business brands.* Heidelberg, New York, 2006.

[6] At this point in time when this book went into press, the future perspective of this industry could not be determined; therefore we based our judgment on 2007 figures.

[7] Willhardt, A.B., and Baumbach, R. „Ingredient branding: Herausforderung für die Markenführung der Automobilzulieferindustrie." 2004.

[8] Jeltsch, M. „Auto 2010: Eine Expertenbefragung zur Zukunft der Automobilindustrie." Accenture-Studie, 2001.

[9] Kalmbach, R., and Kleinhans, C. „Zulieferer auf der Gewinnerseite." *Automobil-Produktion* (2004): 4–8.

[10] Pfoertsch, W., ed. *Living Web: Erprobte Anwendungen, Strategien und zukünftige Entwicklungen im Internet.* Landsberg, 1999.

[11] Voelckner, F., and Sattler, H. „Empirical generalizability of consumer evaluations of brand extensions." Research paper No. 25, 2005.

[12] We have not included the tuning divisions of the various car manufactures, such as AMG from Mercedes-Benz or Ruf for Porsche.

[13] Kasper, E., Klar, J., Renner, D., and Specht, S. „Ingredient branding: Bedeutung des InBranding für Automobilzulieferer." Unpublished working paper January, 2005.

[14] Pfoertsch, W. Ingredient Branding für Automobilzulieferer, Marketing Management Bulgaria (2004).

[15] Bose web content, August 2005, www.bose.de/product/auto, 08.08.2005.

[16] Pfoertsch, W. *Mit Strategie ins Internet.* Nuremberg, 2000.

[17] This applies to the creation of value both within and between companies; see also Porter, M.E. *Wettbewerbsvorteile: Spitzenleistungen erreichen und behaupten.* 4th ed. Frankfurt/Main, New York, 1996.

[18] Brochures from Sympatex Technologies GmbH: Sympatex Press Information, undated.

[19] Ibid.

[20] For a history of the company, see
www.gore.com/de_de/aboutus/timeline/timeline.html.

[21] Vucurevic, T. „Die GORE-TEX® Marke: Eine Komponente wird zum Kaufgrund." In *Jahrbuch Markentechnik 2006/2007,* edited by A. Deichsel and H. Meyer. Frankfurt a.M., 2006.

[22] ibid.

[23] Kevin Keller calls this business model 'self-branding'; cf. Kotler/Keller (2006): p. 391.

[24] Moore, J., and Gore, W.L. „Dry goods." 2005,
http://www.baselinemag.com/article2/0,1397,1817356,00.asp.

[25] www.gore-tex.de (a), 10.08.2008.

[26] www.stern.de/presse/stern/548066.html?q=markenprofil.

[27] www.gore-tex.de (b), 10.08.2008.

[28] Baumgarth (1999), p. 16.

[29] See Bugdahl's four-stage theory, Table 1: Four stages of Ingredient Branding.

[30] Fiesco-Effect: The majority of textile manufacturers use Gore, so differentiation is no longer possible and the competition may take place in the price war in the last stage of trading.

[31] Pinar, M., and Trapp, P.S. „Creating competitive advantage through ingredient branding and brand ecosystem: The case of turkish cotton and textiles." *Journal of International Food & Agribusiness Marketing* 20 (2008): 29–56.

[32] Wedepohl, K.H. *Glas in Antike und Mittelalter.* Stuttgart, 2003.

[33] Stacherl, R. *Das Glaserhandwerk.* Renningen, 2000.

[34] Renno, D., and Huebscher, M. *Glas-Werkstoffkunde.* 2nd ed. Stuttgart, 2000.

[35] Stacherl, R. *Das Glaserhandwerk.* Renningen, 2000.

[36] Schlager, E. „Glas: Ein schwer durchschaubarer Stoff." 2004, www.go.de/index.php?cmd=focus_detail&f_id=181&rang=1.

[37] Pfoertsch/Schmid (2005), p. 125f.

[38] Pfoertsch/Schmid (2005), chapter 2.

[39] Belz, C., and Kopp K.-M. „Markenführung für Investitionsgüter als Kompetenz- und Vertrauensmarketing." In Handbuch Markenartikel, edited by Manfred Bruhn. Stuttgart, 1994.

[40] Belz/Kopp (1994): p. 15.

[41] www.nutrasweet.com, 08.08.2008.

[42] www.dietcoke.com, 03.08.2008.

[43] www.beastpower.de/start.php?nach_marken_sortiert_scitec_nutrition.php, 12.12.2008.

[44] www.aspartame.org, 04.06.2008.

[45] Baumgarth (2001), p. 6f.

[46] ibid, p. 12.

[47] www.canderel.de, 04.08.2008.

[48] www.lebow.drexel.edu, 05.08.2005.

[49] productscan Online Update – December 2004 www.datamonitor.com, 12.12.2008.

CHAPTER 6

Detailed Examples of Successful Ingredient Brands

In this chapter, we would like to present in detail several examples of successful brands of industrial companies that illustrate best practices. The nine cases are (see Table 8):

Table 8. Selected case studies

Case	Principle
TetraPak	**A machine builder becomes household name** "With partnership profit for everyone."
Dolby	**Leading an industry with innovation** "How to successfully maintain customer relevance."
Teflon	**Basics of Ingredient Branding** "How DuPont differentiates and progresses in chemical commodity business."
Bitrex	**Implementing the Network Approach** "Doing good things for the child safety and strengthening the brand."
Shimano	**Implicit Ingredient Branding** "Never ever compete with a customer."
Makrolon	**The High-Tech Material** "Added value in late stages of the life cycle."
DLP	**Pampering the customer** "Big screen HDTVs without the big price."
Schott CERAN	**Differentiating with success** "Ingredient Branding and brand cooperation."
Microban	**Convincing and Measuring** "Ensuring customer attention and price premiums in the value chain."

P. Kotler and W. Pfoertsch, *Ingredient Branding: Making the Invisible Visible*,
DOI 10.1007/978-3-642-04214-0_6, © Springer-Verlag Berlin Heidelberg 2010

6.1   Teflon: Basics of Ingredient Branding

E. I. du Pont de Nemours and Company is one of the early users of the Ingredient Branding concept. The company was founded in 1802 by Eleuthère Irénée du Pont. He had studied explosives with Antoine Lavoisier, a French scientist, and recognized that there was a great demand for gunpowder in North America. He managed to raise capital and imported gunpowder machinery from France. The company quickly acquired a positive image and soon became one of the major suppliers of gunpowder to the USA. DuPont continued to expand, moving into the production of dynamite and smokeless powder. Today DuPont puts "science to work by creating sustainable solutions essential to a better, safer, healthier life for people everywhere. Operating in more than 70 countries, DuPont offers a wide range of innovative products and services for markets including agriculture, nutrition, electronics, communications, safety and protection, home and construction, transportation and apparel."[1]

The company still carries the name of the founder from over 200 years ago. In 1906, the company commissioned artist G. A. Wolf to create the new logo, and in 1909, Wolf designed the oval logo still in use today (see Fig. 45).

Fig. 45. Logo of DuPont de Nemours: early and current version
(All rights reserved by the logo owners)

Since 1955, DuPont is part of the "Fortune 500" list and placed number 81 in 2008 with $30.6 billion in revenues. DuPont led the polymer revolution by developing many highly successful materials based on petroleum-based hydrocarbons. Polytetrafluoroethylene (PTFE) – Teflon – was discovered by Dr. Roy Plunikett at the DuPont research laboratory (the Jackson Laboratory in New Jersey) on April 6, 1938. Plunikett was working with the gases based on the coolant Freon. Upon checking a frozen, concentrated sample of tetrafluroethylene, he and his colleagues discovered that the sample had spontaneously polymerized into a white solid to form PTFE. This is a colorless, odorless powder—a fluoropolymer with completely new properties. Following this discovery, Plunkett was promoted to director of chemistry.

PTFE was first marketed in 1945 under the registered trade name DuPont Teflon. The relative molecular mass of Teflon can exceed 20,000,000 MW (molecular weight), making it one of the largest known molecules. It has a smooth surface, virtually nothing sticks to it, and nothing is absorbed by it. It is therefore not surprising that Teflon was later used as a non-stick coating for cooking utensils. The material was first used by the military as part of the Manhattan Project. After the Second World War, DuPont had ample opportunity to market this new discovery for civilian applications.

Since 1988, DuPont has awarded a research prize to scientists who create new products using Teflon. After the Manhattan Project, DuPont invested continuously in research. Between 1948 and 1962, the company developed fibers such as Orlon®, Dacron® and Lycra®. Since 1961 the company has been expanding continually and developing new products. Scientists have created new materials like Nylon®, Cellophane®, Kevlar®, Nomex® and Tyvek®. DuPont advanced materials were critical to the success of the Apollo space program and their adaptations for consumer use were praised highly.

Ingredient Branding Strategy

One of the challenges faced by the chemical industry is the constant demand to differentiate themselves from the competition and the rise in the requirements of end customers. DuPont created a long list of innovations that improved the life of many people. In the past, the leading chemical companies were able to satisfy consumer demand by offering a **wide product range** based on reliable technology, the result of their world market dominance.

There is another point, which ought to be mentioned: the fact that many retail chains have become enormously powerful in this regard. This is one reason why the manufacturers of consumer goods are under pressure to reinvest considerable amounts of profit in marketing and advertising. Reciprocally, suppliers of product components are sometimes put under pressure by manufacturers to develop their own brands. Thanks to the improved mass communication, particularly the Internet, technical product information is now much easier to find and compare. Customers can research different products online with very little effort before deciding where and when to buy and companies can communicate with the customer directly.

The chemical industry is currently dominated by two European suppliers, two American companies and one Japanese company. These companies have achieved more or less similar rates of growth and their ranking within the market has altered very little. Only those that have chosen to merge have achieved faster growth. For the past few years, the chemical industry has been in a precarious situation. The market share controlled by Asian companies has risen steadily owing to the **cheaper cost structure**. This possesses an enormous challenge to the competition in this sector.

As a way to cope, a number of European firms have decided to relocate production to countries outside Europe to bring down costs. Another possibility is to invest in a marketing or Ingredient Branding strategy. DuPont, the largest and most profitable company in the industry, has registered more than 1,700 brands – Teflon and Lycra to name just two. Other examples are shown in Table 9.

The brand strategy of DuPont was to make the company visible to the end customer through extensive range of innovations, which were trademarked, and the benefits communicated to the final user.

DuPont has been more successful in Ingredient Brand building than any other company in our core industries. From Teflon and Corian® to Kevlar and Nomex, DuPont had carried out some visionary work to pioneer new markets for the "hero" brands, both in the business-to-business and business-to-consumer space. The company created the Branding concept of ingredients with its product Teflon, long before Intel had used the "Intel Inside" campaign. Since starting in 1964, Teflon, today, has 98-percent global brand awareness, according to internal sources.

Table 9. Ingredient Branding examples developed by DuPont

Brand Name	Material	End product examples
CoolMax	textile fiber	sports apparel
Cordura	textile fiber	duffels, tents
Corian	solid surface material	kitchen counters
Dacron	polyester fiber	clothing
Kevlar	brand fiber	safety clothing, safety equipment
Lycra	spandex fiber	clothing, sports apparel
Mylar	polyester films	lightweight applications for aerospace
Stainmaster	stain-resistant fibers	carpets
Teflon	resins	non-stick surface for cooking utensils
Tyvek	protective material	flexible sheet structures for packaging, house insulation

With Ingredient Branding, they overcame the limitations and risk inherent in a too limited, one-way customer-supplier relationship. They also led the customers into new product areas and applications through their vast new innovations. By offering product enhancements and innovations, extra services, faster and more reliable delivery policy and even lower prices, DuPont created advantages for the direct customer and **differentiate itself from the competition**.

In addition, they promoted their corporate brand. After adding the tagline – *The Miracle of Science* – DuPont invested in a 12-page advertisement segment in *The Wall Street Journal* in April 1999 and announced its new corporate brand identity[2]. **The Wall Street** Journal provided a glimpse into **the new** Branding focus for **DuPont**, highlighting the company's nearly 200-year history of product innovations in areas such as aerospace, agriculture, apparel, electronics and pharmaceuticals. It also alludes to the next generation of **DuPont** innovations. Teflon's Ingredient Branding communication is shown in Fig. 46.

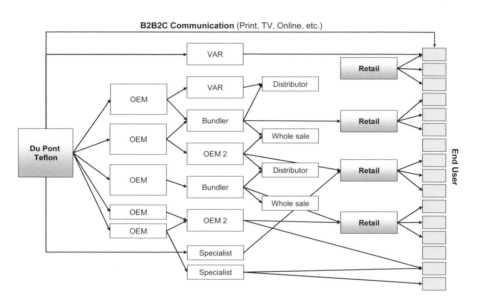

Fig. 46. Teflon's Ingredient Branding communication

In the same year, they launched a global TV advertisement series with the title: To Do List for the Plant. In 2000 DuPont used the first chemical company online advertising by targeting chemists with micro websites that did not appear as banner in order to not offend their high valued target group. Also many product specific promotions were organized. For Teflon they created their claim:

"Teflon – only from DuPont"

Various product applications have been developed under the **Teflon** brand name:

- Fluoropolymer textile fibers
- Medical products
- Cookware and saucepans

The various ranges are now marketed under the name Teflon, and occupy a place in the brand hierarchy are shown in Table 10:

Table 10. Teflon product rang

DuPont® Autograph
This range is aimed at professional chefs. The cookware and saucepans have a special coating designed to last a long time.

- -

Teflon® Platinum Pro
This brand is aimed at young customers who do not cook often. However, the range is of a high quality, including stainless steel as well as aluminium.

- -

Teflon® Select
This range is designed for families who like doing a lot of cooking. It was designed so that the whole family can get involved in cooking, adults and children alike.

- -

Teflon® Classic
The basic version of Teflon.

DuPont expanded its cookware product range in the early 2000, and it became a global business. The market applications delivered solutions for its application areas where other product ingredients could not perform. The application include paint in harsh environment, such as marine coatings, clear coated lenses, wiper blades, advanced carpet protector, lubricants, sporting goods, personal care products, flexible films for photovoltaic, and many more.

In 2003 DuPont Textiles & Interiors division was placed due to strategic reasons in a separate division called Invista. In 2004 this division generated a turnover of USD 6.3 billion and employed over 18,000 people producing a wide range of different materials. That year Invista was sold to Koch Industries. DuPont kept the industrial applications, which was in line with the new company direction to focus more on downstream activities than on applications. Koch Industries is also the parent of polyester supplier KoSa. Koch Industries is the largest private company in America, according to Forbes magazine[3]. Based in Wichita, Kan., Koch Industries owns companies involved in refining and chemicals; process and pollution control equipment and technologies; minerals and fertilizers; polymers and fibers; commodity and financial trading and services; and forest and consumer products. With approximately $100 billion in revenue, Koch companies have a presence in nearly 60 countries and employ about 70,000 people. The company is focusing on long-term success and believes in creating real value, rather than just the illusion of value. With the deal they bought brands such as Lycra, Stainmaster and Teflon.

With Invista's involvement the Ingredient Brand management of the brand reached new highs. They continued to innovate and introduced Advanced Teflon to the market. Lisa Pfrommer, who represented Teflon in her position as North American textile effects manager for Invista, said[4] residential furnishings applications for Advanced Teflon will include washable textiles used for removable slipcovers. She also said Teflon's brand recognition is more than 98% globally with consumers. In order to carry the Teflon brand and hangtags, fabric has to meet three criteria: fluorochemical products (Zonyl/Oleophobel) from Ciba Specialty Chemicals must be applied to the fabric; global performance specifications for fabrics treated with Teflon fabric protector must be met; and the mill or finisher must sign a licensing agreement for Teflon fabric protector from Invista.

Invista ran television and print ads in North America showing the advantages of Teflon in a variety of home textile and apparel applications and highlighting how the product "can make everyday easy." The campaign continued from 2004 till today and included tailored promotions with Invista's industry partners Quaker Fabric, Laura Ashley, American Textiles, Louisville Bedding, Pacific Coast Feather, Springs and others.

The Example of Laura Ashley

Invista Apparel introduced another product to the market: a new type of DuPont Teflon for use in the home (for example to cover sofas or cushions). It offers a higher level of protection against substances like grease and dirt, and is known as Teflon fabric protector.

British brand **Laura Ashley** has been using the Teflon fabric protector ingredient since April 2004. Laura Ashley specializes in luxury home furnishings. The special Teflon material makes the fabric repel dirt and is easy to care for, durable, long lasting and hardwearing.

These were the reasons behind Laura Ashley's decision to use Teflon fibers. The material represents a combination of classic style and modern technology. "Teflon fabric protector offers two major benefits we feel are important in the upholstery market: high performance and easy care," said Meri Stevens, Creative Merchandising Director at Laura Ashley Home Fabrics Customers today want to wear easy-care fabrics that can be washed in the washing machine and do not require ironing. Teflon fabric protector fibers make this possible.

The partnership has been in place since September 2003 and the special materials have been on sale since autumn 2003. Invista spent 7 million Euros on the "Make Every Day Easy" campaign in order to market the materials[5]. The statement "The Teflon brand is closely linked with the promise of ease of care in the minds of consumers" comes from Invista, the company is known for its innovations, and works with a number of successful brands such as Lycra, Stainmaster, Antron, Coolmax, Thermolite, Cordura, Supplex and Tactel.

Invista Apparel uses the know-how of Advanced Teflon to improve the quality of its products. The company has integrated the fibers developed by Teflon into its fabrics. This "product/brand partnership" enhances the value of the new product in the eyes of the consumer because of the special material properties and quality image of Teflon. The surface of the fabric feels smooth and even, despite the different thicknesses of the special Teflon fibers. The fabric is "kind to the skin" and feels soft and velvety. The marketing department at Invista Apparel discovered that customers prefer easy-care products that are pleasant to the touch. By using products from Invista, textile companies can exploit the latest technological developments and give the consumer a positive impression with innovative end products.

An interesting anecdote is that Teflon has become a nickname given to persons, particularly in politics, to whom criticism does not seem to stick. The term honors Teflon, the unique brand name of a "non-stick" chemical used on cookware, and was first applied to the American President Ronald Reagan. He was called the "Teflon president" in 1983 by Patricia Schroeder[6], a then Democratic Congresswoman from Colorado.

6.2   Dolby: Leading an Industry with Innovation

Another example of successful Ingredient Branding is **Dolby Laboratories**. This company is responsible for excellent sound effects in various branches of the entertainment industry. Dolby Laboratories, Inc was founded by an American, Ray Dolby, in 1965. He wrote his doctoral thesis in physics at Cambridge University in 1961. In addition to various consulting jobs in England and India, Ray Dolby made his name by developing the Ampex video recorder system. He got famous by taking the "hiss" out of the analog music cassette recorder systems. In the beginning, Dolby produced professional recording system for studios that created the professional segment of their offerings. Their consumer product offering was licensed out to companies who manufactured analog tape recorder equipment at that time, first on open-reel tape and then cassette recorders in 1970.

This Dolby feature instantly changed the customer experience in listening to recorded music. The modest license fee, which was linked to the final product and its shipment were charged per quarter. This license structure supported the rapid increase on licensees. The next step was the incorporation of the noise reduction system into Integrated Circuits (ICs). Again, Dolby Laboratories developed the system and supported the manufacturer, but the royalty fees were only charged when products were sold to the final customers. Another offering of Dolby came with the sale of prerecorded cassettes. Customer preferred to purchase these cassettes, even when they had to play them on cassette recorders that were not Dolby. The cassettes were clearly marked with the DOLBY SYSTEM logo.

Today, in addition to analog noise reduction and home theater surround sound technology, licensed technologies include many digital technologies, such as Dolby Digital®, the multi channel digital surround sound format adopted for use with DVD, digital broadcast TV, digital cable, and direct satellite broadcast (DSB). The recent push of Dolby's success came from the development of sound technology into computer chips. Here, the same licensing and branding principles were applied and the growth demonstrated again Dolby's large-scale consumer acceptance. Fig. 47 shows the Dolby System and Dolby Digital logos.

 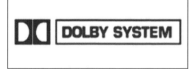

Fig. 47. The Dolby system and Dolby Digital logo
(All rights reserved by the logo owners)

Dolby Laboratories also develops sound editing systems and supplies solutions for film, radio, DVDs, PC games and cinemas. Its licensed technologies are designed to reduce background noise[7] and are integrated in many applications in the entertainment industry. Today, the Dolby name enjoys a global reputation as a synonym for a unique sound experience. In 2008, the company employed 976 people around the world. Also in 2008, it increased its turnover by 38.7% compared with the previous year. Last year, the company turned over around $482 million. The profitability is extremely high, larger than 29%, 80 % comes from licensing royalties. See Table 11 for key financial data from Dolby Laboratories Inc.

Table 11. Key financial data from Dolby Laboratories, Inc.

Annual income statements (all amounts in millions of US Dollars)					
Year	Revenue	Gross Profit	Operating Income	Total Net Income	Diluted EPS (Net Income)
Sep 07	482,0	407,8	186,9	142,8	1,26
Sep 06	391,5	315,5	129,6	89,6	0,80
Sep 05	328,0	247,8	84,1	52,3	0,50

The American company is based in San Francisco, California, where it has offices, laboratories and production facilities. The European market is served from London, and the company operates other offices in New York, Los Angeles, Hong Kong, Shanghai, Beijing and Tokyo. The company deliberately chose these locations in order to respond to the different requirements of regulatory bodies in the US, Europe and Asia.[8]

The company currently owns some 780 patents and 770 trademarks. Analog technology is now being superseded by digital technologies, both in the professional environment and amongst home users. We will take a closer look at a number of these areas and the Dolby technologies most frequently used in these fields. Fig. 48 shows the Dolby Digital principle.

Most feature films and DVDs on the market today rely on a technology first introduced worldwide in 1992. It signaled the beginning of a new digital age. The first DVD with Dolby Digital technology

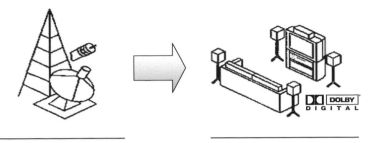

Over-the-air, satellite,vor cable transmission   DTV broadcast via set-top box or DTV receiver

Fig. 48. Diagram showing Dolby Digital principle

appeared on the market in 1997[9]. Well-known and therefore successful examples include: "Manitou's Shoe" and the "Terminator" series.
Dolby Digital is a surround sound technology. The 5.1-channel
sound produces a direct, clear and very realistic sound effect. Dolby
Digital is the most widely used technology to come off the Dolby
production line. It is also found in:

- DVD players
- PCs
- Games consoles
- Digital TV
- Film soundtracks

In addition to Dolby Digital technology, consumers can also use
Dolby Headphone technology, which maintains the quality of the
film sound experience. Dolby Digital technology is also dominant in
the field of games consoles. Well-known console products (the Microsoft X-Box, Sony Playstation and Nintendo Game Cube) use the
technology to create a unique visual experience for video game
fans. PC games with surround sound transport the gamer into another world, making them feel as if they are part of the action.

Here are some of the companies who use Dolby technology in their
hardware and software solutions:

- Ahead Software

- Apple

- Dell

- Fujitsu-Siemens

- HP

- Logitech

- Microsoft

- Sony

- Toshiba

Dolby currently enjoys a dominant position in the global **entertainment industry** with its sound technologies. Evidently the company can afford to virtually dispense with end consumer marketing. The company website features the slogan "Technologies that define entertainment"'[10], but otherwise, Dolby makes almost no efforts at self-marketing. Cinemas equipped with Dolby technology provide the company with a certain amount of advertising (e.g. through the use of short trailers) to highlight the unique sound experience to the audience. Spots where the Dolby logo is displayed are shown in Fig. 49.

In all other respects, it is primarily left to the manufacturers to highlight the use of Dolby technology, since using the Dolby name in

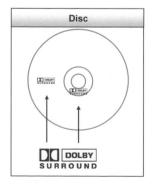 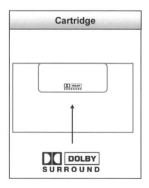 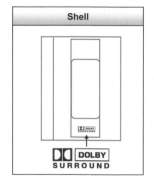

Fig. 49. Spots where the Dolby logo is displayed
(All rights reserved by the logo owners)

their advertising brings additional benefits. Dolby's positive image and technology have a positive effect on the image and profitability of the manufacturer's own brand. Moviegoers often prefer films shown in Dolby surround® or Dolby Digital sound® (indicated by the double D symbol). Licensees who use Dolby technology as an integral component often use the special technology or simply the double D logo to advertise the Dolby[11] branded house. In late 2007, Dolby Laboratories, Inc. announced that the first mobile phone with Dolby Mobile technology, an audio processing technology platform designed to enable high performance playback of entertainment on mobile phones, will be introduced in a handset from Japan's NTT DoCoMo, thereby expanding its offering into the mobile communication world. We will probably see how the Dolby experience will change customer perception of good sound quality in this market.

Dolby's first global Branding director Andy Smith was appointed in 2001. He had worked as strategic marketing director at Intel and influenced the marketing and Branding efforts in the company. Dolby is recognized world wide as a successful example of Ingredient Branding, although it never formulated an Ingredient Branding as part of their strategy. They admit that their "Dolby audio technologies are an essential ingredient of a great entertainment experience, whether people are going to the cinema, watching movies on DVD". Although they have experienced the pull effect on many occasions, they never refer to it in their management statements. Throughout the world the Dolby brand is also recognized as standing for the best in cinema sound. To help that recognition pay off at the box office, the company provides a variety of marketing programs and materials, including one-sheets and trailers, to all theatres with Dolby equipment. These activities approach the final customer and help Dolby system equipped cinemas and the motion picture industry to prosper.

A very impressive and entertaining trailer was developed for North America in cooperation with DreamWorks Animation. It demonstrated the power of the Dolby sound (see Fig. 50).

Fig. 50. End user promotion in cinemas

This kind of direct approach to the consumer created the pull, which is regarded as the power of "Branding an ingredient"[12] as a key to better marketing a more complex product or service. Dolby's business model is shown in Fig. 51.

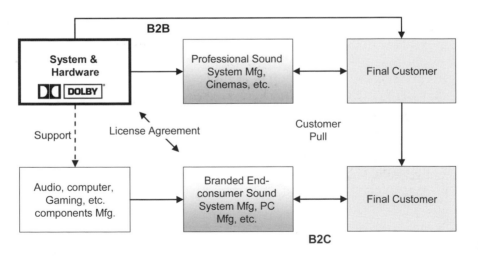

Fig. 51. Dolby's business model

In Dolby's case, no final product or service provider had to compromise its own brand-building to add the Ingredient Brand on the package as well as in advertising. What they provide are:

1. An ingredient that is highly differentiated, supported by patent protection, and thus adding an aura of quality to the overall product.

2. The ingredient is central to the functional performance of the final product by enhancing the sound system and the sound experience.

3. In contrast to most other Ingredient Branding examples, the final products are well branded themselves. However, the product categories where Dolby applies their technology is evolving, and the customer is experiencing performance enhancement with Dolby in each category: from audiocassettes to CDs, DVDs, and new mobile devices.

4. The final products are complex, assembled from components supplied by multiple firms who may sell the "ingredients" separately in an aftermarket.

Based on their business model and their grasp of identifying their final customer, Dolby is able to apply their strategy to future innovations and continue to enjoy the success they have experienced so far.

6.3 Tetra Pak: A Machine Builder Becomes a Household Name

"Tetra Pak. More than just packaging." The story of Tetra Pak began in 1943[13], when Dr. Ruben Rausing developed an economical and hygienic type of milk carton.[14] The essential aspects of Tetra Pak were innovative technology and the use of a tetrahedron, then a completely new shape in packaging. The tetrahedron would later inspire the company name.

The Swede invented a revolutionary new **coating** made of paper and plastic and a special technique for sealing the carton. Starting in 1951, AB-Tetra Pak worked continuously on this principle in Lund, Sweden. In 1963 the **Tetra-Brik** was launched, followed in 1965 by the Tetra-Rex packaging concept. The brick shape of the Tetra-Brik was specially designed to be stacked on Euro Pallets and is still un-beaten in terms of optimum use of space.

1961 saw the introduction of the first packaging systems for the aseptic filling of pasteurized milk in Switzerland, because Rausing recognized the need for "ready packed goods"[15] in Europe and a number of developing countries. The focus during the 1970s was on boosting production and development to the extent that, in the early 1990s, Tetra Pak had a presence on the international arena.

Today, Tetra Pak is represented in 165 countries around the world. Tetra Pak is one of three independent industry groups belonging to the Tetra Laval Group.

Tetra Pak now offers plastic packaging as well as packaging made of cardboard. The company's wide portfolio includes systems for food processing, packaging materials, the manufacture of cartons and plastic bottles, and filling machines and outer packaging. In other words, Tetra Pak supplies food manufacturers with a complete system, tailor-made for their requirements and products.

The road to becoming the world market leader in packaging technology was a long one. Alternative packaging manufacturers and ecological interest groups made it difficult for Tetra Pak to rise out of anonymity and achieve **differentiation from the competition**. So in 1993 the company launched the "Somehow smart" campaign in a bid to establish a sympathetic, reliable image of quality and recyclability in consumers' minds.[16] The first stage of the campaign was to make the brand name well known and give it a profile. This stage was aimed at politicians, teachers and journalists. Only emotional brand advertising was used, taking the form of magazine advertisements. The primary aim was to advertise the product using the key concept of recycling. The brand was given added **presence** through the sponsorship of the Eintracht Frankfurt soccer ball club in Germany. After just two years, the brand policy was so successful that Tetra Pak had become a synonym for carton packaging, so that most Germans do not know the word "carton" and say "Tetra Pak" instead, unaware that it is a brand name.

Quality Assurance Through Partnership

The partnership with Tetra Pak's industrial customers is character-ized by openness to new ideas. In other words, the company is by its customers' side at every stage of the process: developing new products, breaking into new markets, processing, packaging, mar-keting and recycling drinks packaging. Tetra Pak keeps them in-formed about **trends in the foodstuffs market**, for instance, and analyses evolving consumer requirements. Using all of this infor-mation, the company then works with its customers to develop the appropriate packaging for their drinks.

Tetra Pak packaging material is constantly being tested and fur-ther developed. The company operates its own research centre in Stuttgart for this very purpose, where scientists and technicians perform **long-term testing** to examine how the material and con-tents tolerate one another. They study questions like how edible oil reacts with a carton's inner coating over long periods. They also collaborate on the development of new packaging products. The development process involves close partnerships with univer-sities and research groups, keeping the company informed about the newest scientific and technological trends so it can pass these on to its customers.

To sum up, Tetra Pak maintains close **partnerships** with its suppli-ers and customers all over the world to deliver successful, innova-tive solutions and environmentally friendly products of high qual-ity for the benefit of the end consumer.

Trademark

The **brand label** serves to present and identify the brand. Tetra Pak developed a symbol that has come to stand for quality and safety in packaging. Initially the trademark was printed on the underside of the packaging, than on the side; it now appears, clearly visible, on the top of Tetra Pak packaging.[17] The tag line used is: PROTECTS WHAT'S GOOD (see Fig. 52).

Fig. 52. Tetra Pak logos
(All rights reserved by the logo owners)

Pull Effect and Differentiation

Everything revolves around the principle idea of the founder, Dr. Ruben Rausing: "The packaging should save more than it costs". In other words, the packaging should deliver more in terms of cost-effectiveness and environmental considerations than it costs, using fewer resources and being kinder to the environment. Tetra Pak packaging offers a great deal and therefore enhances the value of the manufacturer's product.

The company has another philosophy: "Tetra Pak. More than just packaging", means developing innovative products and systems that turn visions into competitive advantages".[18] Tetra Pak's successful **strategic differentiation** is constantly reducing the **replaceability** of the brand in direct customer-supplier relationships. In addition, we can observe a pull effect whereby consumers will specifically demand Tetra Pak packaging. They associate Tetra Pak with quality and will resist second-choice packaging. Consumer loyalty grows, and as it grows the competition has less and less chance of breaking into the market.

Communication Activities

The Tetra Pak strategy depends on partnerships and a perpetual dialogue with its customers, because the company pursues a shared goal with it: "the maximum market success for their products!"[19] **Joint communication activities** with the manufacturer of the end product are extremely important to Tetra Pak. Procter & Gamble, for example, advertises Tetra Pak in connection with its Valensina fruit juices: "The time is ripe for Tetra Pak". Drinks company Apollinaris & Schweppes now packages its "Silence" still water in Tetra Prisma packaging from the world market leader. The synergy effects resulting from the combination of two strong brands create a significant edge over the competition.[20]

Tetra Pak also runs what it calls **business development programs**, where it works alongside the manufacturer even during the development phase for new drinks. The company helps the manufacturer carry out market analyses and establish consumer preferences. The two partners jointly design the product packaging in the same design studio. Once the drink is in the right packaging, Tetra Pak helps its business customers to market the new product with joint advertising, consumer information and campaigns. For example, the Joe Clever school milk program was intended to offer children a healthy, balanced playtime snack.[21] A number of appealing events were also organized to link in with school milk (e.g. the "Let's make paper" activity day), the objective was to show children how drinks packaging is recycled in a fun and entertaining way.

Partnership – Profit for Everyone

"To take on the challenge of the markets you need conviction, imagination and a partner you can rely on: Tetra Pak. More than just packaging".[22] Before installing a system for an industrial customer, for example, Tetra Pak works with the customer to draw up the technical plans in line with their specific needs and requirements. The appropriate packaging system is then selected and the processing equipment, filling equipment and packaging material are made available. At its training centre in Hochheim, Tetra Pak can train the customer's employees in the theory and practice of operating the filling machines. To ensure that **production runs smoothly** at all times, technicians and engineers are on call round the clock. The foodstuffs market is becoming increasingly international. Tetra Pak helps its customers market their products beyond national borders using its own global presence and by providing contacts in and knowledge of international markets.

"Tetra Pak protects what's good" – The New Campaign

This is Tetra Pak's new corporate motto and also the slogan for the new advertising campaign since 2004. The campaign is intended to highlight the **packaging manufacturer's** commitment to the issue of **protection**. Tetra Pak protects the contents against light, keeps in

Fig. 53. Photographic ad by Tetra Pak (2009)

flavor, is good for the environment, retains freshness and prevents breakages (see Fig. 53).

For this campaign the company designed four TV advertisements with short, whimsical stories, which are broadcast by all the major channels. These are accompanied by advertisements in consumer - magazines. The advertisements feature various target groups describing themselves as people who protect milk, vitamins or flavor.

Tetra Pak has announced its new advertising campaign for 2006 in various parts of the world. The emphasis is on "value for money" concept without compromising on health benefits. The television commercials were on air from early July across India. The campaigns ran for 12 weeks and featured two commercials. The commercials focused on the benefits of UHT Milk set in two different environments. To support the television campaign Tetra Pak also ran a "retail activation" program in Mumbai and Bangalore. For this activity, 300 outlets were chosen in each city. Similar programs were brought to the market in other countries. In 2008 major emphasis was given to China and Latin America. Fig. 54 shows photographic advertisements by Tetra Pak in 2009.

Fig. 54. Photographic ad by Tetra Pak (2009)

With these consumer communications the Tetra Pak Company steps out of the realm of B2B competitors. Unlike the other machine builders they supply complete systems for processing, packaging and distribution. Their processing and packaging systems try to make economical use of resources. And the processing systems are developed to treat the products gently, and consumption of raw materials and energy is minimal during the manufacture and distribution of packages. Their packages fulfill the main purposes of packaging, namely to:

- maintain product quality

- minimize waste

- reduce distribution costs

But they also assure the customer that the company behind these products care and understand the customers need. Since the quality and shelf life of the products are extended the intermediaries of the value chain benefit also from the increased use of Tetra Pak products. Both effects create a pull-effect that clearly benefits Tetra Pak's market performance. Today, the company plays a dominant role in the huge worldwide market for food packaging, but there are many more regional markets to concourse and the company has a good chance to be more successful with its Ingredient Branding concept.

6.4   Bitrex: Implementing the Network Approach

Cameron Smith, the newly appointed business unit manager was sitting in his Edinburgh office overlooking the majestic skyline of Edinburgh. The company at which he was working was almost as old as the castle. Founded in 1815, J. F. Macfarlan has been in the pharmaceutical business ever since. The company was prosperous in many ways, but now there was a new challenge on his desk: expanding the Ingredient Branding concept of the chemical Bitrex – or, to be more precise, **"the most bitter substance in the world"** – to his customers around the world. This was not an easy task, especially as there were many other players involved in the business. He and his predecessor, Peter Mackenzie had achieved a lot in the year after their company started to brand this product.

In 1958, while carrying out development work, laboratory staff at Scottish firm Macfarlan Smith Ltd. discovered an extremely bitter substance: denatonium benzoate. Laboratory staff noticed that the powdered form of denatonium benzoate was extremely bitter. Prepared in solutions, it was found to be much more potent than the standard alcohol denaturant at the time, Brucine. In the same year the chemical was registered as a brand under the name "Bitrex" in the UK, Canada and the USA. The bitter agent was launched on the UK market two years later and it has been used in a wide range of products since the early 1980s.

A very small amount of this additive is sufficient to make a product unpalatable. Because children are particularly sensitive to bitter tastes, which act as a natural warning, Bitrex is a very effective way of preventing them from swallowing harmful household substances. Another advantage, and a decisive competitive advantage for Bitrex, is the fact that it does not alter the properties of the main product, which retains its full original quality. Hence, the substance is often used as a selling point for the end product. Fig. 55 shows the chemical formula and logo of Bitrex.

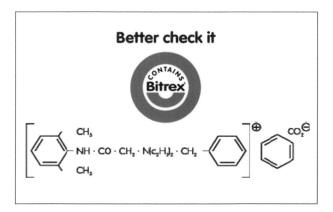

Fig. 55. Chemical formula and logo of Bitrex

The original application for denatonium benzoate was the industrial denaturation of alcohol. Large amounts of this anesthetic lidocaine derivative are used in the denaturing alcohol market – making it legally unfit for consumption. It is now added to a wide range of household cleaners, pesticides, and DIY (do-it-yourself) as well as automotive products. Since being approved in the UK and US in the early 1960s, Bitrex has been officially recognized as the denaturant of choice in more than 40 countries worldwide. The industrial alcohol formulation, SDA40-B (B for Bitrex) is a lasting testimony to this.

This approval process is necessary because in all countries, government revenues from alcohol taxes exclude fuel and non-consumable alcohol — and as a result, these kinds of alcohol have to meet very strict criterion by the authorities. This application has grown recently with bio-ethanol, which is used as a substitute for petrol in cars.

The Company Macfarlan Smith

Founded in 1815, Macfarlan Smith is one of the world's oldest pharmaceutical companies and has over 200 years of experience in natural product extractions and chemical synthesis, specializing in opiate narcotics such as Codeine and Morphine. Over the past two centuries, the company has gone through several changes. J.F Macfarlan founded the company and was followed one year later by D. Flockhart and then T & H Smith in 1827. Discoveries during this time included the isolation of morphine in 1816 and the first liquid essence of coffee in 1840. Duncan Flockhart also supplied chloroform to Sir James Simpson in 1847.

During the 1840s, Blandfield Chemicals Works, Broughton Road, Canonmills, Edinburgh, was acquired by the firm, and a London branch was established in 1848, from which essence of coffee was also manufactured. In 1919, the company acquired the business of Glasgow Apothecaries Co, which had been established at Virginia Street, Glasgow in 1805 by a group of general practitioners who wished to establish an efficient dispensary for their prescribed drugs. Shortly afterwards, Glasgow Apothecaries Co began distributing wholesale to retail druggists. In 1926, T & H Smith Ltd. acquired John Mackay & Co, Edinburgh, and incorporated a number of colonial subsidiary companies to form Edinburgh Pharmaceutical Industries Ltd. This group was, in turn, acquired by Glaxo group Ltd. in 1963, when the name Macfarlan Smith Ltd came into existence.

In 1989, Meconic Ltd was established, and in 1990 bought Macfarlan Smith Ltd from Glaxo holdings through a management buyout, which at the time was the largest of its kind in Scotland. In 1995 Meconic Ltd. was floated on the London Stock exchange and became Meconic Plc. In 2001, Johnson Matthey Plc acquired Meconic Plc and incorporated Macfarlan Smith into the Pharmaceutical Materials Division, under the name of Johnson Matthey Macfarlan Smith, retaining the original company identity.

The Brand Bitrex

"The bitterest stuff on earth", as it is recognized by the Guinness book of records, when added to a liquid renders the substance so unpalatable that anyone trying to drink it will reject it immediately. [23] Prof. Dwyler of the Department of Psychology of the University of Cardiff[24] demonstrated how effective Bitrex could be against the phenomenon of accidental child poisoning. Only a tiny amount of Bitrex is required and it readily dissolves in household and gardening products to give stable formulations. Bitrex is also effective for many other mammals, including dogs, cats, rats, mice, etc.[25]

Child safety is the number two motivation in purchasing decisions.[26] These findings were derived from in-depth focus group analysis in Great Britain and around the world. It is one of the surprising benefits of enhancing product safety. Safety concerns really make consumers with children or pets consider buying a product with Bitrex.

Worldwide, the Bitrex logo has helped products to differentiate themselves from the competition. The product categories range from cleaning, agrochemical, industrial, and automotive.

Macfarlan Smith advocates Bitrex as the 3rd line of defense against accidental poisonings.

1. Safe Handling – It is vital that all household chemicals are stored correctly, out of the reach of inquisitive hands and preferably in a locked cupboard. It is also well known that you should not decant chemicals into other containers that are not labeled correctly.

2. Child Resistant Closures – Child-resistant packaging reduces child-poisoning rates. However, they are not always effective. Possible reasons for the failure of re-closable child-resistant packaging, includes the following:

   • Some children are able to open a properly closed CRC

   • Misuse of the container, including adults failing to close the CRC properly (leaving the lid loose or off) or transferring the contents to a non-CRC container

   • An older child opening the container and giving the contents to a younger child

   • Closures that do not continue to function as designed over the period of use

   • A broken or faulty container.

3. Purchase products containing Bitrex provides that additional peace of mind, that should a household product get into a child's hands, it has the added safety measure of being exceptionally unpalatable. One would be surprised at how attractive some household products are (sweet smelling/brightly colored) and every product displaying the Bitrex logo has passed through the standardized taste testing protocol to determine the effective Bitrex dosage.

Bitrex can be added to a variety of cleaning products, including:

   • All Purpose cleaners

   • Kitchen cleaners

- Bathroom cleaners

- Liquid Laundry Detergents/Capsules

- Fabric softeners

- Washing-up Liquids

All of these products are routinely stored around their point of use. **Bitrex** is therefore an essential part of the three-tier safety program – storage, child resistant cap and **Bitrex**.

Rodenticides & Insecticides

Agrochemical products such as Snail & Slug Baits are available with Bitrex. Both Professional and Home & Garden use baits can be extremely harmful to non-target species through ingestion. Many meta-metaldehyde and methiocarb based pellets are brightly colored to discourage birds from feeding on them, and contain Bitrex to avoid accidental consumption by field wildlife. This also helps prevent poisonings with domestic animals, such as dogs. Consumers are encouraged to look out for the Bitrex logo as a sign of added security on products.

Baits designed to target species such as rats and cockroaches are commonly placed in areas accessible to children and pets. **Bitrex** allows the product to be effective for its intended purpose, while helping prevent accidental ingestion by humans.

Bitrex can be used in many automotive products to help prevent accidental ingestion, protecting both humans and pets. Monoethylene Glycol (MEG), the main ingredient in anti-freeze, is highly toxic and small amounts can cause blindness, physical handicap and even death. It is also exceptionally sweet to the taste.

There have been many cases of dog and cat deaths after licking split anti-freeze from driveways and garage floors. There was even a recent case of the attempted murder by a wife on her husband in the UK, when she laced his dinner with anti-freeze in order to claim life insurance. Many US states are passing laws that all MEG based anti-freeze contain Denatonium Benzoate to help reduce these occurrences. France passed a law in 1997 to the same effect. Automotive screen wash is another product that can be extremely harmful through accidental ingestion. Many products are brightly colored, fragranced, and sold in clear plastic containers. Screen wash can have a high methanol or ethanol content, which makes it ideally suited for Bitrex inclusion to help prevent ingestion. Some retailers include Bitrex as a safety additive throughout the whole automotive range. Bitrex can be added to a variety of other products, including brake fluid, insect cleaners and tire cleaners.

The largest application in volume for Bitrex is in industrial alcohol that is destined for industrial use and must be denatured, removing it from the food chain. Denatured Ethanol-B is the standard denaturant in the industry. Industrial alcohol was originally denatured with Brucine, a natural product, which was subject to large fluctuations in price. Macfarlan Smith's chemists discovered Denatonium Benzoate in 1958 and by the early 1960s; it was approved in over 40 countries including the USA. As well as being synthetic, giving it the advantage over Brucine, as it wasn't subject to the large fluctuations in price, it was also significantly bitter.

A new area for Bitrex is bioethanol & renewable fuels. The British Renewable Transport Fuel Obligation (RFTO) Program will, from April 2008, place an obligation on fuel suppliers to ensure that a certain percentage of their aggregate sales are made up of biofuels. The effect of this will be to require 5% of all UK fuel sold on UK forecourts to come from a renewable source by 2010. Bioethanol falls under the UK Customs & Excise Denatured Alcohol Regulations 2005. All bioethanol must be denatured with a blend of Methanol and Denatonium Benzoate, at the rate of 1% methanol + 10mg/L (10ppm) Denatonium Benzoate. This market is just starting to develop and may become a major application for Bitrex.

Retail Dissemination

Many retailers have understood the concept of Bitrex and use it to differentiate their offerings (see Fig. 56). Tesco was a forerunner in this field and uses also other Ingredient Brands such as Microban to add value for their clients. The French retailing group Carrefour and the German dm – drogerie markt are leading the way in their countries and carry the offerings to other countries during their international expansion.

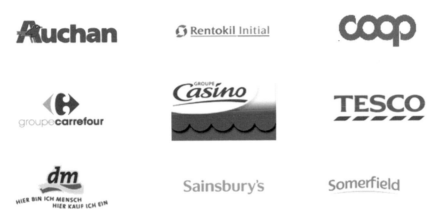

Fig. 56. Logos of large retailers using Bitrex
(All rights reserved by the logo owners)

Network Activities

In every country, Macfarlan Smith works with organizations and institutions that are experts in safety, like the Child Accident Prevention Trust in Great Britain or the German Green Cross. These organizations have self-interest in helping to create a safer environment at home and in the public.

The British Royal Society for Prevention Accidents was instrumental in the 1960s in reducing accidents related to car products, and, in 1984, identified Bitrex as a major tool to increase children's safety at home. With this organization and their local agents the company implements royal society of the prevention of accidents. In 2008, the

German agent, AE Tiefenbacher supported a child safety day nationwide. Also inn 2008, the German Green Cross teamed up with retailers such as Kaufland and dm – drogerie markt to become official supporters of the effort to increase awareness of child safety and protection against poisoning.

A pod cast "Child Safety News" is downloadable from the DGK website. It covers information concerning the risks of poisoning in the household, methods to prevent it and includes interviews with experts for child safety.

A new audio book for children has been developed and introduces "Agent Bitrex" as "Security Detective on Tour". In 2008, it started with two sequences – kitchen and bathroom. In these two little stories, the children can follow Agent Bitrex from room to room where they can hear about safety risks and how to behave. It supports the educational approach of the Bitrex story and the responsible approach of the sponsors. In a joint effort, the ingredient suppliers, the security organization, various retailers and sometimes single-product companies, are working together to reach the final customer and try to increase the awareness about child safety and poi-

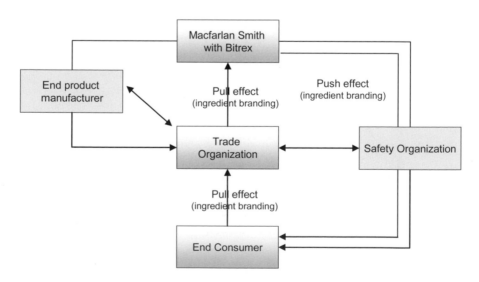

Fig. 57. Network constellation for Bitrex

soning prevention. The recorded poisoning accidents in the UK have fluctuated. From 1989 to 1998, it decreased from 50,000 to around 40,000[27] and continues to fall. This illustrates that the joint efforts of the various parties involved are being successful. The network constellation for Bitrex is shown in Fig. 57.

Reaching Out to the Customers

Macfarlan Smith is putting even more effort into the promotion of Bitrex to the final customers. Their targets are the mothers and fathers of this world. In North America, they developed a unique promotion campaign to increase awareness.

The Sourpuss Photo Contest™ is an interactive safety promotion which educates consumers about the Bitrex solution, showcasing a specific product such as Bug-Gela, a snail and slug killer. The theme behind the promotion is product integrity and innovation. This dedicated promotion leads not only to more awareness, but also to increased sales because it works on the consumer level, at the trade level and on the internal sales motivation level.

This is a feel-good-do-the-right-thing promotion that creates retail traffic, public relations opportunities and sales increases. As an example in the northwest of the USA, sales were increased 25% during one month for a product, which was previously a commodity and found the opportunity to differentiate itself using Bitrex. Literature from the National Safety council complemented the information offering and built trust. Fig. 58 shows retailers promotion with Bitrex.

Fig. 58. Retailers promotion with Bitrex
(All rights reserved by the logo owners)

dm-Drogerie Markt: Bitter Is Safer

German pharmacy chain, dm-drogerie markt has also recognized the benefits of the bitter agent. Since April 2003 they have been adding it to around 40 of its own-brand "denkmit" products. "Adding this bitter agent to our cleansing and cleaning products will give our customers added confidence in the safety of our products and offer preventive protection," explained Ulrich Maith, a member of management at dm-drogerie markt with responsibility for the chain's own brands.[28] This move enabled dm-drogerie markt to enhance the value of its products and also raise consumer awareness of Bitrex. Therefore, both products and both companies benefited in a "win-win" situation.

As far as Bitrex is concerned, a combination of specialization and the Ingredient Branding has enabled Macfarlan Smith Ltd. to break out of the anonymity of a supplier and establish a global market presence. A policy of actively communicating with end customers has generated a pull effect, overcoming "…the limitations and risk inherent in a too limited, one-way customer-supplier relationship", which is of particular importance with regard to "more educated customers". The company addresses a relatively large customer base and still has an opportunity to increase its market potential even more with the aid of the Ingredient Branding strategy. Before a manufacturer can use the Bitrex logo on its product, it must sign a licensing agreement with Macfarlan Smith Ltd. This comprises the following key points:

- The business customer's products must be tested by Macfarlan Smith Ltd.

- Agreement must be reached on the appropriate minimum quantity of Bitrex.

- The business customer must submit samples of the product on request to ensure the right level of bitterness.

- Any changes to the ingredients or design of a product that features the Bitrex logo must be approved by Macfarlan Smith Ltd. before the product is introduced.

If a business customer fulfils the conditions of the licensing agree-ment, it is given permission by Macfarlan Smith Ltd. to use the Bitrex logo. The customer is also offered technical support and assistance with marketing their product. It is in Bitrex's advantage to leverage the most fundamental issue, concern for children safety and create increased sales. In 2008, Macfarlan Smith celebrated 50 years of Bi-trex and more than 30 years of cooperation with national safety or-ganizations which made the world a better place by reducing poi-soning accidents.

"Campaigning for Safety"

In line with this motto, Macfarlan Smith Ltd. aims to raise the global profile of Bitrex amongst business customers and end consumers, of whom the key target audiences are parents with young children.

To achieve this aim, Macfarlan Smith Ltd. has established links with organizations that specialize in children's safety. The company maintains active partnerships with organizations such as the Royal Society for the Prevention of Accidents in the UK, the National Safety council in the USA and the German Green Cross. Macfarlan Smith Ltd. also presents Bitrex at fairs and exhibitions for trade and the public and is a sponsor of Child Safety Week. Bitrex is now sold in over 40 countries around the world, mainly in Europe.

The product has many possible applications including household products (such as washing-up liquid), cosmetics, skincare and hair care products, pesticides, pain and car care products such as wind-screen wash. Macfarlan Smith Ltd. primarily markets Bitrex to busi-ness customers in the B2B sector who want to make their product

Fig. 59. Safety organizations support the usage of Bitrex

(All rights reserved by the logo owners)

safer by adding a bitter agent. Occasionally, there is also a demand from private individuals. Cameron Smith needed to know how to bring this wonderful success story to other markets. Safety organizations that support the usage of Bitrex are shown in Fig. 59.

6.5   Shimano: Implicit Ingredient Branding

Tour de France, the world's largest cycling race, is the global annual top event for every cycling enthusiast. Every summer since 1903[29] around 200 professionals agonize roughly 2,000 miles over some of

Fig. 60. Route of the Tour de France 2009

the highest Alpine and Pyrenees mountains (see Fig. 60). They cycle at nearly 35 miles per hour through the streets crowded with hundred thousands of spectators. The fans often wait for hours in the hot sun and some even arrive days before just to see their idols passing by for a fraction of a second.

What inspires the spectators is the fight between the racing teams at the edge of their physical limits. The cyclers are riding for 20 days, climbing snow-capped mountains while spending more than 5 hours on the saddle per day. This is much more than anyone could expect of a normal human being. However, it is not only muscle power that enables the cyclists to put on a show of this magnitude. Equipment also plays a crucial role. It has therefore become routine for commentators and journalists to report not only about the training methods and the individual strengths and weaknesses of the favorites, but also to discuss in detail the equipment of the cyclists. In fact, in addition to the list of Tour de France winners, there is another list of the winning equipment used each year since 1903.

Today, in the competition of professional cycling equipment, the two giants in contention are Shimano and Campagnolo[30]. The debate between fans has raged for decades about which brand is superior in the bicycle component group. Shimano is the leading brand for bicycle components such as gears wheels, breaks and ball gears. With a 70 percent market share, they not only dominate the whole market, their brands, especially the Dura Ace and the XTR[31] also have become a synonym for high-end quality peak performance and leading edge technology.

Shimano Inc. is also a leading producer of fishing equipment, and since the late 1990s, Shimano has begun selling equipment for golf as well as snowboarding and other sports. However, bicycling is the major business unit. This results from their business history on the one hand, but on the other hand, their bicycle components have become such a success because of a simple reason: superior quality. More importantly, they used the right strategy to promote their goods.

Shimano is an example that marketing makes the difference. To find quality components in the high-end market is not difficult. There is at least a couple of producers like Campagnolo (Italy) or SRAM (USA) which also provide top quality. But Shimano has pushed them into small niches and made them marginal in the overall bicycle market. Shimano didn't do this with just higher quality; they simply had a better Branding strategy. To understand their approach, we must regard the Shimano brand as an Ingredient Brand.

The Global Bicycle Market

The world market for bicycles developed from the Second World War to the 1970s roughly in the same scale as the car market (see Fig. 61). By that time, riding bicycles was an alternative way of transportation and were means of travel for people with lower income. Since biking wasn't a leisure sport but more an inconvenient must if a car wasn't affordable, a market for special component frames and equipment did not exist. If people had the means, instead of buying a high quality bike, they preferred to spend their money on a first small car.

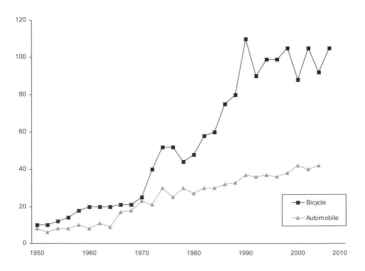

Fig. 61. World bicycle and automobile production (1950–2003)

Source: Earth Policy Institute from Worldwatch, BRIN

These attitudes didn't change with the oil crisis and the rising prices for petrol in the 1970s. In fact, sales of bicycles increased dramatically because driving cars became even more expensive for a lot of people. However, at the beginning of the 1980s the culture of riding bicycles changed. The transportation aspect stepped into the background and people started to use bikes as a sport instrument.

Riding bikes nowadays is a matter of health awareness. This change in consciousness opened new interests into different technical possibilities for the bike. Customers started to identify themselves with their products and this opened up the way for strong brands in the bicycle market. Not only did the demand for special brands come up, different types of bikes were created for variety of needs. Today, a special bike is available for every terrain. Some of these bikes cost more than small cars, and ironically, people spend miles and miles on their bicycles after they drive home from work in their cars.

In the years before this change in the bicycle market, national brands were selling complete bikes: Mead, Sears Roebuck, Montgomery Ward, and Schwinn in the USA; Hercules or Sachs in Germany; Flying Pigeon, and Phoenix in China. These brands still exist today but with a much smaller market share. The rise of Shimano meant the decline of their leadership.

According to Global Industry Analysts Inc. the global market for bicycles is expected to realize a Compound Annual Growth Rate (CAGR) of 5.28% over the 2001–2010 periods.[32] The sales volume will reach around $61 billion by 2010. Asia-Pacific, with a share estimated at 47.36% in the year 2007, forms the largest bicycles market worldwide. The region is also slated to record the fastest growth with a CAGR of over 6.33% during the aforementioned period. The U.S. bicycle industry was a $6 billion industry in 2007[33], including the retail value of bicycles, related parts, and accessories through all channels of distribution, according to research funded by the National Sporting Goods Association.

The bicycle market can be divided into many segments. The most common segmentation is adults and children bikes, and further on into what they are used for. Bicycles for adults form the largest segment in the global bicycles market, accounting for an estimated 44.17% of the total. Sub-categories analyzed under adult bicycles include mountain bicycles, hybrid bicycles, touring bicycles, and specialty bicycles. Sport bicycle segment is forecast to grow at a strong of 6.15% p.a. over the 2001–2010 periods.

The industry usually splits the market into three main segments:

(1) the low-end market (below $300),

(2) the mid-class market ($300-$500), and

(3) the high-end market (from $500 to well over $4,000).

Low-end bikes include children bikes and bicycles used for basic transportation, while the high-end segment includes those used for rigorous recreational activities.

Around 100 million bicycles are sold globally each year. The biggest domestic market is China, accounting for 30 percent of unit sales. The U.S. bicycle market constitutes approximately 17 percent of unit sales, and the European and Japanese markets are about two-thirds and one-half the size of the U.S. market respectively.[34]

Although bicycles are produced in dozens of countries, the top five producers – China, India, the European Union, Taiwan, and Japan – are responsible for 87% of global production. China alone had some 58 percent of the global market in 2004. The following year, 2005, was a record year for the production of bicycles in China with a 16% increase in the production of bicycles and electric bikes to a total of 80,430,000 units produced, of which about 65% were exported. The People's Republic of China today produces over 60% of the world's bicycles. 86% of the bicycles sold in the US are imports from China. However, cycle use in China was decreasing sharply, down to 20% of all trips, compared to 33% in 1995. In Beijing, only 20% of commuters rode bikes in 2002, compared to 60% in 1998.

The bicycle industry has gone through several booms, slowdowns, and consumer interest shifts. Technology improvement spurred the

1970s bike boom. In the 1980s, high gasoline prices encouraged a further increase in bike sales. Then there was a surge in mountain bike sales in the 1990s (almost entirely displacing road bike sales). And in the 2000s, Lance Armstrong's Tour de France victories helped to revive public interest in road bikes, particularly in the United States where mountain bikes had dominated in the prior decade.[35]

The world major companies (components, frames and whole bicycles) covered in "Bicycles: A Global Strategic Business Report"[36] include the following companies: Accell Group N.V., Amer Sports, Bell Sports Corporation, Caloi USA Bicycle Company, Campagnolo SRL, Cannondale Bicycle Corporation, Currie Technologies Inc, Cycleurope AB, Giant Bicycle Inc, Hero Cycles Ltd, Huffy Bicycle Company, Merida Industry Co. Ltd., Miyata Industry Co Ltd, Pacific Cycle Inc., Raleigh UK Ltd., SRAM Corporation, Shanghai Phoenix Company Ltd., Shenzhen China Bicycle Co. (Holdings) Ltd., Shimano Inc, Specialized Bicycle Components Inc., Sunn Bicycle, Tandem Group PLC, Trek Bicycle Corp, Tube Investments of India Ltd, and Yuh Jiun Industrial Co. Ltd, among others.

Shimano: History and Present

Shimano dates back to 1921, when Shozaburo Shimano founded Shimano Iron Works in Sakai City, near Osaka. The town was a legendary blacksmithing centre known for its swords and gun barrels. Rather than follow his father into farming, Shozaburo had apprenticed at an iron works after high school. Later, he started his own company, and the first product it made was a single-speed bicycle freewheels. In ten years, Shimano was exporting freewheels to China. The business was incorporated as a limited corporation in January 1940 under the name Shimano Iron Works Co., Ltd. In 1951, it was renamed Shimano Industrial Co., Ltd. Shimano began making its famous derailleur in 1956. Also called external speed changers, these were the mechanisms that moved the bicycle chain from gear to gear on ten-speed bikes and the like.

The next year, the company began producing an internal, three-speed gearing mechanism that was enclosed in the hub of the rear wheel. This internal speed changer was introduced to the U.S. market a few years later and soon became the standard for three-speed bikes. In 1960, Shimano installed a cold forge that enabled stronger products to be made in a more efficient fashion. Shozaburo Shimano eventually turned over management of the business to his three sons. Though the company made brakes and other components, Shimano refused to produce complete bicycles. "Our founder said, "never ever compete with a customer", remarked one of Shimano's sons to the *Straits Times*[37]. A U.S. subsidiary, Shimano American Corporation, was set up in January 1965. Shimano launched into the bike-crazy European market in the same year.

By 2006, Shimano had become the major brand in bicycle components with sales around the world (Japan: 25 percent; the Americas: 22 percent; Europe: 34 percent; Asia: 19 percent). Shimano did business with almost every major bicycle manufacturer including Trek, Giant, Bridgestone Cycle, National Bicycles in Japan, and Cycleurope in Europe, but not a single manufacturer accounted for more than 10 percent of its sales.[38] Bicycle manufacturers that relied on Shimano components had merely become distributors, according to Cannondale founder and CEO, Joseph Montgomery.[39] Some bike manufacturers such as Cannondale, Trek, and Specialized had begun to manufacture their own components in the late 1990s, but few had major success, as home-produced components were often pricier than Shimano's components. In fact, by 1997, over 90 percent of bicycle manufacturers produced no part beyond the frame by themselves and 90 percent of part manufacturers produced only one type of bicycle part.[40]

Product quality and technological superiority were always key components of Shimano's strategy. Shimano's successful execution of its strategy has allowed it to have a powerful brand, consisting of top quality products, with a global presence, three of the company's mantras as stated in its 2004 Annual Report.[41] Shimano's rise could be traced to several developments. Its earliest big break came 40 years after its founding when it developed a three-speed gear that U.S. manufacturers became strongly interested in. Shimano progressed to making 10-speed drive trains, which allowed it to prosper during the U.S. bike-racing boom of the 1970s and the rise of triathlon. In the mid-1980s, the company developed and packaged/integrated professional-quality road-racing components, allowing it to compete more directly with Campagnolo (the only major player in that category at the time).

At the same time, Shimano completed development of its index shifting system (SIS or Shimano Index System), a technological breakthrough, which made shifting easier and more efficient. The shifting gave riders more confidence and reliability during races because racers could lose important seconds during a race using the old system of shifting. STI was a mechanical integration of shifters into the brake levers. This innovation allowed racers to accurately shift without letting go of the handlebars. The birth and rise of mountain biking helped to fuel resurgence in the popularity of bicycling in the United States.[42] Shimano completely redesigned its gearshift so that it suited mountain bikes after noting that fanatical California mountain bikers were racing specially geared custom-made mountain bikes. Shimano emerged with 15-speed mountain-biking components in 1982 and later 21-speed versions, mainstay of modern mountain bikes. Other innovations included a computer-designed elliptically shaped chain wheel, which increased pedaling efficiency and reduced biker fatigue.[43]

The Business Strategy

In 1970, Shimano built what was then the largest bicycle parts plant, located in Yamaguchi Prefecture, Japan. Later in the decade, according to Design Week, Shimano began hiring engineers to create a unified look among component systems as well as elevating their performance.[44] A European unit, Shimano (Europa) GmbH, was established in Düsseldorf in 1972 with just two employees. The company's shares began trading on the Osaka Securities Exchange the same year and were also listed on the Tokyo Stock Exchange in 1973.[45] Shimano's first manufacturing plant abroad was set up in 1973 in Singapore. Opening a sales office in California in 1974, the company was well placed to ride the booming bike market in the United States during the 1970s.

Shimano's path to success was not without its bumps. As Yoshizo Shimano later told the Asian Wall Street Journal, the company made a huge investment designing, developing, and testing a series of aerodynamic bicycle components in the late 1970s.[46] They were well ahead of their time and took several years to catch on.[47] Shimano had also begun to diversify into tackles for fishing, another sport whose tools required precision mechanisms. However, it did not become a major force in this industry until the late 1970s. Shimano's Bantam reels were introduced in 1978, followed by X-line rods in 1981.[48]

Developing new products with superior quality was always one principle of the Shimano business model. However, their new products were supported by a special strategy. First, their design gave the users the chance to remember the company behind the product. Second, their products were used in the high-end market especially in racing. Together, they gave users the chance to see the Shimano products on the bicycles of professional racing teams as well as on high-end quality bikes on the street. This development fell together with the launching of Shimano's Dura Ace product series. People recognize these products, while the design helped them to remember them. The hobby cyclist starts asking for the Shimano products when deciding to buy a new bicycle. Bit by bit the component becomes a sign of quality for the bicycle. The bicycle producer quickly recognizes the new demand; they start to provide their products with Shimano components. In the 1980s an aftermarket began to establish. Small bike shops provided the Shimano components to replace broken parts of existing bikes. In this way, without knowing it, Shimano established an Ingredient Branding strategy.

The Value Chain for Bicycle Components

With the rising interest in Shimano components, a new way of producing bikes was established. First, different parts of the bikes were sold to the frame producer who produces the whole bike and sells it

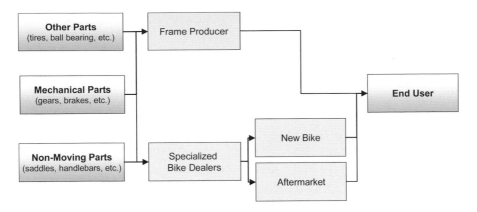

Fig. 62. The value chain for bicycle components

via the retail to the end user. At the same time, when biking became a leisure sport, specialized bike dealers offered customized bicycles. These dealers sold directly to the end user and provided components for the aftermarket (see Fig. 62).

These market structures gained an enormous potential for Ingredient Branding. To start with, Shimano offers its products to the frame producer and specialized bike dealers. At the other end, users ask for the Shimano components in the new bike so that the push effect from Shimano gets supported by the end user's pull. The aftermarket gives the end user the chance to replace the broken parts of the bike, but more importantly, the end user gets the chance to replace the competitor's product with one from Shimano. These chances fall together with rising brand awareness by the end user. Shimano built the foundation for its success while benefiting from the value chain. Theoretically, end users had the chance to choose from many component producers but only one had a strong brand, Shimano. Thus, Shimano's implicit use of Ingredient Branding strategy was the basic for their success.

Ahead of the Pack in the 1980s

Shimano continued to refine its biking products, creating new market leaders. The AX line of components for bicycle racing came out in

1980, followed two years later by a series for mountain bikes dubbed Deore XT. Annual sales exceeded ¥50 billion in the mid-1980s. At this time, Shimano employed 1,500 people around the world. Shimano beat its European competitors to the mountain biking craze, observed the Far Eastern Economic Review.[49] By the late 1980s, Shimano was considered the standard for mountain bike components. The range of Shimano's cycling offerings expanded throughout the 1980s.

The company began selling a line of bike shoes in 1988. In the same year Shimano set up a UK subsidiary that focused on fishing tackle sales. Moreover, Shimano shifted some of its fishing reel production to Singapore, which, due to the rise of the yen, was producing about ¥4 billion ($26 million) worth of bike parts a year. In 1989, Shimano established three subsidiaries in the Netherlands that sold an array of products. Sales were ¥84 billion in 1989. Exports of Japanese bicycles and components as a whole grew furiously in the late 1980s, reported the Asahi News Service, reaching ¥115.4 billion ($848.7 million) in 1990. By now, one-third of Shimano's production went to Europe.[50]

Global Expansion Continues in the 1990s

Shimano opened a plant in Malaysia in 1990. In the same year, the company bought an interest in Alfred Thun S.p.A. This was re-named Shimano Italia S.p.A. after the rest of the stock was acquired. A fishing equipment unit was also set up in Italy in 1990. In addition, Shimano was expanded its Singapore operations. The company also set up subsidiaries in Belgium and Indonesia in the early 1990s. The parent company's name was changed to Shimano, Inc. in 1991. The proprietary SPD (Shimano Pedaling Dynamics) line of quick-release "clipless" pedals was introduced in 1990. Evolution of the fishing tackle line soon saw the introduction of the Stella reel and the SHIP (Smooth and Hi-Power) system. In 1995, Shimano rolled out its Nexus line of seven- and four-speed internal hubs for cruiser bicycles, which were growing in popularity in the United States due to their retro styling and simplicity of operation.

Shimano also developed an in-hub gear system that could be locked to prevent theft. It was introduced to the Japanese market in 1997.

Competition in Asia increased towards the end of the decade as European manufacturers entered this market. Bicycles had long been a staple form of transportation in China, and, as its economy grew, so did the demand for high-end bikes. The Far Eastern Economic Review had observed that most of China's 320 million bicycles did not have gears in the early 1990s.[51] However, this was changing rapidly, and Shimano claimed a 50 percent market share on gears there. After reports of cyclists being injured by broken cranks, Shimano recalled more than 2.5 million of them in 1997. It was the largest recall in the bike industry to date, reported the Los Angeles Times, and cost the company $15 million or more.[52] Due to the popularity of Shimano's mountain bikes, the affected parts had been installed in about 50 different brands over the previous three years. But the recall and the service provided reduced the negative effects.

In 1997 Shimano acquired G. Loomis Inc., as it launched an Action Sports Division offering products for growing new sports such as snowboarding. Shimano set up a Golf Division in 1999 and continued to develop new products in other areas, such as a wobble-free fishing rod.

2000 and Beyond

Shimano became more visible than ever on the global stage as long-time user Lance Armstrong began his winning streak at the Tour de France in 1999. While overseas production accounted for 30 percent of production in 2000, exports accounted for more than 80 percent of revenues of ¥141 billion. As the Japanese bike market stalled, the Nikkei Weekly reported Shimano was shifting the focus of its overseas plants to supplying local bike manufacturers rather than producing parts to export back to Japan.

At that time, Shimano was investing ¥1 billion to boost production at its Shanghai plant by 60 percent and was adding a three-speed gear line there to meet new demand. In 2001, the company set up a ¥5 billion factory in the Czech Republic to meet booming bike demand in Eastern Europe, as well as building a plant in mainland China. A Taiwanese unit was established in 2002, and a second, ¥2 billion ($17 million) factory opened in the People's Republic of China in 2003. Shimano also opened a ¥500 million ($4 million) fishing rod production facility on the site of its Kunshan, China, bike parts complex. The company was aiming to increase overseas production to half of total production by 2004, reported *Asia Pulse*.[53]

After extensive design and testing, an automatic gear shifter for bicycles was announced in late 2003. The device used magnets and other sensors to determine a bike's speed and make shift adjustments accordingly. Shimano was hoping to sell 50,000 units a year at ¥200,000 ($1800) each. Yoshizo Shimano told the Financial Times that the motivation for the idea was to allow bike commuters to concentrate on traffic by freeing them from the distraction of selecting gears.[54] Shimano continued to innovate as a manufacturer of fishing gear as well. In late 2001, it introduced the Dendomaru 3000SP, an electric reel with an LCD screen displaying the length of line cast as well as other data to give novices feedback on their technique. A few years later, Shimano developed an underwater fish detector in partnership with Furuno Electric Co., a maker of navigation instruments. Sales for its fishing gear were growing at the rate of 6 or 7 percent a year, reaching ¥143.7 billion in 2003. Net income grew more than 50 percent to ¥12.3 billion. As it proceeded into the first decade of the 21st century, the company had an estimated 70 percent share of the world market for bike parts.

The Distribution Channels

According to the National Bicycle Dealers Association (NBDA) bikes are sold through four primary and distinct channels of distribution:[55]

- The specialty bicycle retailer,

- The mass merchant

- Full-line sporting goods stores,

- Others, which is comprised of a mixture of retailers, including multi-sport stores such as REI, outdoor retailers and mail order[56].

Department, discount and toy stores sell mostly price-oriented products. Approximately 75% of bicycle units were sold through the mass merchant channel in 2006, but this represented 37% of the dollars due to the declining average selling price of $72. The specialty bicycle retailers feature higher quality merchandise, and also rely on adding value through added customer services such as bike fitting, expert assembly and repair. This channel commanded approximately 17% of the bicycle market in terms of unit sales in 2006, but 48.9% of the dollars, a dominant dollar share. Dealer price points generally start at around $200, with the average at approximately $422, though prices can range into the thousands. While the number of specialty bicycle stores has declined in recent years due to consolidation, this is the only distribution channel that maintained or increased average retail bicycle selling price. The recent trend has been for mass merchant gains in unit sales market share, but stability in dollar market share due to declining prices in the mass segment.[57]

The Purchase Process

The purchase process for bicycle changed with the new interest in cycling as a leisure sport. While in the 1950s to 1980s customer bought a complete bike at their dealer, today, the specialized dealers

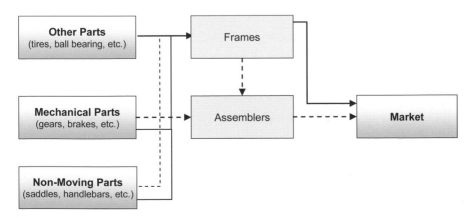

Fig. 63. Material flows in the bicycle industry[58]

are the targets for high-end bicycles. The pre-assembled bikes offered minimal chances to customize the bike so consumers had to take what they got offered. At this point, the component supplier wasn't a counterpart to the consumers.

Before the 1980s, suppliers delivered only to the OEMs and to a small after sales market. With the change in biking culture, big biking events attracted a wide public interest where people came in touch with the idea that leading edge performance needs leading edge equipment. It was at this time that the first brands became known by the masses. In particular, two components suppliers could be identified; Campagnolo and Shimano. The big change in the purchase process started when people replaced their broken component. Cyclist asked for specific parts at their bicycle dealers, and in particular, they wanted branded products. Since Shimano already had a relationship with the dealers because of their aftermarket service, it was natural for them to promote their products. Some of the dealers developed to become bicycle assemblers by providing customized bikes for their customers. The role of the assembler increased particularly in the USA, Japan and Europe, catering to the mid and high-end market[59]. The material flow in the bicycle industry is displayed in Fig. 63.

Customers go to their specialized bike dealers and choose their frame brand from **Specialized, Giant or Bianchi** as well as the components from **Shimano** and some other brands. In the USA, approximately 6,000 independent bicycle dealerships exist, with 1,500 dealers accounting for 60 percent of all unit sales.[60] But that retail environment has begun to change in the 2000s as dominant bike manufacturer players began to rise. Now, the three big final product companies spend a lot on product development and marketing. They are looking for a "concept store" experience, with better support for the brand and retail exchange with the consumer. In essence, they are looking for a vertical alignment to create more secure networks for each brand.

What's Next?

Shimano has reached a leading market position for bicycle components throughout the world. Over the years, they have developed a strong Ingredient Brand with a reputation for reliable and high-quality products. But they know that they cannot rest on their laurels if they are to remain the number one mid to high-end component player in the world. At all times, companies with new technologies such as SRAMs road bike components and Specialized (and other bike manufacturers) own mechanical components threaten to eat into Shimano's market share. Today, as the major brands (Trek, Specialized and Giant) all have complete product ranges that cover virtually every cycling experience, the basis for competition globally is shifting to distribution. The major brands are all working on exclusive concept stores, dealer penetration, and ways to manage the retail channel.[61]

Shimano and the mountain bike success changed the bicycle industry completely. Schwinn, once the biggest US bicycle manufacturer lost its leading position, filed for Chapter 11 twice and is today just one of many players. Cannondale reacted to Shimano's dominance by producing its own components and bicycles to the high–end market. Campagnolo, the famous Italian bicycle parts manufacturer, retracted from the mountain bike industry and focused on the high-end road bicycle market. Marketing has given the importance of quality and quality control at Shimano. All such challenges force Shimano to innovate technologically, look for new markets to enter (often in conjunction with OEMs), and continuously become more efficient on all fronts. As the Shimano team looks to the future, they are both wary and excited at the prospects.

Shimano has achieved its success by implicit Ingredient Branding. Two main factors are responsible for pulling off this strategy. First, Shimano used a well-known sport event related to bicycles, the Tour de France, to communicate the superior quality of their ingredients to bike enthusiasts. Second, they distributed their products to special retailers who offered bicycles that are exactly designed to meet individual customer wishes. The pull effect caused by the reputation existing in sport competitions led to a high demand for Shimano's quality components at retailers. Thus, a well-balanced mix of product, communication, and distribution strategies of Shimano made the Ingredient Branding approach successful.

6.6   Makrolon: The High-Tech Material

People all over the world come into contact with polycarbonates every day. Ever since 1953, this plastic has built an impressive array of success in many different product areas: eyeglasses, medical equipment, safety helmets and visors, automotive glazing and headlights, water bottles and solar modules, floor mats, sheeting for carports and greenhouses, and many other applications. Today, countless producers all over the world rely on the properties of polycarbonates. And more products and applications are constantly being added. It is impossible to imagine the future without polycarbonates.

One of these polycarbonates is Bayer's Makrolon. An estimated 45 billion of CDs have been produced with Makrolon since the birth of the compact disc in 1982. They would create a belt about 10,800,000 kilometers long, roughly equivalent to 28 times the mean distance between the earth and the moon.

Today Makrolon has a brand awareness of 31% and is absolutely the best-known polycarbonate in the market place in Europe. Lexan® from GE Plastics has the leading position in the USA.[62] The following case study describes Bayer's Ingredient Branding strategy for Makrolon in Europe. We focus on the rise of Makrolon and we broach the issue of developing this strategy for the future. Finally, awareness is not everything. Does Branding pay off? What are the conditions that determine the benefit Bayer can achieve with Makrolon? All these questions are existential successful management issues of the Makrolon brand.

When the Bayer Corporation from Leverkusen invented the polycarbonate Makrolon in 1953, it did not cause any particular shockwaves. Bayer patented the invention in the same year. In the early days Makrolon was primarily used as an insulating plastic, for example for switches and fuse boxes, but it is now recognized as a highly versatile material that can be used in many areas of life. With its high transparency, impact strength and dimensional stability, even at high temperatures, Makrolon is suitable for virtually any application. Makrolon continues to be used in electrical engineering applications but also, for instance, in headlamps and interior fittings for cars, transparent roofing for carports and swimming pools, ideal UV protection for sports goggles and sunglasses, and packaging for reusable milk bottles and water dispensers. When Polygram, a subsidiary of Philips, made the first compact disc, they used Makrolon, which is now used by renowned manufacturers as a fixed component of many CDs, CD-ROMs and DVDs. Recently they also applied it for Blue-Ray discs.

Bayer Polymers did not pursue an Ingredient Branding strategy until 2000, when it began marketing Makrolon as a brand in its own right and bringing it into the public eye (see the Makrolon logo in Fig. 64). Prior to this, it was largely unknown to consumers and only marketed to the business partner as an application chemical.

Fig. 64. Makrolon logo
(All rights reserved by the logo owners)

Bayer clearly selects Ingredient Branding partners to use and process the product, given that Makrolon has had a good reputation in the plastics processing industry. The strategy aims to make the consumer aware that both the manufacturer of the end product and the company that make the most elementary component of the product which stand for **flawless quality** and that the customer can trust this product. However, being a processor of Makrolon does not necessarily mean that an end product meets the same quality standards or reflects Bayer's level of prestige. The polycarbonate could be simply an ingredient, which cannot compensate for a manufacturer's poor reputation or the inferior quality of other ingredients used in the manufacturing process.

Bayer uses brand usage agreements to ensure the required level of quality and assumes the right to take samples during production to offer end consumers assurance of consistently high quality. But Bayer does not only consider a company's products when choosing its Ingredient Branding partners: it also scrutinizes the company and its image as a whole. When it comes to Ingredient Branding the Leverkusen firm wants to know exactly with whom they are associating in the public eye and who is allowed to use the **Bayer cross** for their own marketing purposes. Bayer does not want to be **visible** with a high-tech brand on low price/no name products in order to avoid damage to the image of the brand Makrolon.

Becoming an Ingredient Branding partner is a coveted position amongst companies that process Makrolon. As a result, Bayer is signing brand usage agreements with more and more firms. At the present time, cycling, skiing and sports goggles from UVEX Sports GmbH & Co. KG, CD-ROMs and DVD-ROMs from MMore International BV and ampoules for a needle-free injection system from Rösch AG all carry the Makrolon seal of quality.

The **Ingredient Branding family** also includes CDs and DVDs from other manufacturers (regionally separated), protective floor mats, water dispensers, flexible solar modules and many other products. What Bayer and its partners are both aiming to achieve is to differentiate themselves from the competition and competing products by means of the Branding strategy. It is important to highlight the advantages of Makrolon and transfer this positive image to the end product with the help of brand name. This differentiation gives the ingredient a **unique selling proposition** or USP, and encourages the end customer to give preference to products with the Makrolon logo or even keep a lookout for this particular product when looking to make a purchase. The potential customer then may ask for a product manufactured with Makrolon.

However, the pull effect cannot be achieved simply by adding the Makrolon quality seal to product, packaging and advertising material. Quality and credibility must also be conveyed to the consumer, who must be able to build up a familiarity with the Makrolon brand. Bayer's Ingredient Branding partners label their products and brochures all over Europe with the words "made of Makrolon" and the Bayer umbrella brand (branded house). The partners explain the advantages of this special polycarbonate and why customers should choose products with this ingredient in print advertisements, brochures, and catalogues, on their websites and at trade fairs. To initiate the **pull effect**, Bayer uses advertising campaigns to appeal directly to (potential) end consumers, and in 2000 it began targeting individual audiences with appropriate motifs, giving the brand the right emotional associations for the particular segment. Bayer used PR (public relations) in the print media and on television to convey its messages. The "fastest" and most conspicuous advertising medium was the intercity locomotives operated by Deutsche Bahn. Bayer was the first company to use intercity locomotives as advertising space, which criss-crossed Germany.

The Makrolon brand was given five different motifs, which were partially oriented towards Bayer's partners UVEX, Legoland and MMore. These locomotives proved extremely popular with railway fans, and a dedicated website set up by Bayer attracted huge numbers of hits. Model railway maker **Märklin** currently stocks a model of the locomotive featuring partner MMore, which is delivered with a computer mouse made of Makrolon. This is another example of Bayer seeking to demonstrate the versatility of its plastic, by partnering with Märklin.

The Ingredient Branding partnership between Bayer Makrolon and its customers is balanced because of its interdependence. The principle is based on synergies, i.e. each partner integrates the other and refers to the partnership in their advertising, brochures, catalogues, websites and even plastic locomotives (see Fig. 65). This does not result in advertising cost allowances or similar benefits and concessions for either side.

Fig. 65. Makrolon locomotive

As a relative newcomer to Ingredient Branding, Bayer is still in the early stages of establishing its high-tech plastic Makrolon as a brand with the user. Establishing a brand that has hitherto been completely unknown to consumers is an extremely difficult task and often associated with considerable advertising costs. So Bayer exploited its well-known name and reputation and incorporated the Bayer cross into the Makrolon logo. This had the effect of making consumers associate the plastic from the outset with the Bayer corporation, which already represents tradition and quality, and has proven it with brands such as Aspirin®. The positive image of the company can thus be transferred to the new Bayer brand. Demonstrating the link between the two brands cuts down on costs for introductory and ongoing advertising, partly because Makrolon benefits indirectly from product advertising for other Bayer products.

Background on Bayer AG

The History: The partnership "Friedrich Bayer et comp." was founded on August 1, 1863 in Barmen – now a district of the city of Wuppertal – by dye salesman Friedrich Bayer (1825–1880) and master dyer Johann Friedrich Weskott (1821–1876). The object of the company was the manufacture and sale of synthetic dyestuffs.

Between 1881 and 1913, Bayer developed into a chemical company with international operations. Although dyestuffs remained the company's largest division, new fields of business were joining the fold.

Of primary importance for Bayer's continuing development was the establishment of a major research capability by Carl Duisberg (1861–1935). A scientific laboratory was built in Wuppertal-Elberfeld – which was also the company's headquarters from 1878 until 1912 – that set new standards in industrial research. Bayer's research efforts gave rise to numerous intermediates, dyes and pharmaceuticals, including the "drug of the century," Aspirin, which was developed by Felix Hoffmann and launched onto the market in 1899. The First World War interrupted Bayer's dazzling development. The company was largely cut off from its major export markets, and sales of dyes and pharmaceuticals dropped accordingly. Bayer was increasingly integrated into the war economy and began to produce war materials, including explosives and chemical weapons. In 1917, during the war, Bayer launched its third production site in Dormagen.

A community of interests had already existed between Bayer, BASF and Agfa since 1905. In order to regain access to the vital export markets, these and other companies of the German tar dyes industry joined together to the IG Farben AG in a larger community of interests in 1915/16 on the initiative of Carl Duisberg. After the Second World War in November 1945, the Allied Forces confiscated the operations of IG Farben AG and placed all its sites under the control of allied officers. The company was to be dissolved and its assets made available for war reparations. Yet the British permitted Ulrich Haberland (1900–1961), who had been in charge of the Lower Rhine consortium since 1943, to remain in his position. Soon they allowed production to resume as well, as the chemical industry's products were essential to supply the population. In the years that followed, Haberland worked to build up a new and competitive company in the successful Bayer tradition. The allied military governments had initially planned to break up the IG Farben AG into as many small companies as possible. Yet these companies would hardly have been able to survive on the world market or even in

Germany itself. The allies finally came to this realization as well, and thus – on the basis of allied law – 12 new thoroughly competitive companies were created in the Federal Republic of Germany. Thus in 1946, while still under allied control, Bayer began to reestablish its sales activities abroad. By the 1950s, the company was allowed to acquire foreign affiliates as well. At first, the United States and Latin America were the focus of these activities.

The reconstruction of Bayer was closely linked with the "Wirtschaftswunder" (economic miracle), in the Federal Republic of Germany. As a result of World War II, Bayer for the second time had lost its foreign assets, including its valuable patents. It was clearly vital to rebuild Bayer's foreign business. Farbenfabriken Bayer AG was newly established on December 19, 1951. The Leverkusen, Dormagen, Elberfeld and Uerdingen sites were allocated to the new company, and in 1952 Bayer also received as a subsidiary the newly established Agfa "joint stock company for photo fabrication," but lost their foreign subsidiaries.

The first mild recession in the Federal Republic of Germany occurred in 1966, but it was the oil crisis of 1973/74 that ended the "economic miracle". By the time Herbert Gruenewald succeeded Kurt Hansen as management board chairman of the Bayer AG following the 1974 annual stockholders' meeting, the global economy was undergoing a radical transformation. Within just a few months, prices for chemical raw materials based on oil had risen astronomically. Makrolon was affected by these developments as well. The crisis reached its apex in the early 1980s as a severe global recession set in, and unbranded communities came under heavy price pressure.

The 1990s saw another major structural transformation, with Bayer, like other companies, facing the challenge of globalization. In the wake of the radical political changes that took place in Germany and Eastern Europe after 1989, the company increased its focus on these promising markets. As early as 1992, Bayer broke ground on a new site in Bitterfeld in East Germany, where production of Aspirin began in 1994. The importance of North America to the Bayer Group continued to increase. In Canada, Bayer acquired Toronto-based Polysar Rubber Corporation in 1990 — the most significant acquisition in the company's history up to that point. The transaction made Bayer the world's biggest supplier of raw materials for the rubber industry.

Under the leadership of Dr. Manfred Schneider, Bayer acquired the North American self-medication (over-the-counter drugs) business of Sterling Winthrop in 1994 — a milestone in the company's history, as the purchase also allowed the company to regain the rights to the "Bayer" company name in the United States. For the first time in 75 years, Bayer could operate in the United States under its own name and with the Bayer Cross as its corporate logo. In 1995 U.S.-based Miles Inc. was renamed Bayer Corporation, and Makrolon could also use the Bayer cross in their logo.

To better equip itself for the challenges of the future, Bayer set up a third pharmaceutical research center, this time in Japan, in addition to the locations in Europe (Wuppertal) and North America (West Haven, Connecticut). In 1995 the research center of Japanese pharmaceutical subsidiary Bayer Yakuhin Ltd. was dedicated at Kansai Science City near Kyoto. This marked the basic completion of Bayer's Europe/North America/Japan "pharmaceutical research triad." In the years that followed, these operations were supplemented by alliances with numerous innovative biotechnology companies. In the year 2001, Bayer acquires Aventis CropScience for €7.25 billion, making it a world leader in crop protection. In December of the same year, the company's management announces plans to establish independent operating. One year later Bayer CropScience AG was launched as the first legally independent Bayer subgroup. In 2003, the subgroups Bayer Chemicals AG and Bayer HealthCare AG and the service company Bayer Technology Services GmbH gain legal independence as part of the reorganization of the Bayer Group. The subgroup Bayer MaterialScience AG (which produces Makrolon) and the service companies Bayer Business Services GmbH and Bayer Industry Services GmbH & Co. OHG followed.

In 2005, Bayer completes the acquisition of the Roche consumer health business, advancing to become one of the world's top three suppliers of non-prescription medicines in the same year. Lanxess AG was spun off from the Bayer Group. This company continues Bayer's chemicals business and parts of its polymers business.   In January 2005, an extraordinary stockholders' meeting of Bayer Schering Pharma AG resolves to affect a "squeeze-out" of the remaining minority stockholders. Bayer Schering Pharma AG, headquartered in Berlin, now operates together with Bayer's existing pharmaceuticals business as a division of the Bayer HealthCare subgroup. Bayer is now one of the global leading enterprises with core competencies in the fields of health care, nutrition and high-tech materials.

Organization

Bayer AG defines common values, goals and strategies for the entire Group. The three subgroups (HealthCare, CropScience, Material-Science) and three service companies Business Services, Technology Services, Industry Services) operate independently, led by the management holding company. The Corporate Centre supports the Group Management Board in its task of strategic leadership (see Fig. 66).

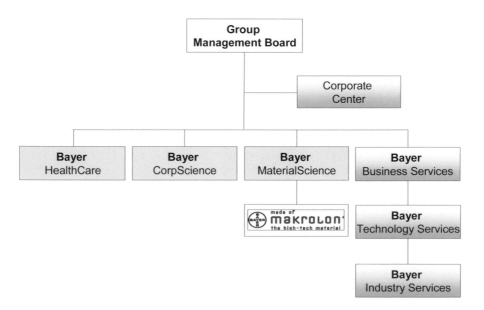

Fig. 66. Bayer Group organization

Bayer MaterialScience AG

Bayer MaterialScience is a renowned supplier of high-performance materials such as polycarbonates and polyurethanes, and innovative system solutions such as coatings, for a wide range of everyday uses. Products holding leading positions on the world market account for a large proportion of its sales. The business unit of Bayer MaterialScience holds five subdivisions. Collectively, the subdivisions provide the basis for Bayer MaterialScience's operations. They develop and manufacture products within their focus. The subdivisions are the following:

- **Coatings, Adhesives, Sealants (BU CAS)**
  This business unit is responsible for the development and production of a broad range of raw materials for coatings, adhesives and sealants.

- **Polycarbonates (BU PCS)**
  Makrolon polycarbonate is a classic among Bayer Material-Science's products.

- **Polyurethanes (BU PUR)**
  Polyurethanes are one of the major materials used in the manufacturer of foams for padding, furniture, and so on, and also of many durable industrial and commercial coatings.

- **Thermoplastic Polyurethanes (BU TPU)**
  Thermoplastic polyurethanes have become simply indispensable. They make sure, for example, that a car functions properly.

- **Inorganic Basic Chemicals (IBC)**
  IBC is responsible for worldwide chlorine supplies at Bayer MaterialScience.

The revenues of each business unit in the revenue of the whole Bayer Group is shown in Fig. 67.

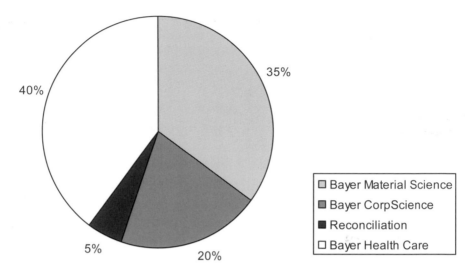

Fig. 67. Revenues per business unit of the Bayer AG 2007

Background on Makrolon

Today's Makrolon production has reached an every day use of more than 500 tons and a capacity of more than 1,200,000 tons in four existing subsidiaries. Bayer MaterialScience is increasing its market share based on high investments and focusing on China in the future.[63] With an expected growth of more than 8% p.a. in polycarbonates Bayer chose China with Shanghai as the main location to strengthen their competitive advantage. Bayer MaterialScience is investing more than €720 million up to 1.1 billions from 2006 to 2012 in projects including polycarbonates. Makrolon has been crowned with success and is used by different segments, ranging from roofing, surface coating, and medical technology to car windows. Because of the great success and diversity Bayer has had with Makrolon, they opted for the marketing tool "Ingredient Branding". The key of Bayer Makrolon's new Ingredient Branding concept was the requirement that the component was used for high-class core products, labeled with the Makrolon logo. The new instrument "Ingredient Branding" puts both the product and the component in an excellent competitor position as well as creating added value.

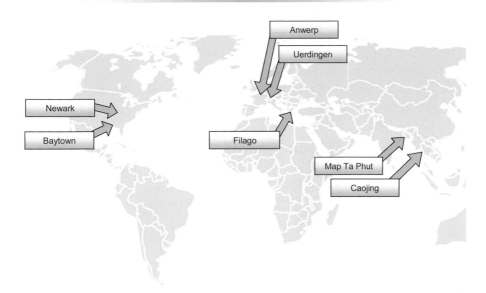

Fig. 68. Local production of Makrolon

The locations for the Makrolon production are organized globally. There are seven production places: Baytown in the USA, Uerdingen, Antwerp and Filago in Europe and Caojing and Map Ta Phut in Asia (see Fig. 68).

The Market for Polycarbonate

Polycarbonates (PC) were first prepared by Einhorn in 1898 and extensively researched until 1930 when they were discarded. Research was then re-started in the mid 1950s by General Electric, and in 1958 the Polycarbonate popularity expanded to a global community. Today, approximately 75% of the Polycarbonate market is held by Bayer and GE Plastics, now acquired by Saudi Basic Industries (SABIC)[64].

Experts predict that the demand of computers and home appliances will continue to grow in the next few years, and the demand for polycarbonate (PC) from this sector will increase at an annual rate of 10%-12%. For the railway, highway, airport and urban construction sectors, it is expected that there will also be a strong demand for hollow sunlight panels. In the past few years, enterprises located in the YRD (Yangtze River Delta) and PRD (Pearl River Delta) regions that use PC to manufacture panels greatly outperformed those enterprises that produce panels from other resins. Hollow sunlight panels are semi-structural, corrugated (much like cardboard) panels that take advantage of the clarity and toughness of Polycarbonate. They are often used instead of glass for greenhouses and other similar structures, as they are virtually unbreakable. Bayer pioneered this application in the 1970s in Europe, bringing the application to the U.S. by the early 1980s. GE entered the market in the middle of the decade, but this application has remained a major one for Bayer.

It is anticipated the demand for PC from the hollow sunlight panels manufacturing sector will grow at an annual rate of 12%-15%. Moreover, experts forecast that PC-based blend alloy composite material suppliers to become some of the largest consumers for PC, as the automotive industry has a great demand for their product.[65] The main competitors in the market place for Bayer MaterialScience polycarbonate are:

- SABIC (GE Plastics Lexan®)
- Dow (Calibre®)
- Teijin
- Mitsubishi Chemical Group
- Idemitsu
- Sam Yang
- Chi Mei
- Formosa
- Policarbonatos do Brasil

Bayer's Branding Strategy for Makrolon

To get in touch with consumers and retailers, Bayer started with Ingredient Branding campaigns to inform end users about Makrolon. Bayer's multi stage marketing differs from "Intel-Insides" strategy. Whereas Intel is using brand advertising and cooperation advertising, Bayer is almost solely using cooperation advertising; both partners are advertising together. Interesting is the fact that Bayer is not paying any advertising grants to advertise with partners. Cooperation advertising in terms of Bayer means that each partner has to finance his own part. This form of a partnership results in a "win-win" situation for both sides, with added value for both without sharing costs. Bayer is furthermore expecting good reputation with high quality and good image of the end product. When signing license contracts, the partner has to agree with pre-product tests before labeling the ingredient on the core product, the allowance of samples taken by Bayer to secure the quality.[66] The Makrolon logo is labeled on the core product or packages. The integration of the Bayer Makrolon logo is further extended to exhibitions, advertising campaigns, event and sponsoring activities.

With Bayer's Ingredient Branding campaign of cooperation advertising from 2001, Bayer targeted the selected end user groups for products groups, CD/DVD, sunglasses and medical products. Bayer and partners were pushed the message to consumers to call attention to Makrolon, the labeled polycarbonate, and created the pull effect. Bayer and its partners communicated the new branded ingredient in magazines, journals and popular magazines. The campaign was launched in Germany, Great Britain, Spain, and other countries. In collateral to labeling Makrolon, the chosen partners educated the end user of the ingredient by advertising campaigns, flyers, websites and exhibitions. A consequent communication concept with the integration of advertising and public relation pushed the message to more consumers' minds. Today Makrolon is a well-known brand to many end users in most parts of the world, with USA still lagging behind. For Bayer Material Science, brand management became an important part not only for B2B customers, but also for addressing end users. Makrolon created a competitive advantage through communication with the end user, and it showed that Ingredient Branding could properly improve the brand value of polycarbonate.

Bayer's aim is to communicate Makrolon's benefit to the end user. This could lead the end users to be willing to pay more for the labeled ingredient, demanding the ingredient in core products. The communication process usually starts with partner campaigns, using the Bayer cross and "made of Makrolon". The communication process also includes "point of sale" marketing activities. In addition, public relations are helping to inform the target customers. End user surveys help to define consumer wants and needs. Partnerships and the resulting "win-win" situation is an important step in implementing an Ingredient Branding strategy. The "win-win" situation can occur through reduction of prices for the core product manufacturer or support in advertising campaigns.

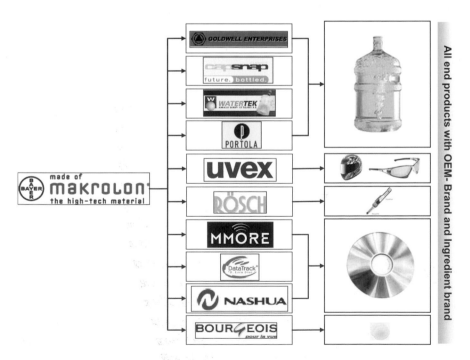

Fig. 69. OEMs using Makrolon for their end product

(All rights reserved by the logo owners)

Different partnership campaigns made the ingredient as well known as the core product. The IC advertisement on train locomotives had been a communicator in pushing the messages and strengthens Makrolon profile.[67] Through compact discs, automotive headlights[68], eyeglass lenses, helmets, household appliances and water bottles – almost everybody comes into contact with Makrolon at least once a day. Makrolon is about to become a well-known brand, like Aspirin. Bayer and its partners who use Makrolon to manufacture their products began publicizing the brand name and the outstanding properties and qualities of this polycarbonate to the final consumers. Throughout Europe, these co-Branding partners label their products with the "made of Makrolon" logo and the Bayer cross. By applying this seal of quality, Branding partners like MMore, HiSpace, and Data Track convey the message that the material used for their recordable CDs and DVDs guarantees optimum storage quality and security.

To accompany the labeling of their products, the partners also use ads, flyers, web sites and exhibition stands to draw attention to Makrolon. Other co-Branding partners include water bottle producers Capsnap in Austria and Watertek in Turkey, and Makroform GmbH, a member of the Bayer Group whose products include polycarbonate sheeting for high-quality roofing.

The following Fig. 69 shows selected OEMs, which uses Makrolon in their end product. All these companies show the ingredient by using the Makrolon brand on their final product.

The Example UVEX

UVEX was one of the early participants of the Ingredient Branding activities of Makrolon. Since the company's foundation in 1926, UVEX has always focused on its mission "Protecting People" – at work, sport and leisure activities and Makrolon was the perfect material to help to achieve this mission. UVEX WINTER HOLDING comprises four international subsidiaries under one roof:

- UVEX SECURITY, for protection at work: eyewear, helmets, gloves, hearing protection, foot and work wear.

- UVEX SPORTS, for sport and leisure: helmets for skiing, cycling and motorcycling, sunglasses and goggles for skiing, cycling, motorcycling and fun sport, protective clothing and boots for motorcyclists.

- ALPINA, for sport, leisure and the optical trade: ski and cycle helmets, ski goggles, cycle and sports sunglasses, optical frames and sunglasses.

- FILTRAL, fashion sunglasses and reading glasses.

Bayer's partner for the Ingredient Branding strategy is UVEX SPORTS. This business unit offers products for motor sports, cycling and skiing, which are sold in specialist shops throughout the world. As well as distributing to all major world markets, the company has subsidiaries in Switzerland, Austria, the Netherlands, the USA and Japan.

UVEX SPORTS is known as a professional supplier of protective equipment in international top-class sports. Far-reaching sponsorship activities in bobsledding, tobogganing, snowboarding, downhill,

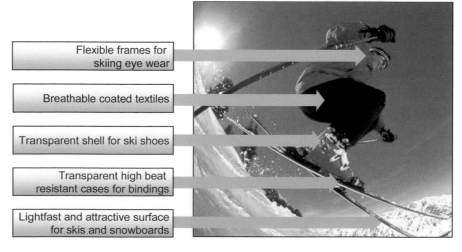

Fig. 70. Possible application in ski equipment for Makrolon®

and cross-country skiing increase the company's market presence and significance. Top professionals such as ski jumpers Janne Ahonen, Sigurd Pettersen and Kazujoshi Funaki; racing skiers such as Michaela Dorfmeister, Renate Goetschl, Sonja Nef, Fritz Strobl, Andi Schifferer and Sammi Uotila; tobogganist Georg Hackl and bob sledder Christoph Langen and many more represent the UVEX winter sports team. Makrolon can be transparent or opaque, is resistant to impact and weathering, and withstands high and low temperatures. These attributes linked to the Makrolon brand are major aspects for high quality sport products. The partnership between these two brands embodies the similar or complement attributes to the end user. Ski equipment is a good example. Starting with the eyewear, where Makrolon can be used to build flexible frames, breathable-coated textiles, transparent shells for ski shoes, transparent high beat resistant cases for bindings and lightfast and attractive surface for skis and snowboards as possible applications (see Fig. 70). All these end products are part of UVEX's product portfolio.

Table 12. OEMs using Makrolon for their end product

OEM	End product brand	Product categories
RS Office	Rollsafe, Roll-o-Grip u.a.	Floor cover mats
BNL Eurolens	BNL Eurolens	Eye glasses
Euro Digital Disc Manufacturing	Data Track	CDs
MMORE	MMORE	CDs / DVDs
Tera Media Corporation	Nashua	CDs / DVDs
Videolar	EMTEC / Nipponic	CDs / DVDs
Luceplan	Constanza	Design lamps
Salman Plastik	Salblend, Salflex	Electronic
Spirit of Golf	Laser Line Tee	Golf equipment
Matsuzaki Industry Co. Ltd.	Maruem	Suitcases
G+B Pronova	Holo Pro	Holographic projection disks
Geomag SA	Geomag	Magnet-Toys
Societe Bourgeois	Galaxy	Optical Lenses
Alurunner GmbH	Alurunner	Sleighs
Sunovation	Sunovation	Solar modules
UVEX	UVEX	Sports equipment
Goldwell Enterprises Inc.	Goldwell	Water bottle
Watertek	Watertek	Water bottle
Capsnap Europe	Capsnap	Water bottle
Portola Packaging Inc.	Portola, Garafón	Water bottle
OEM	End product brand	Product categories
RS Office	Rollsafe, Roll-o-Grip u.a.	Floor cover mats

Bayer and UVEX have created a promotion campaign together. Both companies communicate the brands not only on the products but also on sport events or in image brochures. Both companies perform together on fairs and show therefore not only the raw material polycarbonate but also a possible application for Makrolon. UVEX Sport products are made for high performance sportsmen. These products symbolize the high performance standard that brings the consumer closer down to the ingredient Makrolon thereby enabling companies to achieve a win-win situation. OEMs using Makrolon for their end product are shown in Table 12.

6.7   DLP: Pampering the Customer

Texas Instruments Incorporated, better known in the electronic industry as TI, is an American company based in Dallas/Texas, founded in 1930 as a geophysical exploration company that used seismic signal processing technology to search for oil. In 1954, TI entered the semiconductor market with its introduction of the first commercial silicon transistor (see Fig.71 for DLP logos).

Fig. 71. DLP logos
(All rights reserved by the logo owners)

From the company's earliest days, the objective has been to use the company's unique technical skills to fundamentally change markets and create entirely new ones. A constant thread throughout TI's history has been their use of progressively more complex signal processing technology – with advances ranging **from the incremental to the revolutionary** – to literally and repeatedly change the world. TI provides innovative digital signal processing (DSP) and analog technologies help create the world's most advanced electronics. The real-time signal processing technology permeates daily life in many different ways, from digital communications and entertainment to medical services, automotive systems and wide-ranging applications in between.

The company's core business today is semiconductor with total revenues of $12 billion in 2008, accounting for 96 percent of the revenue. The education technology business, representing 4 percent of the revenue, designs and develops calculator and technology solutions that help educators and students in their math and science learning. TI received the award of **the Fortune's "Most Admired Companies" – ranked No. 1** in the semiconductor industry – 2008 for the 5th consecutive year.[69] The following chart shows the position in the memory chip industry (see Fig. 72). This chart highlights that their position is justified.

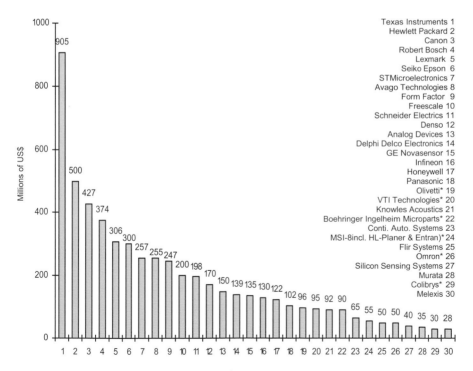

Fig. 72. Largest memory chip manufacturer 2006

DLP – A History of Innovation

DLP (Digital Light Processing™) is a trademark owned by Texas Instruments representing a technology used in projectors and video projectors. The story of DLP begins in 1997 when Texas Instruments scientist Dr. Larry Hornbeck starts to explore how principles of light reflection can be used to manipulate light. Ten years later, in 1987, he develops the Digital Micro Mirror Device (DMD), an optical semiconductor capable of steering photons with unparalleled accuracy. In 1992 TI forms the Digital Imaging Venture Project to explore the commercial viability of the DMD. One year later the Digital Light Processing™ technology is named; the Digital Imaging division (later to become the DLP Products division) is established to unlock its potential for commercial projection display applications. In the mid-nineties, TI announces its first customer agreement and in 1996, the first commercial DLP systems are shipped to InFocus, nView and Proxima. In Europe, Liesegang was the first to get on board and in Japan, PLUS Corporation made the debut. In 1997, the Motion Picture Academy of Arts and Sciences chooses DLP technology to project the Oscars; DLP technology has been used at the Academy Awards ever since. In 1998 came the first award for them. DLP Products receives an Emmy award for outstanding achievement in engineering development from the Academy of Arts and Sciences. Dr. Larry Hornbeck also receives an Emmy for inventing DLP technology.

One year later the DLP Cinema® projector technology is publicly demonstrated for the first time on two screens in Los Angeles and New York for the release of Lucasfilm's *Star Wars: Episode I – The Phantom Menace*. International field-testing of DLP Cinema technology began. The new millennium starts with the introduction of the world's first sub-3-lb. DLP projector by PLUS Corporation, demonstrating DLP technology's capability to lead the market in portable projectors. The same year, Digital China launches the first China-branded DLP projector. In 2001, TI announces the first 16:9 projector, greatly anticipated by home theatre enthusiasts. Additionally, InFocus announces the first sub-2-lb.projector with its groundbreaking LP120 DLP.

The following year is marked by other companies entering the DLP markets. In January, Samsung announces their first DLP HDTV, priced at $3,999. HP enters the projector market with DLP technology in April. One month later Dell follows. In June NEC is named the third DLP Cinema manufacturer partner. In 2004, DLP becomes number one supplier of micro display technology, according to TSR. InFocus becomes first TI customer to ship 1 million DLP projectors. This year LG Electronics and Toshiba introduce DLP HDTV.

The year 2005 started with HP, Optoma and Radio Shack introducing the first "Instant Theater" projectors, incorporating sounds system and DVD player with DLP projection into one, consumer-friendly unit. Besides, the first sub-1-lb.projectors are announced and introduced by Mitsubishi, Toshiba and Samsung. The "Pocket Projectors" create new category of micro-projection. In October, Dell introduces the first high resolution (SX+) at mass market prices ($3499) and Samsung ships 1 million DLP TVs.

In 2006, the year of its 10-year anniversary, DLP technology achieves greater than 50% market share in the worldwide front projection market for the first time and DLP Cinema projectors surpass 1,000 deployed milestone; 1,200 projectors deployed worldwide. TI announces 10 Million DLP systems shipped in 10 years. In 2007 and 2008 the new application went smaller and handheld projection systems were introduced. Samsung launched the DLP Pico Projector Phone, as small as a regular mobile phone. The Pico Projector will enable the user to view various image sizes, a maximum of up to 50 inches depending on ambient light conditions. The device includes Texas Instruments' DLP Pico chipset for media viewing.

Today, Dr. Larry Hornbeck is on his twenty-ninth patent and going strong. And the DLP Products division is shaping the digital future with the same dedication to excellence that's made Texas Instruments a world leader in digital signal processing.[70]

The Ingredient Branding Process

For the consumer, the Texas Instruments brand is best known for calculators and early attempts to enter into the personal computer market. Beside that, Texas Instruments is an industrial brand of the semi contactor industry, serving their clients. TI was the first company with global reach, but since the introduction of the DLP chip set, they started a significant campaign to promote its new invention DLP technology to final end user. Today DLP is used in a wide range of projection and display applications by a number of different companies making TVs and selling them to consumers. The consumer television environment has many formats, features and technologies – from HDTV and LCD to Plasma and HDMI, and many more. DLP offers another solution for specific applications: **Big screen HDTVs without the big price!** They offer also projector from large to small, and cinema applications, including 3-D digital cinema.

Texas Instruments is promoting its new product offerings to the end users and takes the opportunity to help their own customers sell DLP products more effectively with a campaign to speak directly to consumers, educating end users about the difference of their technology. With the help of the advertisement agency McCann-Erickson in Dallas, TX Texas Instruments DLP division launched an award winning campaign. They won the 1998 BRONZE Effie award for computer hardware. Texas Instruments was awarded for their "Ingredient Branding campaign that supports the launch of a new technology, DLP"[71].

TI continued to sponsor the Annual Academy Awards with DLP Projectors and TVs since 1998 and decided to boost public attention in 2006. They supported the NASCAR NEXTEL Cup Series racing team and the #96 DLP HDTV Chevrolet. The NASCAR sponsorship was one piece of a nationwide direct–to–consumer marketing effort of DLP technology, which was the first campaign of this type for Texas Instruments. Within a short time, TI saw consumer awareness more than double for DLP HDTV technology amongst NASCAR fans that attended the races. Overall on–air TV network brand exposure

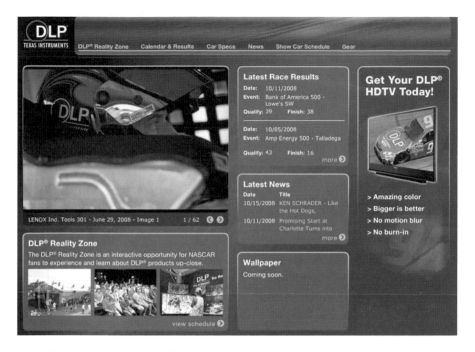

Fig. 73. Screenshot from DLP racing homepage

for DLP technology was in the top 10 of all competing NASCAR sponsored cars during the entire 2006 season, which placed DLP Products' first–year team in the same league as the top performing veteran sponsored racing teams such as Budweiser and Home Depot[72]. A screenshot from the DLP racing homepage is shown in Fig. 73.

With this considerable investment, DLP raised its awareness, and the attention of the top management. Revenue increase did not happen immediately, but this was a smart approach for a company like TI, with no infrastructure to sell to consumers and no driving need to take on the likes of LG, Samsung and Panasonic. Instead of competing with them, TI has focused on selling them the technology and partnering with all of them to market it. TI has over 50 partners selling DLP products. Each of these partners likely contributes financially to support marketing behind the DLP ingredient. And each of these partners offers their own communications support of DLP in their product literature, advertising and retail displays. For a publicly traded company like Texas Instruments, the boost to familiarity among investors that comes from this type of exposure can even drive a higher stock price. For TI, Ingredient Branding became a compelling solution for selling a strongly differentiated component.

DLP – How It Works

Inside of every DLP projection system an optical semiconductor known as the DLP chip is placed. Larry Hornbeck's DLP chip is probably the world's most sophisticated light switch. It contains a rectangular array of up to **2 million hinge-mounted microscopic mirrors**; each of these micro mirrors measures less than one-fifth the width of a human hair. When a DLP chip is coordinated with a digital video or graphic signal, a light source, and a projection lens, its mirrors can reflect a **digital image** onto a screen or other surface. The DLP chip and the sophisticated electronics that surround it are what it's called DLP technology. A DLP chip's micro mirrors are mounted on tiny hinges that enable them to tilt either toward the light source in a DLP projection system (ON) or away from it (OFF)-creating a light or dark pixel on the projection surface.

The bit-streamed image code entering the semiconductor directs each mirror to switch **on and off up to several thousand times per second**. When a mirror is switched on more frequently than off, it reflects a light gray pixel; a mirror that's switched off more frequently reflects a darker gray pixel. In this way, the mirrors in a DLP projection system can reflect pixels in **up to 1,024 shades of gray** to convert the video or graphic signal entering the DLP chip into a highly detailed grey scale image. The white light generated by the lamp in a DLP projection system passes through a color wheel as it travels to the surface of the DLP chip. The color wheel filters the light into red, green, and blue, from which a single-chip DLP projection system can create at least **16.7 million colors**. And the 3-chip system found in DLP Cinema projection systems is capable of producing no fewer than **35 trillion colors.**

The on and off states of each micro mirror are coordinated with these three basic building blocks of color. For example, a mirror responsible for projecting a purple pixel will only reflect red and blue light to the projection surface; our eyes then blend these rapidly alternating flashes to see the intended hue in a projected image.

1-Chip DLP Projection System

Televisions, home theatre systems and business projectors using DLP technology rely on a single chip configuration like the one described above. White light passes through a color wheel filter, causing red, green and blue light to be shone in sequence on the surface of the DLP chip. The switching of the mirrors and the proportion of time

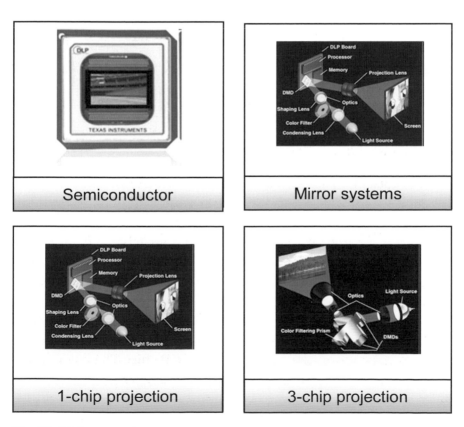

Fig. 74. DLP principles

they are on or off are coordinated according to the color shining on them. The human visual system integrates the sequential color and sees a full-color image.

3-Chip DLP Projection System

DLP technology-enabled projectors for very high image quality or very high brightness applications such as cinema and large venue displays rely on a 3-chip configuration to produce stunning images, whether moving or still. In a 3-chip system, the white light generated by the lamp passes through a prism that divides it into red, green and blue. Each DLP chip is dedicated to one of these three colors; the colored light that the micro mirrors reflect is then combined and passed through the projection lens to form an image.[73] The DLP principles are shown in Fig. 74.

LCD vs. DLP

The DLP systems have a very strong technological competitor. Despite their similarities, these two technologies are very different in the way they deliver the image to the viewer. LCD (liquid crystal display) projectors usually contain three separate LCD glass panels, one each for red, green and blue components of the image signal being fed into the projector. As light passes through the LCD panels, individual pixels ("picture elements") can be opened to allow light to pass or closed to block the light, as if each little pixel were fitted with a Venetian blind. This activity modulates the light and produces the image that is projected onto the screen.

As described above DLP works quite differently than LCD. Instead of having glass panels for passing light, the DLP chip is a reflective surface made up of thousands of tiny mirrors. Each mirror represents a single pixel. In a DLP projector, light from the projector's lamp is directed onto the surface of the DLP chip. The mirrors wobble back and forth, directing light either into the lens path to turn the pixel on, or away from the lens path to turn it off. [74]

Both technologies have great advantages:

DLP

Highest contrast ratios: DLP home theatre projectors normally have contrast ratios from 2000:1 up to 5000:1 or more, and generate the best "black levels" – which means more detail in very dark areas "shadow details".

Longer life of DLP: In contrast to LCD, in DPL technology replaceable light sources are used which lead to a longer life of the product. Very often the parts are user-replaceable which increases the comfort for the customer. DLP Projectors have a **lighter weight** that LCD or Plasma TV.

Less "screen door effect" than LCD: One of the main goals the inventors of these technologies have is to limit the pixel visibility for the viewer. In these areas DLP projectors have a distinct advantage over LCD projectors. A DLP projector allows you to sit about 25%-40% closer to the screen.[75]

No possibility of phosphor **burn-in** – unlike CRT and plasma systems, a DLP HDTV and projector simply has no tube, phosphor or other elements to burn in. This means no worries of video games and network logos burning in on screen. HDTVs and projectors with DLP technology use a single-panel system (vs. a three-element system) and will not suffer from mis-convergence or degradation of video.[76]

LCD

Better color saturation than DLP technology: Inside most single-chip DLP projectors, a clear (white) panel is included in the color wheel along with red, green, and blue in order to boost brightest or total lumen output. Though the image is brighter than it would otherwise be, this tends to reduce color saturation, making the DLP picture appear not quite as rich and vibrant.[77]

LCD projectors don't have a spinning color wheel. This results in a very **low level of noise.** LCD projectors usually produce significantly **higher ANSI lumen**[78] outputs than do DLPs with the same wattage lamp.

Pampering the Customer

At the end of the day the consumer has to decide which technology in which product he or she prefers. So the question was: how to attract the customer? With the campaign launched in 2006 Texas Instruments wanted to turn HDTV consumer's attention away from plasma and LCD and towards their DLP technology. The theme of the campaign was **"It's amazing. It's the mirrors."** This was in reference to the millions of tiny mirrors that make up one of the chips used in a DLP display. The theme lends its name to the website for the campaign **itsthemirrors.com.** The campaign included four television ads directed by frequent Spike Lee cinematographer Mayik Sayeed, and involves a girl and her elephant (really) sharing the wonders of DLP technology with everyday folks and celebrities.

In 2007 TI announced the largest campaign ever supporting DLP-based micro display HDTVs. The $100 million dollar marketing investment includes a new campaign anchored by three major sports sponsorships and kicks off the peak fall 2007 HDTV buying season. As a part of the new campaign, DLP Products became a prominent sponsor of ABC and ESPN's Monday Night NFL and college football programming, as well as those stations' Nextel Cup NASCAR programming.[79] The new spots point out the key advantages that DLP's advanced display technology hold over the competition. The spots, created by JWT Communications, Entertainment and Technology Practice and shot in California, bring young Bella and the elephant back to share the magic of DLP technology and builds on the **"It's amazing. It's the mirrors."** campaign. In 2007 it introduced the Internet basketball sensation "Mr. 720," one of the only people in the world to successfully complete two revolutions while dunking a basketball. Mr. 720's incredible feat was caught in high definition for one dramatic spot that will highlight the lack of motion blur and fast action enabled by DLP technology.

Market research showed that a HDTV buyer is a tech-savvy and sport enthusiast. Therefore TI focuses on sports including DLP's ongoing NASCAR sponsorship, online, retail and promotional elements. "In 2006, we associated DLP technology with millions of mirrors and saw awareness of the relationship rise nearly 200 percent. This year we're focusing on benefits of DLP micro mirror technology and closely targeting areas where the typical DLP buyer, spends most of its time – watching football," noted Jan Spence, manager of corporate Branding, TI DLP Products. "DLP technology has inherent advantages over other HDTV technologies," said Doug Darrow, brand and marketing manager for DLP Products. "This new campaign sets out to help educate the consumer on those advantages so that they can make an educated buying decision for their HDTV. Research shows that when consumers research their buying decision they have a much higher likelihood to purchase DLP than other HDTV technologies."

Market Share

The campaigns are paying off. Although LCD is still the best-selling HD technology on the television market, DLP is gaining fast. According to a report released in May 2007 by the NPD Group[80], sales of HD DLP sets with 50 inches and larger grew 63 percent between December 2005 and the end of 2006. "DLP was successful in claiming a significant amount of market share in 2006, particularly in the larger screen sizes, 50 inches and above" said Stephen Baker, vice president of industry analysis with The NPD Group. "Even during the holiday season when the so-called 'flat-screen war' was at its peak for the year, DLP proved to be a viable competitor against not only other micro displays, but also against plasma and LCD."[81]

And it's the big screens that are making the difference. In 2006, more 50-plus-inch DLPs was sold than any other competing technology, capturing 28.9 percent of the unit market, according to NPD. DLP also accounted for more than one quarter of all 1080p HDTVs sold in December 2006. Demand for 1080p technology, DLP and non-DLP alike, increased almost seven times between December 2005 and 2006, a trend that NPD expects to continue. "We're extremely pleased by the progress DLP has made during the past year and see further growth in 2007, thanks in large part to the innovations of our customers and our supporting brand and marketing efforts," said Adam Kunzman, business manager of DLP HDTV Products with Texas Instruments[82].

Until 2009, Texas Instruments remained the primary manufacturer of DLP technology, which is used by many licensees who market products based on TI's chipsets. The Fraunhofer Institute of Dresden, Germany, also manufactures Digital Light Processors, under the name of Spatial Light Modulators, for use in specialized applications. For example, Micronic Laser Systems of Sweden utilizes Fraunhofer's SLMs to generate deep-ultraviolet imaging in its Sigma line of silicon mask lithography writers. They did not have the guts or the funds to battle with its competitor Texas Instruments. Through Ingredient Branding, DLP technology has quickly gained market share in the front projection market and now holds roughly 50% of the worldwide share in front projection.

Over 30 manufacturers use the DLP chipset to power their projectors, but what are the challenges ahead, is it a new technology or the power in the market structure. The answer could possibly be found in the new activities of TI DLP.

A new loyalty program for schools, which uses multiple systems in their premises, has been started. The program targets K-12 school districts in the United States and offers them loyalty points, which they can use with new purchases of equipments. This is another way to connect directly with the customers (see Fig. 75 for logo of new educator loyalty program).

Selected DLP manufacturers are shown in Fig. 76.

Fig. 75. Logo for new educator loyalty program

Fig. 76. Selected DLP manufacturers
(All rights reserved by the logo owners)

6.8   Schott Ceran: Differentiating with Success

Glass-ceramic cook top panels from Schott Ceran have achieved the status of a high-quality household staple by offering considerable benefits to customers. With experience of more than 30 years and more than 75 million units sold, the Schott Hometech division is market leader for glass-ceramic cook top panels worldwide.[83]

This section will discuss the Ingredient Branding strategy that has been implemented by the Schott brand management. Company background and the way to success will be described in detail, and in particular, Ingredient Branding implementation will be analyzed critically[84]. Schott AG, a non-listed stockholding company, super-vised by a foundation, is a multinational, technology-based group developing and manufacturing specialty materials, components and systems for nearly 125 years to improve how people live and work[85]. Schott has manufacturing sites and sales offices close to its customers on all major markets. For the systematic improvement of efficiency and customer satisfaction, management and employees align themselves to Schott's core values: accountability, market-driven innovation, technological expertise, integrity and reliability, entrepreneurship. Sales increased in recent years greatly due to in-ternational expansion and the involvement into new technological areas such as solar panels and medical devices.

The story of the multinational, technology-based group started in 1884, when Otto Schott, Ernst Abbe, Carl Zeiss and Roderich Zeiss founded the Glastechnische Laboratorium Schott & Genossen (later: Jenaer Glaswerk Schott & Genossen) in Jena, Germany. Five years later, Ernst Abbe founded the Carl-Zeiss-Foundation. After the conversion of the foundation enterprise into a stock corporation, the Carl-Zeiss-Foundation became its sole shareholder (2004). The main markets of Schott are household appliances, optics, electronics, pharmaceutical industries, automobile, and solar energy. The company employs about 16,800 people worldwide; Germany's share is 7,200 people. In the financial year 2005/2006, Schott realized sales of 2.23 billion Euros worldwide and an operating profit (EBIT) of 193 million Euros.[86]

The brand structure of Schott is dominated by a typical umbrella brand strategy (branded house). On top of the brand pyramid is the Schott corporate brand, representing all majority participants. For joint ventures, there are different company brands and there are so-called designed product brands[87], such as Schott Ceran, where the corporate brand backs the product brand (see Fig. 77).

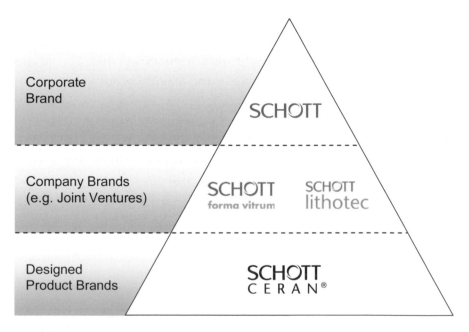

Fig. 77. Brand pyramid Schott (source: internal presentation, Schott AG)

Market and Competition

The Schott Ceran ceramic cook top panel is a component of cooking surfaces and is usually bought together with cooking stoves and ovens. For this reason, the market for "white goods" (comprising major household appliance) will be considered here in more detail.

The German market for white goods (39 million households) is the largest in Europe. Market saturation for electric kitchen stoves and ovens was 84 percent in 2004 (83 % in 2000)[88], indicating weak growth potential. This industry realized positive growth rates between 1998 and 2000. Since then, the first year with positive growth was in 2006.[89]

As for competition, Schott has to deal with two main competitors who also focus on specialty glass but have not established own brands for their products. An exception is "Eurokera", although not a serious threat, due to its low investment in their brand. Thanks to the weak competitive environment, Schott was able to achieve a first-mover-advantage and succeeded without much hardship in differentiation from its competitors.[90] Remember that Ingredient Branding is likely to be more successful when the number of competitors is low while the number of OEMs is high.[91] Given that Schott has only two main competitors, the situation is a good one for following an Ingredient Branding strategy. On the other hand, the industry of household appliances is highly consolidated with only a few OEMs present in the market. This complicates the execution of an Ingredient Branding strategy, as communication is likely to be restrained and the brand might be suppressed by OEMs, especially if host brands are very strong.

Brand Strategy

Building up long lasting partnerships is an important part of the Schott corporate culture. Confidence and reliability with the target group to realize a win-win-situation are more important than short-term sales increases. Continuous investment in R&D further characterizes the strategy of Schott. Partnerships also offer the opportunity to share knowledge and to exchange information and can culminate in collaborative product development. This approach can also be found in brand management activities. Marketing measures are planned and finalized together, as it happens with Schott and Rinnai in Japan or Haier in China.[92]

The Success Story

The success story of Schott Ceran started with the decision to develop glass-ceramic cook top panels. Today, Schott Ceran is considered to be the most important product in the Schott portfolio. Due to a high customer satisfaction, the rate of repurchase for glass-ceramic cook top panels is 96 percent. In Europe, more than 50 percent of all new electric stoves are equipped with Schott Ceran.[93] The production started in 1971 when the first glass-ceramic cook top panels were sold under the brand name Schott Ceran. Ceran glass-ceramic cook top panels are featured with high heat transmission and low thermal expansion. The benefit for the end consumer is a smooth, non-porous surface, which is easy to clean, and helps to maintain the cook top panel in good condition for a long time. Ceran cook top panels are four millimeter thick, offer thermal stability and resist thermal shocks of up to 700° C with almost no heat loss.[94]

Important milestones in the success story of Schott Ceran are the continuous optimization and advancement of manufacturing technologies. In 1971, Ceran was first represented by stove manufacturer Imperial at the household appliances fair Domotechnica. In 1976, the company became active in consumer and market research and in 1980, sold one million cook top panels. Introducing Schott Certificates for cookware (1983) and winning the German Marketing Award (1984) were further cornerstones in the success story of Schott Ceran (see Fig. 78).

Originally driven by innovation technology, Schott is now increasingly concentrating on a market-oriented strategy.[95] In 1997 a new brand architecture was established. Before this point in time, Ceran appeared basically as a product brand, with the brand name "Schott" that was not easy to recognize. Within the scope of a common new

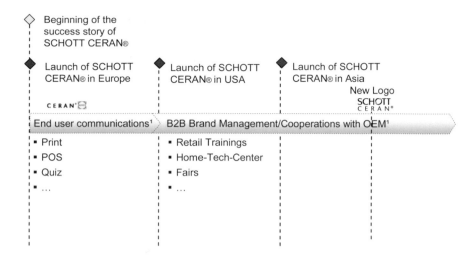

Beginning of the
success story of
SCHOTT CERAN®

Launch of SCHOTT
CERAN® in Europe

Launch of SCHOTT
CERAN® in USA

Launch of SCHOTT
CERAN® in Asia

New Logo
SCHOTT
CERAN®

CERAN®

End user communications¹   B2B Brand Management/Cooperations with OEM¹

• Print
• POS
• Quiz
• ...

• Retail Trainings
• Home-Tech-Center
• Fairs
• ...

¹Refers to the launch of SCHOTT CERAN® in Germany

Fig. 78. Schott Ceran success story

strategic alignment, the new logo was introduced in 1997, emphasizing both brand names, "Schott" and "Ceran". The aim in doing this was to let the product brand benefit from the good reputation and image of the corporate brand "Schott". Conversely, Schott could benefit from the well-established brand image of Ceran.[96]

Branding a corporation is commonly known as Corporate Branding. Ingredient Branding and Corporate Branding overlap when the brand is advertised towards the consumer and promoted as an institution. The example of Intel demonstrates this, as the Intel Corporation is communicated as a Corporate Brand towards the consumer and is promoted as a component of personal computers as well. Schott also decided to follow this strategy to let Ceran benefit from the strength of the Corporate Brand.[97]

Based on a consumer study conducted by a market research institute, the presence of glass-ceramic cook top panels was identified as the second most important criterion to determine the buying decision of end customers. Price was the most important criterion, the brand name ranked fifth. The finding shows that Schott Ceran is more than an ingredient with functional property and benefit for consumers. In fact, it can be considered a very important component to influence the buying decision of consumers, as it adds significant value to the host product.

The Value Proposition

The brand promise of Schott Ceran consists of three pillars: unmatched experience, innovation partnership, and customer care.

"Unmatched experience" is characterized by the long lasting experience for more than 30 years, coupled with continuous research and development investment amounting to six percent of the turnover per year. "Innovation partnership" is also based upon continuous investment in new technologies and further includes focusing on different target groups. Partnerships give the opportunity to share knowledge and to identify the customers' specific needs. The third pillar, "customer care" is characterized by direct customer orientation.[98] The strategy is to direct the main focus on B2B-customers while brand awareness advertising and B2C-marketing are only applied in the beginning of a product launch in a specific market. The value proposition of Schott is shown in Fig. 79.

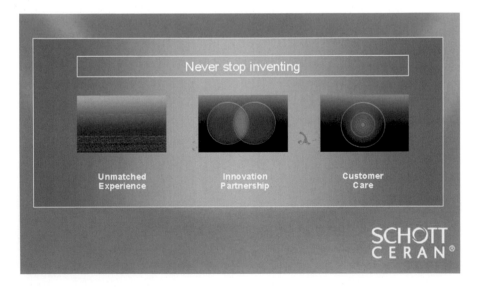

Fig. 79. Value proposition

Marketing Activities

Promoting the Ingredient Brand towards downstream customers, such as retail and end users comprises the following core benefits:

- Easy to clean

- Additional surface space

- Lower boil-up times

- Energy-saving due to modern heating system

- Beautiful modern design

- Variety of shapes and designs

These benefits are integrated in promotion communication, depending on their relevance and importance for the specific target groups. Training for retailers is of particular importance, as they act as an intermediary between the manufacturer and end user. Cooking events, point of sales measures as well as end customer services such as call centers have been elements of the Ingredient Branding campaign. Furthermore, end user studies are utilized as a means to identify the customers' needs and to develop appropriate measures.[99] As already mentioned, Schott only promotes the brand proactively towards the end consumer at the beginning of a product launch in a specific market. After having achieved a certain level of brand awareness, marketing activities are mainly concentrated on OEMs (see Fig. 80).

Fig. 80. Selection of OEMs

Cooperation with OEMs is established to get the opportunity to start unified marketing activities and to share knowledge. Reaching the end consumer with Schott Ceran is mainly implemented by OEMs.[100] The establishment of partnerships with OEMs to increase the proper brand awareness is, according to Pfoertsch/Mueller, considered a crucial step in developing an Ingredient Branding campaign. The supplier usually awards a grant for the advertising cost of the OEM, rewarding him for the visualization of the brand label and the communication of the benefits of the ingredient. The supplier pushes the OEM to promote the ingredient by giving him financial incentives.[101] Nevertheless, Schott uses statistics to control sales. Cooperative partnerships and regular consultation give further opportunities to exert influence on communication and media selection.

Ingredient Branding with Rinnai (Japan)

A model example of successful brand cooperation exists between Schott and Rinnai, Japanese manufacturer of household appliance. Rinnai was founded in 1920 and stands for high-quality products and good service, a well established company in the Japanese market. In this collaboration that has existed for more than 25 years, Schott Ceran was able to benefit from the good image and reputation of Rinnai resulting in increased brand awareness and higher popularity.[102] Ceran cook top panels are appreciated due to their modern design, and the smooth and non-porous surface and longevity of the product contribute to an increasing popularity of Schott Ceran in Japan.

A high growth potential can be anticipated for Rinnai gas stoves with Ceran. In the mind of the Japanese people who are very brand conscious, Schott, like other German brands, stands for high quality and reliability. Taking advantage of this, Schott and Rinnai arrange their marketing activities using the German flag as an adhesive label on the Ceran cook top panels[103] (See Fig. 81). Marketing campaigns are planned together, with the vision to realize growth in the market and to attain a win-win situation. The Japanese end user adds more value to the host product and Rinnai benefits from the

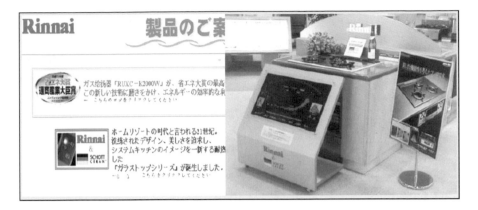

Fig. 81. Downstream marketing activities in cooperation with Rinnai Japan[104]

good brand image of Schott Ceran, which is based on a high degree of innovation. This cooperation has the potential to further develop new Asian markets.

In Asia, the popularity of gas stoves with Ceran is growing, indicated by increasing demand, especially in Japan. The growth potential in China, which could also be high, depends on the establishment of natural gas as an energy source. Due to its considerable purchasing power, South Korea cannot be ignored as an important Asian market. Besides the importance of high-quality products, Koreans increasingly prefer modern and classy design. In general, German brands are equated to constant high quality and technological advance in Asia.[105]

Schott Ceran and Vileda

The cooperation between Vileda and Schott Ceran is another good example of brand alliance. Vileda developed a special sponge for the cleaning of Ceran cook top panels. The persuasive partnership has been established to promote the brand "Vileda PUR active for Ceran" in the form of Schott pushing the Vileda brand by advising consumers to use special Vileda sponges to clean Ceran ceramic cook top panels.

In this collaboration, both brands benefit from the image and brand value of the other brand, both standing for high quality and constant innovation.[106] According to the definition in Pfoertsch/Mueller, co-Branding exists when "two independent brands from the consumer goods or services sector form a brand alliance", whereas Ingredient Branding implies the "cooperation of a supplier and a consumer goods company".[107] From the marketing perspective, the brand alliance between Schott and Vileda, who act independently, can be considered to be a form of co-Branding, as both brands benefit from the brand image and reputation of the other brand (see Fig. 82).

Fig. 82. Cooperation between Vileda and Schott Ceran

The success of Schott Ceran is based upon long lasting partnerships, focusing on the realization of a win-win-situation. The main focus is directed to B2B-marketing activities and although end consumers are addressed too, this is done mainly by the OEM. Advertising activities to promote the brand towards end consumers without interaction of the OEM are applied only until a certain level of brand awareness has been achieved.

Common success indicators such as the identification of the Ingredient Brand and significant functional benefits for the customer are given to Schott Ceran. Referring to the 4-step theory of Bugdahl, Schott Ceran seems to be in step four in regards to the German market. As Ceran ceramic cook top panels are used by many OEMs, the differentiation potential becomes increasingly insignificant. It can also be concluded that local brand adaptation is necessary for Ingredient Brands, depending, among others, on the product lifecycle and customers' specific needs.

6.9 Microban: Convincing and Measuring

Changing markets through technological innovations have been the pattern of success for many generations of companies, but changing markets with knowledge management is an emerging pattern. Companies that can create value for a business partner through not only technological innovation, but also successful Branding are able to create enhanced value through improved market knowledge. It is that value creation that lies at the core of the Microban International business model.

Microban is the global leader in built-in antimicrobial protection, engineering safe, durable and effective antimicrobial solutions for con-

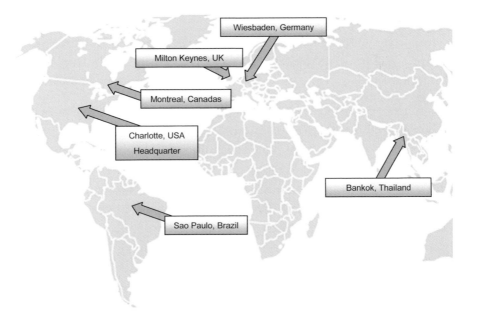

Fig. 83. Microban international locations

sumer products, textiles, building materials, commercial and health-care products. The company's experienced team of formulation chemists, polymer engineers and microbiologists have engineered antimicrobial solutions for a breadth of materials including: polymers, textiles, coatings, ceramics, paper and adhesives. The company utilizes a broad portfolio of antimicrobial technologies to provide its business partners with the optimal antimicrobial solution for each of their unique product applications.

Today, Microban is a global company with over 150 partners manufacturing more than 750 products with Microban antimicrobial protection in countries around the world (see Fig. 83).

In the Beginning

It started with a phone call; William L. Morrison[108] thought he was simply returning a routine call to a physician who was looking for help designing a system to keep disposable medical products clean and fresh longer. As they talked about infection control in the medical environment, the M.I.T. – trained entrepreneur noticed the telephone receiver in his hand and thought of the potential for contamination on the average public pay phone and how it might be controlled. This one question led to the development of the first antimicrobial polymeric products for both medical and consumer applications.

Over the years, Morrison's original concepts have undergone significant refinement and have made the transition from the laboratory to the "real world". Inspired by the original work of W. L. Morrison, Microban was founded by three engineers with a background in biomedical product development. Through proprietary processes they developed a way to engineer antimicrobial additives into a breadth of products. The result was the development of antimicrobial solutions that provided products with an added level of protection against damaging microbes such as bacteria, mold and mildew.

These early founders knew they had found a way to deliver an important and compelling benefit to a broad range of products. They also realized the importance of Branding as a way to protect their intellectual property and quickly hired a team of former NutraSweet marketers with experience in Ingredient Branding. And so in 1996, the company first began leveraging the "Microban" trademark with manufacturers as an effective tool for communicating the benefits of built-in antimicrobial protection to their customers.

In 1994, **Microban** was incorporated, and in 1999 Microban Products Company was purchased partially from Sprout Group[109] creating one global company. Under Bill Rubinstein's leadership, former Chairman and Chief Executive Officer of **Microban,** the Sprout Group of DLJ's (Donaldson, Lufkin & Jenrette, Inc.) venture capital affiliate invested $23 million into the company. Then in 2005 TA Associates[110], a leading private equity and buyout firm completed a minority investment in **Microban**, and named David Meyers as the President and Chief Executive Officer.

The Range of Products and Services

Microban is a full service antimicrobial solutions company that offers not only the product. The business concept includes also providing manufacturers with research & development, marketing support, regulatory assistance and quality assurance. Finally, OEMs have the chance to use the Microban brand to show the added value to their end users (see Fig. 84).

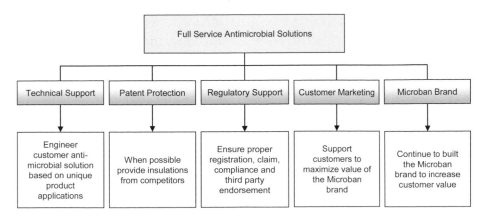

Fig. 84. Products and services from Microban

Partners, Not Customers

The success of Microban lies not only in the compelling nature of antimicrobial protection, but also in its commitment to partnership support. Unlike many ingredient technologies, delivering antimicrobial protection across a breadth of product substrates and industries requires a significant amount of technical and intellectual support. Microban provides its partners with full service support including:

- Technical development

- Regulatory assistance

- Patent counsel

- Marketing support

- Microban brand

Technical Development

Microban technology is built-in to a product during the manufacturing process and becomes an intrinsic part of the product inside and at the surface. When microbes, such as bacteria, mold and mildew come in contact with the product surface, Microban protection penetrates the cell wall of the microbe and disrupts key cell functions so that the microbe cannot function, grow or reproduce. All products engineered with Microban protection undergo extensive testing in microbiology and chemical analysis labs. In addition, Microban technology has been proven effective in over 20,000 tests at over 27 independent laboratories around the world. The Microban research & development staff includes polymer engineers, formulation chemists, microbiologists and analytical chemists. The staff has extensive knowledge and experience in antimicrobial applications development, utilizing a broad range of organic and inorganic chemistries. The onsite microbiology lab provides manufacturers with antimicrobial testing services using industry standard test methodologies. Microban has also many patents for antimicrobial additives.

Unlike some ingredient technologies, Microban engineers must custom engineer an antimicrobial solution that meets the needs of each partner's unique product application. For example, the antimicrobial solution for a cutting board is very different than the solution you might use for paint or a pair of athletic shoes. For each individual product application, Microban engineers must evaluate the following important parameters:

- Antimicrobial Efficacy – Is the intended application susceptible to the growth of bacteria, fungus or both?

- Usage Conditions – Under what conditions is the product used, i.e. contact with food, water, skin, ultraviolet light, etc.?

- Durability Requirements – What is the estimated lifetime of the product?

- Product Compatibility – What substrates and manufacturing processes are being used to construct the product?

- Regulatory Approvals – Do the potential antimicrobial candidates have the appropriate regulatory approvals and safety profiles?

Regulatory Assistance

Microban and its partners manufacture and sell products around the world, so Microban must support its partners with global regulatory assistance. Microban actively engages with the appropriate local regulatory bodies to ensure that all antimicrobial additives are approved for use in an intended application prior to commercialization. In addition, Microban provides guidance on claims development and reviews all partner-marketing claims to ensure compliance with regulatory authorities.

Patent Counsel

Microban has over 75 issued and pending patents pertaining to the use of antimicrobial additives across a breadth of product applications including polymers, coatings and textile finishes. Microban in-house patent counsel provides expert guidance on potential patent opportunities and in some instances provides their partners with insulation from competitors in the market.

Marketing Support

Microban provides extensive marketing support to help ensure the success of its new partners. They provide partners with assistance on product claims, sales training materials. They offer packaging concepts that illustrate how to communicate the benefits of Microban antimicrobial protection, retailer presentation materials, draft press releases and offer additional marketing communication materials. This is designed to help its partners effectively leverage the Microban brand.

Microban also conducts extensive quantitative and qualitative market research across a breadth of product categories and consumer

Fig. 85. Print advertisements of Microban and its partners

groups in order to provide their partners with the knowledge needed to provide expert claims guidance, as well as insight into potential market strategies for leveraging the Microban brand. The Microban marketing team also frequently conducts custom research for partners to acquire category specific knowledge for a new partner and to provide that partner with assistance in selling the Microban brand and benefit to their customers. Fig. 85 shows former examples of cooperative advertising of Microban and its partners.

The Microban Brand

Interest in antimicrobial protection has quickly spread from soaps and detergents to the benefits of built-in antimicrobial protection in solid products. In a recent US survey almost 60% of consumers said they were concerned about their day-to-day exposure to microbes while over 80% of consumers reported usage of four or more antimicrobial products. The Microban brand is an important consumer trustmark that enables its partners to easily and effectively communicate to their customers the benefits of safe, durable and effective antimicrobial protection. Today, the Microban brand has over 41% aided brand awareness in the United States and growing awareness in countries around the world (see Fig. 86 for the Microban logo).

Fig. 86. Microban brand logo

Quality Assurance

The Microban brand promise to consumers is to deliver continuous, durable and effective antimicrobial protection. To ensure **Microban** fulfill that promise, all manufacturers products are subject to extensive testing prior to commercialization and stringent quality assurance guidelines after commercialization to ensure ongoing antimicrobial efficacy and durability.

The Market

The awareness that coming in touch with harmful bacterial in daily life can cause a wide range of diseases has its origin in the USA. Later, this recognition and knowledge also became known in middle Europe and Asia. Today there are three enormous markets with awareness that antibacterial security adds to peace of mind in addition to nutrition, sports and clean environment for healthy living. The look at the market growth promises a still increasing number of customers interested in antibacterial products.

In the USA, there exists a growing interest for products with antibacterial protection with an annual growth rate of around 8%. It is expected that the future growth rate will be as high as or even higher than the years before. These calculations do not include new applications of antibacterial applications and services. Beside the

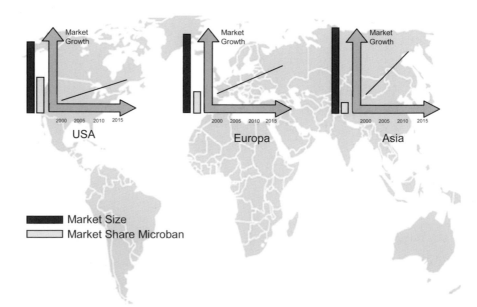

Fig. 87. Market growth and revenues by present location

increasing purchase, new applications are one of the main pillars to assure company growth over the next years.

Europe is also an important market for **Microban**. Currently the market is much smaller than North American, but the growth rate is 11% p.a. Asia has the biggest market potential. However, today only a relative small fraction of the whole revenues of the suppliers of antibacterial protection are achieved in Asia. For the future an increasing importance is expected. Currently a growth rate of around 17% p.a. is projected. Fig. 87 shows the market size, the achieved revenues and the growth rates for Microban's present locations.

Competitors

The potential for added value in antibacterial protection for a wide range of products has been noticed by OEMs as well as competitors and consumers. Today, three main strategies for participation from the rising interest in antibacterial products can be observed in the market place. Ingredient Branding is a strategy other competitors pursue as well. However, no brand is comparable to Microban in terms of strength, awareness or trust. The big chemical companies like DuPont or Dow also offer chemicals that can be built into the manufacturing process. If an OEM decides to add such substances, they have to select the brand that tells the consumer about the ingredient inside. A number of companies pursue this strategy. Others use the support for the chemical companies and add a self-brand as a symbol of quality to their main brand. Samsung can be named as an example for self Branding as differentiation strategy to other end product manufactures. The product portfolio of Samsung's[111] antibacterial line includes air conditions, freezers, laptops, keyboards and other applications that could come in contact with bacteria. For these products, Samsung creates the "**Silver Nano**" brand. The Silver Nano Health System is a trademark name of an antibacterial technology, which uses silver nanoparticles in washing machines, refrigerators, air conditioners, air purifiers and vacuum cleaners introduced by Samsung in April 2003. Samsung home appliances such as refrigerator or air conditioner add silver nano-coating to their inner surfaces for an overall anti-bacterial and anti-fungal effect. As air circulates, the coated surfaces contact with the silver ions[112], which can resist any airborne bacteria, which in turn suppress the respiration of bacteria, adversely affects bacteria's cellular metabolism and inhibits cell growth.

Today, **Microban** provides the strongest brand. The company holds, beside brand leader, also the market leader position. With increasing market volume new competitors can be expected. In 2000 the **Sanitized AG** from Switzerland[113] entered the market with an application developed in 1930 in the USA by expanding its applications to odor reduction, also claiming to reduce the formation of bacteria, fungi and mite infestation. Since 2008 **Sanitized AG** intensifies the activities in the US market and plans to successfully increase brand awareness generally as well as on end consumer level. Stewart Klein, president of Sanitized, Inc. in the US claims that the "existing recognition and the available networking possibilities offered by AATCC (American Association of Textile Chemists & Colorists) supply SANITIZED a strategically important platform for attaining this goal"[114].

For specific applications specialized products are on the market as well: BACTRON antibacterial protection from Champion Technologies and Bio-Pruf™ from Rohm and Haas are designed for paint and wall surface coatings. Maxguard® AB offers gel coat with antibacterial protection. Lecluyse is European market leader in vinyl application. Both companies have their own brand, but use Microban as their ingredient base.

The Value Chain

Microban is not at the beginning of the value chain. The raw materials are provided from approximately 15 different suppliers, large and specialist companies. These substances are processed by Microban International Ltd. They add the microbial protection into the host product for their various OEM clients, providing kitchen utensils, household items, toys etc. With the research and testing, the company makes sure that the offered value-added is fulfilling the expectation of the customers. The logo of the brand **"Microban"** is given for the additional feature of the service offering of Microban so that the end product can demonstrate and make the benefit visible for the end user. This way, **Microban** becomes more than only a name for the substance that is used for making the product antimicrobial. Microban stands for knowledge, expertise, and treatment of the end product material as well as for a complete concept that offers an additional benefit for the end user. Fig. 88 illustrates Microban's position in the value chain. From the processed base materials, many product manufactures (OEMs) are producing finished or semi-finished products, from household appliances to toys to garden equipment. These products then enter the market through distributors, wholesalers and retailers in the market place and get purchased by the end consumer.

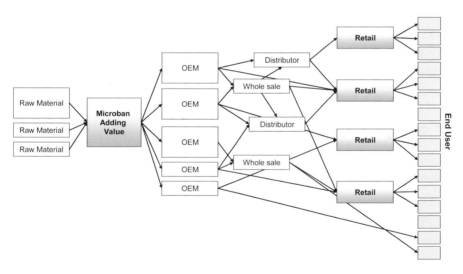

Fig. 88. Microban value chain

In the value chain the brand name **Microban** is first used at the **Microban** stage. **Microban** works together with around 130 OEMs, which produce over 750 different products. Fig. 89 shows a selected sample of companies, which offer their products with the Microban branded ingredient.

Fig. 89. Selected end product brands with Microban as Ingredient Brand

Most OEMs sell their products through wholesale/distributors and retail. The distribution channels the OEMs choose cannot be influenced by **Microban**. A direct communication to the distributor is hindered due to the magnitude of products and distribution alternatives. Also, many retailers are heavily concentrated and have an unchallenged power position in the market. They protect their brand and product offering. Therefore, only a few cooperate with Microban. Home Depot in the USA and TESCO in the UK have established product areas where all their antimicrobial product offerings are displayed in particular areas. In these areas the brand **Microban** is very visible, and these activities are supporting the company's efforts to reach the final customer.

A similar situation can be found between the OEM and the distributor stage. The decision, which products are listed and finally find their way into the shelves, depends on many different factors. The product politics of retailers is influenced by prices, market, competition, region and many more factors. In fact **Microban** has the chance to act on the market side only by showing the end user that the benefit in the end product is important for them.

The end product reaches different categories of end users. These groups can further be divided into the actual user and the maker of the buying decision. Another user group for the end products can be institutions or other companies like hospitals or operating companies for public buildings as well as architects and engineers.

Various different characteristics determine the influence, which Microban has on the end user due to the structure and length of the value chain:

- **Number of stages to the end user:** The shortest value chain exists when only one OEM sells his products directly to the end user. Many existing structures have at least one OEM and many different distributors and retailers. A value chain with several OEMs is also possible and makes the value chain more complicated for the Ingredient Brand provider Microban.

- **End user characteristics:** Is the end product used by a private person or a company that produces an own service with the product (e.g. cafeterias or gyms), and how is the buying process?

- **OEM market structure:** Another important criterion is the market in which the OEM operates. It is also essential in which position and how strong the OEM is in relation to the competition or other suppliers in his market.

These four characteristics determine the success of both parties of this brand alliance in the market place and Microban is evaluating every brand relationship continuously. They put major efforts for the selection of suitable partnerships and the development of the successful ones.

Customer Attitude for Selected Products and How to Manage the Microban Brand

Since Microban solutions can be found in many products, the majority of the products can be categorized into four groups: home products, commercial & foodservice, building products, apparel & textile and healthcare products. Each category has different sub-product groups. Fig. 90 shows an example of product groups and their applications.

Microban has a huge number of applications, which end up in an almost unmanageable number of different products with Microban "inside". To be a value contributor in the value chain, Microban has

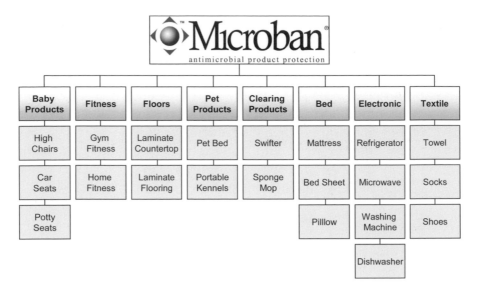

Fig. 90. Selected products groups with sub-products

to manage its benefit to the various players and capture value for itself. There is a need to understand all the various product offerings in the various categories, e.g. baby products: high chairs, car seats, potty seats, and their companies' contribution in the value chain.

By analyzing the value increase from supplier to OEM, distributor, retail and the final customer in a network analysis, Microban can determine their contribution. The value capture is determined by the final customers' willingness to pay a price premium over the unbranded product. With a detailed market analysis the amount can be estimated per product category and application. Microban's own investment and cost structure finally determines their financial success. This integrated process is displayed in an overview chart (see Fig. 91). The various performance measures of the company indicate the management involvement and investment for the various product groups and the selection of new ones.

The most important factor of the analysis is the determination of the quantity and the price premium generated by the ingredient, which is added to a final product. This can be determined by intensive two-stage customer analysis.

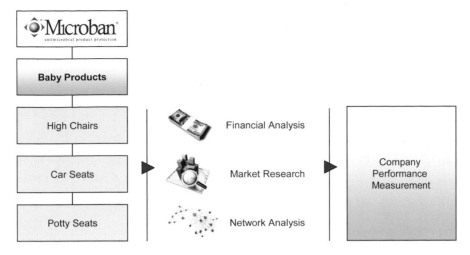

Fig. 91. Managing the added Ingredient Brand value

First, it is necessary to analyze the end users willingness to pay for the end product with and without Microban. Then, it has to be analyzed on various price levels how many people would buy and how many would not. The second analysis is about the price premium at the supplier/OEM stage. The price difference between the ingredient with and without the brand represents the price premium and determines the success of the Ingredient Branding process. Various product applications have various price/sales curves. This is visualized in Fig. 92.

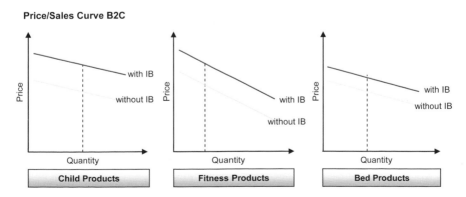

Fig. 92. Price premium and possible sales quantity of selected products with Ingredient Brand (IB) and without

Microban Value Creation

Microban creates value for its host brand partners on three key dimensions.

1. Improving the quality of the host product
2. Creating a point-of-differentiation
3. Providing an alternative market strategy

It should be noted that the value Microban creates for its manufacturing partners increases exponentially as Microban moves from simply improving the quality of the host product, to differentiating their products in a meaningful way and ultimately to providing the partner with a potentially lower cost and lower risk market strategy to improving their business results.

Improving Product Quality

The foundation for value creation for all Ingredient Brands is the delivery of a compelling improvement in product quality that is capable of influencing consumer purchase preference.

Microban technology helps address an important and growing consumer concern about day-to-day exposure to bacteria and mold. Because the benefit of antimicrobial protection is not one that can be observed prior to purchase. Customers might ask, "How do I know that the product will resist the growth of bacteria or mold?" the Microban brand becomes an important communication tool for its' manufacturing partners, a trustmark that signals safe, durable and effective antimicrobial protection to the end user of the product.

Creating a Point of Differentiation

While improving a product's quality is the foundation for developing an Ingredient Branding strategy, the real value creation for the host brand happens when the Ingredient Brand becomes an enduring point of differentiation versus its competitors. This can sometimes put the Ingredient Brand and the host brand at cross purposes, i.e. the ingredient supplier is seeking to maximize its revenue opportunities by penetrating the market, while the value the host brand derives from the relationship diminishes with the successful market penetration of the Ingredient Brand.

For example, early adopters of Stainmaster and Intel reaped larger rewards than late stage adopters who merely adopted the technology in order to level the playing field. Only Ingredient Brand suppliers who have a technology advantage or a strong patent position are able to enter the market and secure utilization of their Ingredient Brand despite the lack of barriers to the host brand's competitors.

Some Ingredient Brands have been able to secure brand utilization through large investments in consumer advertising that generate pull. For example, this strategy has been frequently used by DuPont, i.e. Teflon. The company leveraged their investment in advertising to generate awareness of the ingredient and create pull by manufacturers wishing to leverage the awareness of the Ingredient Brand.

Microban developed a novel and more creative approach, but in doing so created a more enduring point of differentiation for its partners. The company pursued partners across a breadth of industry verticals and product categories where consumers were concerned about bacteria, mold and mildew and offered these partners exclusivity in exchange for brand utilization. In this way, Microban was able to offer its partners a valuable point of differentiation versus their competitors and together the companies grew awareness of the Microban brand in a more natural way based on the marketing activities of the host brands.

The company continued to help build the brand through its own efforts, but by leveraging the marketing efforts of hundreds of partners, the brand was able to grow more quickly and in exchange, the partners were afforded an enduring point of differentiation through exclusivity. This approach has also led to more meaningful and collaborative relationships with its partners. Microban partners were not concerned about sharing marketing information and strategies since Microban was not selling to its competitors. The result was an alliance that was focused on the mutually beneficial outcome of driving increased consumer purchase interest.

Providing an Alternative Market Strategy

In every marketing textbook you'll essentially discover that there are five key levers for strengthening a business:

1. **Pricing Leverage** – One can increase the price of a product and increase revenues and profits. The alternatives is decreasing the price and sell more units, as long as doing so means selling enough incremental units to compensate for the decrease in price (often measured as pricing elasticity).

2. **Market Share** – One can utilize numerous tactics, i.e. new features, benefits, more advertising, lower price, etc. that drives increased purchase interest for a product and steal market share from competitors.

3. **Product Mix** – One can try to drive increased sales of the more profitable items in the product mix thereby increasing total profit.

4. **Distribution** – The three strategies above are irrelevant unless a company is in the game with distribution on the shelf. With massive retailer consolidation, today more than ever manufacturers have the need to differentiate their products to not only secure new distribution, but also to defend their existing distribution.

5. **Grow the Category** – A viable strategy for new product categories where the primary objective is still to bring new users into the segment.

Microban partners have leveraged the benefits of Microban antimicrobial technology and the brand as an important point of differentiation to significantly impact their businesses. In fact, Microban provides counsel to its partners on appropriate go-to-market strategies based on the relative strength of the host brand in the market and the consumer demand for antimicrobial protection within a given category.

Pricing Leverage

Pricing leverage is an important lever, with every penny increase or decrease dropping directly to the bottom line. However, today's manufacturers are at the mercy of retailers where price is "king" and finding an enduring point of differentiation is difficult to impossible. However, those brands that have been able to maintain market dominance may be in a position to potentially gain pricing leverage when introducing Microban protection to the marketplace based on their higher degree of influence with retailers and greater consumer loyalty. In addition, many Microban partners have leveraged Microban to defend their current pricing position and to enhance their reputations as category innovators.

Market Share

One of the most effective market strategies for a host brand leveraging the Microban brand is a market share strategy. Ingredient Brands are extremely effective at influencing brand preference at the point of sale, acting as a powerful endorsement that can reassure the buyer of a desired performance attribute. As anticipated, weaker brands in the category do benefit more substantially from market share shifts with the utilization of an Ingredient Brand. However, the marketers for category-leading brands are often tasked with defending market share and thus, Ingredient Branding are still a viable consideration for those marketers as well.

For example, in a research conducted for the women's reusable razor category, Microban once again did not deliver significant market share for the category leader, but did produce considerable results for the number two brands in the category. These results demonstrate that even for category leaders, Microban delivers significant value by protecting valuable market share with an innovation that's likely to lower cost and risk alternative market strategies.

Product Mix

Thanks to the advent of category management, today's retail shelves are lined with good, better and best alternatives. The problem is that often the only distinguishable difference for the consumer is the price. An Ingredient Brand can be an important cue to shoppers, helping them to distinguish the improvements in features and benefits within a product category. In fact, a compelling feature with the power of an Ingredient Brand can be a powerful tool in trading consumers up and improving the product mix, a win for manufacturers and retailers. However, for this strategy to be effective execution is critical so that consumers are aware of the relative choices and the step up in pricing must also be appropriately reflective of the product improvements.

Microban technology has been used by many of its partners as a product mix strategy. The inclusion of Microban was extremely helpful in a category where there was little observable difference in the products. For example, consumers needed to read the package bullet points to discover that the VF6000 was able to trap smaller particles and thus was a superior filter. The Microban brand became a signal of improved quality, a reason to believe and thus a reason to purchase the more expensive filters in the product mix.

Distribution

With massive retailer consolidation and the creation of the superstore, distribution has become "king". In fact, it is not uncommon for a single retailer to account for over 50% of a company's annual sales. Today, the concept of having all your eggs in one basket has taken on a new meaning.

Every year manufacturers must run the gauntlet known as the "product line review" where only the fittest survive. Even category leaders must keep pace delivering new and improved products, with often little chance of raising their prices.

Many Microban partners have utilized the Microban brand and technology to capture valuable shelf space, increase their facings at retail or even to defend their shelf space. In fact, some Microban partners have opted to leverage Microban technology to gain distribution in lieu of other strategies despite the consumer's willingness to pay more.

Growing the Category

An Ingredient Brand can be an effective tactic for leveraging any of the first four levers, but not for growing a category. An Ingredient Brand identifies an important component or benefit within a product, but it's not capable of driving a consumer to the category. For example, if a customer was in the market for a new pair of sandals, Microban protection might be an important feature that helped him choose to buy brand A versus brand B, but if he wasn't really in the market for sandals the presence of Microban would be irrelevant.

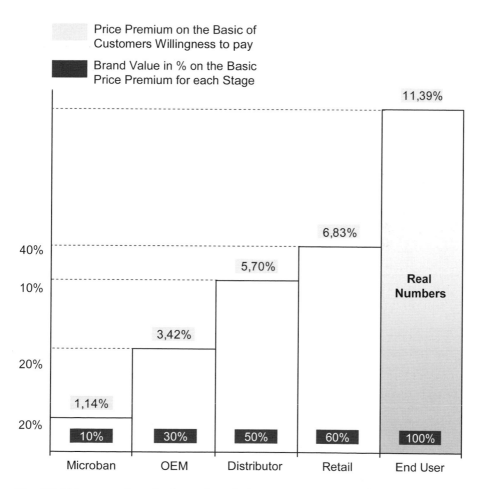

Fig. 93. Price premium in the value chain

These findings are the basis of arguments for finding more OEMs willing to put Microban in their product offering and they are also a prerequisite to determine the price for the supplier/OEM offerings. In many cases the ingredient offers more benefits in terms of value creation for the later partners in the value chain. The following example illustrates the situation on towels with micro-bacterial protections (see Fig. 93).

An implication for OEMs is that strong and suitable Ingredient Brands like Microban are able to complement and positively impact the brand image of the host brand and lead to higher brand equity that manifest itself in a higher price premium. Therefore, Microban's Ingredient Branding leads to a tangible benefit for the OEM.

Ingredient marketers have utilized many strategies to help create consumer awareness of their ingredient technologies. For example NutraSweet used a strong patent position to ensure forced brand utilization of the NutraSweet trademark by Coca-Cola and Pepsi. Dolby and Intel offered incentives such as improved pricing and co-op marketing dollars to encourage brand utilization. DuPont utilized a consumer pull strategy for its Lycra and Teflon technologies to create the desire for brand utilization by its customers.

Microban has created a new and unique Ingredient Branding model that has enabled them to successfully grow the Microban brand into the most recognized and trusted brand for built-in antimicrobial protection. By providing its partners with technical expertise, full-service support and exclusivity, they have created a win-win alliance with their partners that have resulted in successful utilization of the Microban trademark on more than 750 products around the world.

Summary

- Multiple case studies of successful Ingredient Branding implementation have been identified.

- Different industry conditions and company specific situations require unique approaches for Ingredient Branding, as demonstrated.

- Strong strategic brand leadership is required to establish and maintain a lasting InBrand.

- Product and application innovations are required to maintain the competitive edge through differentiation and customer understanding.

- Ingredient Brand management does not end with conventional management knowledge but requires continuous application of innovative concepts and thinking, such as network and value chain analysis

Notes

[1] See company Internet site under http://www2.dupont.com/Our_Company/en_US/.

[2] The Wall Street, April 28, 1999, Insert.

[3] Reifman, S., and Murphy, A.D. „America's largest private companies." *Forbes,* March 11, 2008.

[4] Andrews, S.M. „Invista will tout Teflon at showtime." *Furniture Today,* December 15 2003.

[5] Home Textiles Today, Invista bows new Teflon Monday, September 22 2008.

[6] Scripps Howard News Service. http://www.knoxstudio.com/shns/story.cfm?pk=REAGAN-SCHROEDER-06-09-04&cat=WW. Retrieved on 31.10.2007.

[7] www.hoovers.com, 10.08.2008.

[8] Electrical and electronic engineering for radio, television, video, DVD and so on are governed by industrial standards established by various bodies over the course of the last century in order to protect individual markets. Businesses must respond to these requirements on a local level, otherwise access to the market would be impossible.

[9] www.dolby.com (a), 10.08.2008.

[10] www.dolby.com, 05.08.2008.

[11] Dolby Surround Trademark Placement, 25.10.2007.

[12] See Mike Kohlbrenners Blog http://www.kolbrenerusa.com/blog/index.php/2008/04/14/branding-from-the-inside-out/ seen June 4, 2008.

[13] Tetra Pak brochure: wer wir sind ('Who we are'), undated.

[14] Unnamed author: Wie alles begann ('How it all began'), 20.10.2004.

[15] ibid.

[16] Simon/Sebastian (1995), p. 42.

[17] Simon/Sebastian (1995),p. 42.

[18] Tetra Pak brochure: wer wir sind ('Who we are'), Dr. Ruben Rausing, undated.

[19] Tetra Pak brochure: was wir tun ('What we do'), undated.

[20] Simon/Sebastian (1995), p. 42.

[21] Tetra Pak brochure: Joe Clever – Natürlich Milch ('Milk, naturally'), undated.

[22] Tetra Pak brochure: wie wir arbeiten ('How we work'), undated.

[23] Dwyer, D.M, Hodder, K.I., and Honey, R.C. „Perceptual learning in humans: Roles of preexposure schedule, feedback, and discrimination essay." *Quarterly Journal of Experimental Psychology* 57B (2004): 245–259.

[24] Sibert, J.R., and Frude, N. „Bittering agents in the prevention of accidental poisoning: Children's reactions to denatonium benzoate (Bitrex)." 1854387 (P,S,E,B) *Arch Emerg Med,* 1991 Mar 8, pp. 1–7.

[25] Mundy, M.E., Dwyer, D.M., and Honey, R.C. „Inhibitory associations contribute to perceptual learning in humans." *Journal of Experimental Psychology* 32 (2006): 178–184.

[26] McQueen, M.P., and Spencer, J. „U.s. orders new China toy recall: Aqua dots are pulled off shelves after reports of children falling ill." *Wallstreet Journal,* November 8, 2007.

[27] Department of Trade and Industry: Home and leisure accident report, London 1998.

[28] www.dm-drogeriemarkt.de, 10.08.2008.

[29] There had been some interruptions during the First and Second World War.

30 Bremner, B. „Shimano – The Tour de France's other winner: Japan's leading bike parts maker is also ahead of the pack. But it can't afford to coast." *Business Week,* Aug. 9, 2004.

31 Dura Ace and XTR are both product groups for the high end market.

32 Bicycles – Global Strategic Business Report, Global Industry Analysts, Inc., March 2008.

33 The National Bicycle Dealers Association; http://nbda.com/page.cfm?PageID=34, (seen: Mai, 8th, 2008).

34 Saloner, G., Chang, V., and Shimano, T. „Shimano and the high-end road bike industry." Stanford University case study CASE: SM-150, 2006, p. 2.

35 Saloner, G., Chang, V., and Shimano, T. „Shimano and the high-end road bike industry." Stanford University case study CASE: SM-150, 2006, p. 5.

36 Bicycles – Global Strategic Business Report, Global Industry Analysts, Inc., March 2008, p. 466.

37 „Not a Single Worker Retrenched Since 1973," Straits Times, April 26, 1998.

38 Ibara, Y. „Hub Company in the Global Bicycle Industry." Morgan Stanley Dean Witter, July 18, 2001, p. 14.

39 Kerber, R. „Bicycles: Bike maker faces a tactical shift." *The Wall Street Journal,* October 12, 1998.

40 Galvin, P., and Morkel, A. „The effect of product modularity on industry structure: The case of the world bicycle industry." *Industry and Innovation* 8 (2001)., p. 31.

41 Shimano Annual Report, 2004, p. 1.

42 Isely, P., and Roelofs, M.R. „Primary market and aftermarket competition in the bicycle component industry." *Applied Economics* 36 (2004).

43 Saloner, G., Chang, V., and Shimano, T. „Shimano and the high-end road bike industry." Stanford University case study CASE: SM-150, 2006, 2006, p. 9–10.

44 Vickers, G. „Graham Vickers explains how a Japanese cycle component maker is having a growing impact on the high quality bicycle market." *Design Week,* April 19, 1987, p. 19.

45 Shimano company homepage: www.shimano.com.

46 Voigt, K. „Your life: The interview: Pedal power." *Asian Wall Street Journal*, November 28, 2003.

47 Shimano company homepage: www.shimano.com.

48 http://www.referenceforbusiness.com/history2/30/Shimano-Inc.html.

49 Friedland, J. „Components of success: Japanese bicycle-parts maker Shimano eyes China." *Far Easter Economic Review*, November 18, 1993.

50 http://www.referenceforbusiness.com/history2/30/Shimano-Inc.html.

51 Friedland, Jonathan, (1993), p. 66.

52 Dickerson, M. „Shimano to recall 2.5 million bicycle cranks." *Los Angeles Times*, July 10, 1997.

53 „Japan's Shimano to Invest US $17.1 Million in New Chinese Subsidiary," Asia Pulse, March 11, 2003.

54 Foremski, T. „Fishing gear maker floats a helpful idea." *Financial Times (London)*, February 3, 1999, p. 5.

55 The National Bicycle Dealers Association; http://nbda.com/page.cfm?PageID=34 (Mai, 9th 2008).

56 REI is the global leader in the outdoor gear and clothing category with customers in virtually every country world wide and total revenues in 2007 of $1,2billion.

57 The National Bicycle Dealers Association; http://nbda.com/page.cfm?PageID=34 (Mai, 9th 2008).

58 Galvin, P., and Morkel, A. „The effect of product modularity on industry structure: The case of the world bicycle industry." *Industry and Innovation* 8 (2001), p. 31.

59 Ibara, Y. „Hub Company in the Global Bicycle Industry." Morgan Stanley Dean Witter, July 18, 2001, p. 3.

60 Taylor, R., and Karl, U. „Product variety, supply chain structure, and firm performance: Analysis of the U.S. bicycle industry." *Management Science* 47 (2001), p. 1593.

61 Delaney, B. „Splits with Giant, Specialized." *Bicycle Retailer & Industry News* 14 (2005), p. 1–33.

62 On May 27, 2007 GENERAL ELECTRIC sold GE Plastics to Saudi Basic Industries Corp. (SABIC) for $11.6 billion 2006. The Pittsfield, Mass.-based business employed 10,300 people and generated $6.6 billion in sales and $675 million in profits in that year. In 2002 they had started a branding campaign which improved Lexan's reputation outside America.

63 Bayer also benefited from the sale of its largest competitor, the Plastics Group of Geneeral Electric. GE had been a very strong competitor, dominating the U.S. market with its Lexan® Polycarbonate. In the 1970s, GE considered a consumer branding effort for its Lexan Polycarbonate, including filming of commercials (A Bull in a Lexan Shop) and tagline development (Lexan – A Good Name to Stand On), and logo. Deemed too expensive at the time, the full implementation of the project was abandoned, with a minor effort to tag products with the new logo (an elephant standing on a circus stand of Lexan). For greater understanding of how these companies competed, particularly in the arena for development of new applications of polycarbonate.

64 As mentioned before General Electric sold its plastics division to SABIC. General Electric's plastics unit reached $6.6 billion in revenue in 2006. The division has struggled amid inflation in natural gas and raw materials like benzene, and profits at the unit fell about 22%, to $674 million in 2006, from $867 million in 2005. The sale has always been controversial, but it is not unusual for GE to leave markets when the major offerings reach the mature stage (i.e. consumer electronics, television, small appliances).

65 The 1985 European Ford Sierra and some Fiats were the first to use Polycarbonate blended with polyesters for energy –absorbing bumpers. In 1986, the U.S. Ford Taurus and Mercury Sable used the PC blend for bumpers. These blended ederivatives of PC were developed specifically for these applications by GE Plastics.

66 Horizont 2002, Zeitschrift für Marketing, Frankfurt, S. 26.

67 Ironically, by the 1970s, one of the major U.S. applications for polycarbonate was in commuter train windows, primarily for safety reasons. Though initially more expensive, the lower replacement frequency and added passenger safety overcame the initial costs. Today, polycarbonate glazings (windows) are the standard in all passenger rail applications.

68 See automotive headlamps: The paradigm shift from standardized glass beams to today's plastic custom designs.

[69] See at http://money.cnn.com/magazines/fortune/mostadmired/2008/industries/industry_53.html.

[70] Company website see www.ti.com.

[71] Effie winners represent client and agency teams who tackled a marketplace challenge with a big idea and knew exactly how to communicate their message to their customer. See http://www.effie.org/winners/showcase/1998/284.

[72] Indicar-Net (2007) DLP products races into year two of its NASCAR sponsorship, February 16, 2007.

[73] „How DLP works" see company website http://dlp.com/tech/what.aspx.

[74] Powell, E. „The great technology war." 2003, http://www.projectorcentral.com/lcd_dlp.htm.

[75] dito.

[76] See company website www.ti.com/dlp.

[77] See Powell (2003).

[78] The ANSI contrast is a tool, in which the measurement is done with a checker board patterned test image where the luminosity values are measured simultaneously. This is a more realistic measure of system capability, but includes the potential of including the effects of the room into the measurement, if the test is not performed in a room that is close to ideal.

[79] Texas Instruments press release 2007.

[80] An American market research firm the NPD Group in Port Washington, NY 11050.

[81] Harrison, C. „Big battle over big-screen." *The Dallas Morning News,* May 2, 2005.

[82] Ogg, E. „HDTV's evolving alphabet soup: LED, OLED, LCD, DLP, CNET news." October 11, 2007.

[83] Corporate Information Schott AG, Accessed: February 25, 2007 http://www.schott.com/magazine/english/sol106/sol106_07_colorfulmenu.html?PHPSESSID=91.

[84] The comments are based on interviews with Ruban Harikantha, General Manager Regional Sales and Marketing (Schott Hometech) and

Andreas Uthmann, Corporate Brand Manager (Schott), January 30, 2007 in Mainz as well as on the subsequent telephone interviews.

[85] Information on glass technology and the historical background is available at the company museum and the former founder's private home. See also: http://www.schott.com/english/museum/index.html.

[86] Corporate Information Schott AG, URL: http://www.schott.com/german/company/business_report.html, Accessed: February 21, 2007.

[87] The expression „designed product brand" is based upon a definition of Schott AG.

[88] Gfk Marketing Services GmbH & Co. KG; Hausgeräte-Fachverbände im Zentralverband Elektrotechnik- und Elektronikindustrie e.V.: Zahlenspiegel des deutschen Elektro-Hausgerätemarktes 2004/2005, Accessed: December 8, 2006.

[89] Die Welt: Hersteller von Haushaltsgeräten wollen höhere Preise durchsetzen, Date of publication: June 8, 2006, URL: http://www.welt.de/data/2006/06/08/905982.html?prx=1, Accessed: February 14, 2007.

[90] Interview with Andreas Uthmann and Ruban Harikantha, January 30, 2007.

[91] Pfoertsch/Mueller (2006), p. 33.

[92] Interview with Andreas Uthmann and Ruban Harikantha, January 30, 2007.

[93] Clef, Ulrich (2002): Die Ausgezeichneten – Die Unternehmenskarrieren der 30 Deutschen Marketingpreisträger; Clef Creative Communications GmbH, Munich, p. 174.

[94] Schott AG, Corporate information, URL, accessed: February 17, 2007: http://www.schott.com/hometech/english/products/ceran/generally/material.html.

[95] Clef, U. *Die Ausgezeichneten: Die Unternehmenskarrieren der 30 Deutschen Marketingpreisträger*. Munich, 2002, p. 171.

[96] Expert interview with Andreas Uthmann and Ruban Harikantha, January 30, 2007.

[97] Pfoertsch/Mueller (2006), p. 16f.

[98] Brand Presentation Schott AG, internal information.

[99] Ruebenthaler, K. „Marketing in der technischen Glasindustrie." In *Handbuch Industriegütermarketing: Strategien, Instrumente, Anwendungen,* edited by K. Backhaus and M. Voeth. Wiesbaden, 2004, p. 1195 et sqq.

[100] Internal information, Schott AG.

[101] Pfoertsch/Mueller (2006), p. 63.

[102] Expert interview with Andreas Uthmann and Ruban Harikantha, January 30, 2007.

[103] Odrich, B. „A productive partnership." Schott online magazine Solutions, 2007, http://www.schott.com/magazine/english/info103/si103_05_rinnai.html?PHPSESSID=91.

[104] Brand Presentation Schott AG, internal information.

[105] Odrich, B. „A productive partnership." Schott online magazine Solutions, 2007, http://www.schott.com/magazine/english/info103/si103_05 _rinnai.html?PHPSESSID=91.

[106] Corporate information Schott AG, URL: Accessed: February 15, 2007 http://www.schott.com/hometech/english/products/ceran/dailyuse/vileda_sponge.html.

[107] Pfoertsch/Mueller (2006): p. 20.

[108] Microban Information, further information see also Microban website at http://www.microban.com/americas/about_us/history/?lang=en.

[109] Sprout Group Press Release in: BUSINESS WIRE (NEW YORK)–Dec. 7, 1999.

[110] TA Associates Completes Minority Investment in Microban International TA Associates Press Release, February 17, 2005/BOSTON, MA.

[111] Samsung silver nano health system gives free play to its 'silver' magic – Creating a new era of germ-free home with silver nano home electronic appliances, Samsung press release Mar 29, 2005.

[112] Silver nanoparticles deadly to bacteria in: Nanotechnology/Bio & Medicine March 10th, 2008.

[113] Company information at corporate website http://www.sanitized.com/en/about-us/history.html.

[114] SANITIZED AG to increase brand awareness in US markets, Company announcement published in fibre2fashion.com under http://www.fibre2fashion.com/news/textiles-company-news/newsdetails.aspx?news_ id=60257.

CHAPTER 7

Managing Ingredient Brands and Measuring the Performance of InBrands

In today's fast-changing markets, Ingredient Branding had become a major marketing strategy as demonstrated by the increasing number of products sold with embedded branded components. Despite its success in generating positive effects on participants in the value chain, the effect of Ingredient Branding in business markets has not been evaluated in relation to brand equity[1]. Various academic and consulting organizations are offering different measurement approaches and apply them also to InBrands. Some companies such as Intel and Dolby have developed their own measurement systems and use them as an integral part of their brand management system as highlighted in the case studies. Now, we would like to shed some light on managing and understanding brand evaluation methods, and suggest valuation tools for assessing brand equity from the component supplier's perspective for InBrands.

7.1 Managing Ingredient Brands

After demonstrating the success of various industries and case studies on Ingredient Branding, we think it is necessary to go deeper into the management processes of InBranding. Brands can create market-based assets, because it can be drawn upon as a re-

P. Kotler and W. Pfoertsch, *Ingredient Branding: Making the Invisible Visible*,
DOI 10.1007/978-3-642-04214-0_7, © Springer-Verlag Berlin Heidelberg 2010

source by consumers, component suppliers, original equipment manufacturers and others.

This perspective is based on the newest research identifying the consumer of Ingredient Brands as co-creator in the value chain[2]. This can occur in two ways:

1. The ability and willingness of consumers to pay a price premium for branded ingredients. They signal a strong, favorable, and unique relationship between themselves and the selected InBrands.

2. The consumer integrates branded ingredients into their everyday life; create knowledge and associations of the branded ingredient.

As a result, increasing number of component suppliers realize Branding opportunities for themselves. This inadvertently transforms business markets by increasing demand for the branded ingredients. Furthermore, as the use of branded ingredients diffuses through consumer contexts, the contexts themselves are changing and evolve in such a way that ingredients that were once unfamiliar become familiar and sought after. In this way, the newly evolved contexts become fertile new markets for firms involved in the existing value chains and can be especially fruitful for those ingredients that are already branded[3].

There are also companies who want to brand their ingredient so that consumers are able to quickly process emergent product and service categories because of the salience, recognition, and association of Ingredient Brands.[4] This has the following results:

- A large improvement in downstream value, based on an ingredient from an upstream supplier.

- The benefit is real, visible and important to the downstream end user.

- The benefit might be "invisible" at the point of sale, not easily discerned until the product/service/offering is put into use.

- The firm, manufacturer or OEM, the ingredient "user" is compelled in some way to "call out" this ingredient to the end user to make it apparent at the point of sale that there is a "special ingredient" in the offering that is making it a higher value.

- The benefit is articulated to the consumer in ways that can spell higher prices or higher propensity to buy the product.

Processes and Pre-conditions of Ingredient Branding

For B2B companies, gaining knowledge about the final customers and their desires and need related to their product and service offering puts them in a very favorable position and gives them a competitive advantage over their competitors.

If the component supplier selects an Ingredient Branding approach, the company has various ways to execute the strategy. Before starting this process a preparation phase is needed. A number of companies, which have implemented an Ingredient Branding strategy made themselves familiar with the concept, its challenges and opportunities and often hired experienced professionals from the marketing departments of NutraSweet, Gore-Tex or Intel.

Equipped with this knowledge and manpower, companies set out to scan their product and service portfolio to identify potential In-Brand options as a first step in the InBranding management process. This is guided by the conditions we identified for successful In-Brands:

- High functionality for the final product
- Importance for the total product performance
- Accessible power structure in the value chain
- Potential partner for co-operation

This first step can only identify the possible options. In step two, customer preference clusters and addressable customer need have to be identified. This step clearly gives priority to intensive customer analysis. However, this is often unknown territory for many B2B companies. Since these companies are used to deal with business customers, a new set of instruments have to be applied; from focus group research to panel analysis to end customer testing, many B2C market research instruments have to be applied to create sufficient insights in the final users' understanding and buying behavior.

Step two could last several months and determines the elements of step three: strategy development. The information to the final customer and the investment of the final customer is a crucial aspect of the InBrand strategy, because it determines the approach and the investment for communication.

If an ingredient supplier only wants an access point to the retail level this may be sufficient and the channel partner will then do the communication to the end user. Shimano has implemented such a concept. If the company wants to approach the customer directly they have to communicate with the end user.

Another strategic issue is the relationship of the ingredient provider with the important partner in the value chain. Many factors determine this situation. Factors could be the power structure, the position of leader of innovation in the value chain, or the access points to the final customers. The goal of various steps has to be determined and broken down to manageable elements. The final step of this process is the development of the marketing concepts, which lays out the master plan for the execution (see Fig. 94).

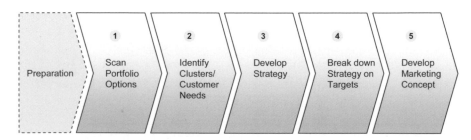

Fig. 94. InBrand management processes

Since the Ingredient Branding strategy is based on a multi stage marketing process, it needs careful planning and continuous monitoring. If a company underestimates this management task, this can lead to negative effects:

- Backlash from the user/OEM and the channel

- Brand conflicts

In practice, the creation of downstream brand equity for the ingredient can happen in several ways, including[5]:

- The ingredient creator invests separately from the ingredient users by making direct investments in communications of the Ingredient Brand and its benefits downstream to the consumer market or segments of the market that are important; (examples: NutraSweet, Intel, Gore-Tex, Makrolon, Microban, etc.) or

- alternatively, by working together with the ingredient user, ingredient creators using differential pricing, price off, or co-op rebates can gain the support of the ingredient user in building the Ingredient Brand (example: Sony supporting Dolby Sound).

Value Flows/Multiple Effects

The injection of a new brand in the process of marketing down the value chain can have a myriad of effects – which sets up a rather complex "effects base," as shown in Fig. 95[6].

As shown, effects can happen between these key players in a myriad of ways, including:

I-1 is direct investment by the creator of the ingredient in building consumer brand equity consists of direct communication, advertising, sampling or other sorts of activity.

R-1 is equity and a direct connection between the consumer and the ingredient creator – creating the anticipation to look for other products with ingredients from the creator, and creating direct consumer

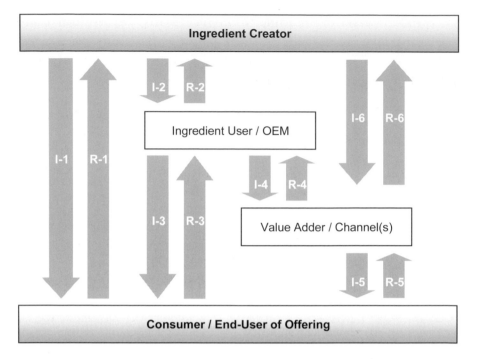

Fig. 95. Ingredient Branding – spectrum of effects

pull for offerings with the creator's ingredients, which can be used to gain power and garner higher prices from the user and through the channel.

I-2 can be direct investments that the creator of an ingredient provides for a user/OEM to utilize the ingredient, (also includes price concessions, or other sorts of inducements the creator might use to get the user/OEM to use and/or promote the ingredient. I-2 might also include negative effects such as the OEM feeling trapped by having to use the ingredient due to consumer demand, or other loss of control.

R-2 is a series of returns the user can provide to the creator, including higher prices, loyalty, deeper partnerships with the creator, the surrender of control, and limiting opportunistic sorts of purchasing practices.

I-3 can be investments that the ingredient user makes in communicating with the consumer that the ingredient is in their product as well as the value it brings. As they do so, they are actually investing in building brand equity for the ingredient creator.

R-3 can mean greater uptake by the consumer, driven by the benefits coming from the ingredient, including higher sales velocity, higher prices, greater loyalty, and greater propensity to advocate the product to others. This also includes brand equity effects for both the user brands and the Ingredient Brand.

I-4 can be a direct investment that the ingredient user makes to the channel, informing the channel of the power of the ingredient, and to enable the channel to better sell their product including the ingredient to consumers[7]. For example: A variety of carpet manufacturers use "Stainmaster" fibers and chemicals, so every carpet manufacturer who helped build the value of Stainmaster actually provided an investment for other user/manufacturers who incorporated those ingredients, as the Stainmaster Ingredient Brand became more well known.

R-4 is return from the channel to the user/OEM –which could mean higher prices, greater up take, greater velocity and turn of product.

I-5 refers to investment that the channel makes with the consumer in raising visibility of the Ingredient Brand, as well as the user/OEM's brand as it sells its product. This can be achieved through a variety of market communications or other promotional activity, incentives, sampling, installation of point-of-purchase displays, etc.

R-5 represents greater channel returns and higher prices, faster uptake, brand loyalty, and the anticipation that more products with the key ingredient might become available.

I-6 represents direct investments the creator of the ingredient might make straight to the channel – in building awareness of the ingredient and advising channel partners to be looking for products from user/OEM's that incorporate the ingredient. By going straight to the channel, the ingredient creator would have the opportunity of gaining additional power over user/OEM's, by creating a channel pull for the product, and an incentive to the channel to look for and stock these products because of the promise of greater product turns.

R-6 represents return to the ingredient creator through channel pressure on user/OEM's to deliver products that use the creator's ingredients.

Relative Brand Power

Additionally, the business of Ingredient Branding incorporates another potential complexity – when considering the relative power of the ingredient creator's parent brand. This means the Ingredient Brand relating to the user's brand[8].

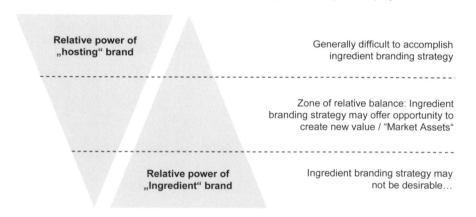

Fig. 96. Relative brand power effects of Ingredient Branding

A visualization that might be used to describe a "zone", where Ingredient Branding is easiest to implement – when the relative consumer equity of the user/OEM's brand and the ingredient creator's brand are relatively well matched – is shown in Fig. 96.

If there is the situation where the creator's Ingredient Brand is relatively unknown but the user's brand is very well known, negotiations will be difficulty and the creator might have to provide significant concessions for getting the user to use its brand to begin building the equity in the creator's Ingredient Brand. An example of this might be Texas Instruments' DLP (Digital Light Processor) ingredient when it was introduced[9]. At that time negotiations with a powerful user/OEM brand such as Sony would have been very difficult. Sony could also explore other technology alternatives for projectors and large-screen TVs. In contrast to Sony, negotiations were relatively easy with Proxima, a less well-known brand, to incorporate the Texas Instruments DLP in its projectors.

If the ingredient creator has a very powerful brand, well known by end users and trusted, and the user has a relatively unknown brand, then negotiations for uptake, pricing, utilization and build of Ingredient Brands and brand marks should be fairly easy for the creator. On the other hand, the user's brand may be lesser known because it is entering the market, or because its products are of relatively low quality – so the creator may not choose to negotiate with those companies.

There is a zone where the brand equity of the creator and user are relatively in balance, and where Ingredient Branding negotiations are more on an "equal partner" footing. Here the dynamics and economics of the Ingredient Branding negotiations between the creator and the user/OEM can explore the opportunity for real brand synergy with both market-based assets of the creator and user/OEM increasing as they work together.

Relative Relationship Power

Another approach to analyzing the space of Ingredient Brands and how they might be negotiated can be viewed in Fig. 97. It outlines a "space" where the relative brand power of the user/OEM is on the horizontal axis and the relative brand power of the creator's Ingredient Brand is on the vertical axis, dividing the "space" into four quadrants.

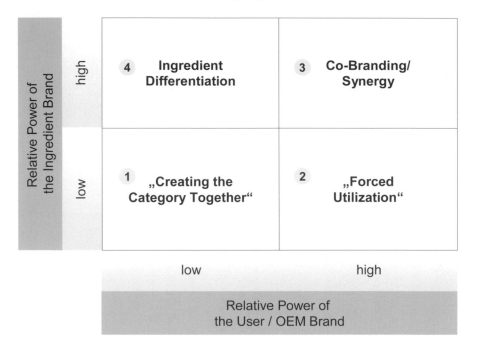

Fig. 97. Relative power relationship between Ingredient Brand and user/ OEM brand

Quadrant 1 might be viewed as a space where the ingredient creator and the ingredient user, both with low power, are "creating the category together." In this case, if the creator has come up with a high value but little known ingredient, and the user's brand is also relatively unknown, the two could work together to open a new category. So both brands would create brand equity simultaneously and synergistically in the new category.

Once again, an example of this might be TI's DLP ingredient in Proxima projectors, or historically, the efforts Dolby labs put into helping to build portable cassette players with lower hiss because of their technologies. At the time of introduction of Dolby, cassette players were relatively new and Dolby was virtually unknown. Tape players developed progressive amounts of "hiss," adding noise to the taped signal every time the tape was played. Dolby, by providing a technology that eliminated this, and Sony, by miniaturizing cassette players, worked together to create what became a powerful category: personal, portable, high-quality music.

Quadrant 2 – In this situation the creator has a relatively unknown Ingredient Brand, and is negotiating with companies of user/OEM brands of high power at the point of utilization. In this case, negotiations for the creator will be difficult unless the ingredient is truly revolutionary and serves a significant un-served downstream demand hitherto unreachable by the user/OEM. If the user/OEM needs the ingredient badly enough, even an unknown ingredient can create a "Forced Utilization" situation. The ingredient creator would essentially say: If you want this ingredient, help me build the brand for it.

An example of this might be NutraSweet's negotiations with Coca-Cola in developing the Diet Coke brand. NutraSweet was in a very strong position to bring its Aspartame sweetener to Coca-Cola and enable them to serve a significantly large market. NutraSweet, with strong patent protection and a "killer ingredient," was able to negotiate to get Coca-Cola and Pepsi to adopt the NutraSweet brand mark, and basically endorse and create the market based asset for NutraSweet.

Quadrant 3 – There is high brand equity of both brands – the creator's and the user/OEM's. This is a situation where co-Branding would be the right choice for creating synergy – when each brand brings its own power to the end user for combined sales. An example of this might be Eddie Bauer and "Jeep." Both of these already have strong brand associations, and the combination in natural synergy creates a greater pull downstream in the market.

Quadrant 4 – In this case there is high brand power for the ingredient creator and low brand power for the user/OEM. The ingredient may be the only thing differentiating what essentially is – or is becoming – a commodity category populated by user/OEM brands of similar brand equity. An ingredient creator can move into an essentially commoditized consumer category and go straight to the end user and take responsibility for de-commoditizing the category, giving it great power over the user/OEM brands and great consumer franchise and brand equity[10]. This was viewed earlier as a case of DuPont with Stainmaster. Relatively undifferentiated carpet brands were being sold in a non-differentiated way through a variety of channels. DuPont, by building direct franchise with the consumer – and owning that entire franchise – essentially had great power over the ingredient user/OEMs, such the carpet manufacturers Shaw or Mohawk.

The Execution of an InBranding Strategy

For executing an Ingredient Branding strategy from a supplier perspective the company and its management has to be very clear about its strategic options. The purpose of InBranding strategies is differentiation[11]. All of our examined InBranding cases (see previous chapter) started with a narrow focus. The companies had a very specific idea that was clear and simple, which could separate them from the competition: bittering agent – Bitrex, synthetic leather – Alcantara, natural soluble fibers – Oliggo, natural laxative – Senokot, just to name a few. With this differentiation supplier companies have the credentials or the product/services that make the product offering trust worthy, real and believable. This ability to differentiate and offer a unique benefit to the final user is the basis for awareness creation. Therefore the companies have the opportunity to make the customers and prospects aware of this difference. Each industry has specific technological and market conditions. Every Ingredient Branding supplier has to have a full understanding of his role in the industry value chain and the amount of his influence. As stated in Chapter 2 there may be three, five or even seven layers of value creation, till the consumer benefits from the ingredient's strength. Various value adders may help the OEM to manufacture the final product and various value adders may support the channel efforts. The closer the ingredient creator can get to the final consumer the better.

Product categories such as dietary supplements or fibers have the most number of Ingredient Brands. We identified about 20 fibers and about the same number for dietary supplements with rising numbers. In both areas there are many innovative start-up companies, that apply this concept, but also some brand minded multinationals with very professional brand management. The companies Cargill Inc. and Invista Inc. are both very secretive about the marketing and branding methods.

Invista's products include brands such as Lycra fiber, Stainmaster carpeting, Cordura durable fabrics, Tactel nylon fiber, and Antron commercial carpet fiber as well as a variety of polyester resins and specialty intermediates. Invista launched a new advanced Teflon fabric protector for use in bedding and other washable home textiles. The stain-repelling agent in the finished product causes liquid spills to bead up and rolls off fabric, and also prevents fibers from holding stains and soil, according to the company. Invista is working with its mill partners and also supports the consumer launch with a $7 million "Make Every Day Easy" ad campaign. Invista also announced its official sponsorship of the "Show Me Your sloggi" contest hosted by leading underwear manufacturer Triumph. The grand finale of this men and women international contest took place in Paris, on November 12, 2008.

With an unparalleled heritage within the intimate apparel sector, the Lycra fiber brand was the perfect partner for this exciting competition. Integral to modern underwear and committed to constant innovation, the brand continues to offer consumers improved fit, comfort and shape retention. This exciting and interactive partnership with Triumph fully highlights Invista's continued mission to introduce more consumer-focused activity within the marketplace, creating stand out by accessing and leveraging new media channels.

Lycra fiber is the only fiber brand recognized and valued by consumers worldwide with 83% of women aged 18–49 acknowledging the Lycra brand in garments. 67% of consumers are willing to pay more for garments with Lycra fiber proving that the Lycra brand is at the forefront of many consumers' minds as a key ingredient when it comes to purchasing fashion items. With this kind of marketing and success Invista has established a great position in the fiber market place and uses InBranding and sometimes co-branding

Fig. 98. Brand development alternatives

to push its sales premium and price premium to create more healthy cash flows or increase its market share. These alternatives are shown in Fig. 98.

Cargill Inc. has not clearly committed itself to InBranding. This company still relies heavily on their B2B relationship and occasionally steps out of the dark to approach the final customer. One example of their offering is CoroWise, the cholesterol reducer. But with many of their natural sweeteners, barley beta fibers, and functional carbohydrates, they pursue InBranding activities, but don't state it publicly or sometimes don't have a consistent execution. The reasons for this may lie in the power constellation of the industry. Due to the globally fragmented "hosting brands" and the different needs of the final customers in the various areas of the world it may be very difficult for many dietary supplements providers to apply a consistent Ingredient Branding strategy. Solae from the DuPont/ Bunge joint venture is trying to establish an InBrand for soy protein, and success may be possible.

Other InBrands have been struggling, such as Olean from Procter & Gamble and NutraSweet. Splenda, Xglit, and Isomalt are driving strong, and there is more room in the market. Specialty applications are in high need, brands such as Ocean Spray, Senokot and Z-trim

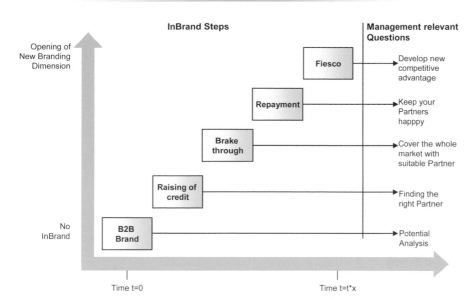

Fig. 99. InBrand development steps

are increasing their marketing efforts, and others are looking for their chances. All of them have their chance for creating an own brand for final partners; the most artful Branding effort may be the InBranding. InBrand development has to go through various steps over time as shown in Fig. 99.

Coming from a B2B brand, a positive potential analysis leads to the decision that the brand should be developed. First of all, the right partners have to be found and convinced of the potential and bene-fits for them. This could be seen as the raise of credit.

The next achievement is the coverage of the whole market with suitable partners, which marks the breakthrough if it is successful. After that the InBrand strategy should pay off at least for the part-ners to keep them happy. The ultimate goal is developing competi-tive advantages like a better marketing position, which leads to tangible benefits in form of a price premium or sales premium.

In the computer industry the InBrand development steps could be noticed easily. Intel and Microsoft went through all stages and developed finally more to a master brand concept. Other component suppliers like nVidia, ATI or MSI are in the breakthrough phase. Most of the analyzed InBrands are still in the phase of raising credits. Some industries like automotive and electronic components have difficulty industry conditions, so only a few InBrands made it to the repayment phase. Dolby and Shimano are two of them. If their logo is on a final product "the magnifying effects" are taking place[12]. Particularly weak or unknown brand capitalize on the benefits of this effect very much. For example, many Chinese heavy construction equipment companies use Perkins, Cummins or Deutz diesel engines. Moreover, they use Siemens controls or Rexroth hydraulic systems to boost their final product performance and perceptions of customers.

With a conscious and consequent InBrand management the component supplier's success can be enhanced. As illustrated by Invista, who sell their brand management also as a consulting service, these skills could be developed. A prerequisite for this is consistent brand identity management, with clear stated Ingredient Brand guidelines. The brand design has to be implemented visually and verbally consistent in the host and Ingredient Brand messages to the final user. A company with many Ingredient Brands is 3M. It has implemented these kinds of regulations recently and achieved increased brand recognition. They understand the InBranding process and do the necessary preparations. Moreover, the company has a consistent strategic development concept in place, and executes it accordingly with the steps, which we provided with the InBrand management processes (see Fig. 94). Every component supplier can start changing its efforts from B2B to B2B2C. After identifying the position of their offering to the market and the current stage in the product life cycle, the innovative product with a high impact to the customers' benefits should be selected. Of course older products with high impact could be selected, too. In case that the existing market structure has to be changed and the customer audience is already big, the marketing communication spending may have to start with large investment. An example for this is Makrolon from Bayer. This case demonstrates that an InBranding attempt in a later stage of the life cycle is possible.

Bayer did thorough analysis to identify customer needs of customers. By understanding the importance to the customer and the existing knowledge about the Ingredient Brand product features, the company could determine their actions to the customer. They also had to consider the total complexity of the product offering. The polycarbonate high-tech material Makrolon is used in sunglasses for bicycling and other outdoors sports. The material protects the eye, can be coated easily and has to be suitable for contemporary design. The educated customer may prefer the material, but may also consider the design aspects.

In this complex relationship, quality perception, trust and performance recognition are relevant dimensions. The more clearly they could be identified and put into addressable segments the easier they are to communicate and get the customer pull started. Shimano showed how this was done in the bicycling market, but they also transferred this concept to their fishing rails. Recaro car seats and Brembo performance brakes were targeted initially to the car racing enthusiasts to start the hype. Tetra Pak led the retail organization help them to initiate the pull.

Many roads are possible to success, and after a company has successfully developed an application they could branch out. Shimano started with racing bicycles gear, now they provide all kind of components. Dolby reduced the hiss in recording, now even mobile phones have Dolby sound-enhancing applications engineered in. We expect similar development for InBrand applications in dietary supplement, material applications, systems, and possibly even with automotive components one day.

For making an Ingredient Branding strategy work, a clear "front to back" responsibility has to be established. This means that brand management is an integrated part of marketing and all activities around R&D, manufacturing and market delivering has to be coordinated from there. It is also necessary to establish intermediary steps with clear targets and the establishment of a final customer response system.

Companies who have achieved this are the InBranding champions. They understood the conditions in the market, judged their strength correctly and started championing the market. As shown in the case studies, it was not always a smooth ride and many setbacks occurred. Companies who analyze the conditions properly and ask the following questions have great chances to succeed:

- Which are the right OEMs to choose?

- What's my brand value today, and after 5 years?

- How does my InBrand help the OEM and other partners?

- How can the most positive impact for my cash flow/sales be created?

- What kind of partnership arrangements and involvement of third parties are required?

- How will the competition react?

- How to maintain the competitive advantage?

- Which OEM/channel partner benefits the most?

- How do customers judge the InBrand?

- How is the pull effect from the consumer to the OEM measured?

- What is the OEMs price/sales premium with the InBrand?

- Does the price/sales premium reach me through the network?

These kinds of questions about the product offering, the market conditions and the appropriate management action can steer the InBrand management through the various phases of the life cycle and the competitive challenges. Certain conditions for the InBranding success apply to all these kinds of attempts. As stated before the product offering has to be highly differentiated and the functional performance of the ingredient has to be important for the final user. With complex products and weak OEM brands the initial start may be easier. Companies may also use the aftermarket to start the customer recognition for their brand to become a leading industry application. It helps to start in early life cycle stages and to learn from other InBrands. The best way of doing so is to imitate or hire some of their marketing managers. Growing with the industry from the beginning or even branching out into other applications can help to secure solutions for the whole industry.

The most important aspect of InBranding success is the constant feedback of the customers and the way they use the product with the ingredient. Companies have to innovate and establish such kind of information flow. Gore-Tex consistently interviews customers; they sponsor competitions and collect feedback. Shimano monitors component sales all around the world and has established recently shop-in-shop concepts in their most important markets. Dolby has a license system in place, which collects the use of their application per product of the OEM brand. This gives Dolby a knowledge advantage over every OEM in their industry. Microsoft is on the forefront of customer insights. With the interconnectivity over the Internet the use of any system components and configurations can be monitored. With this kind of information product development and promotional activities could be directed and used for strategic Branding decisions.

Increased quality perception, improved trust and better judgment of the component performance lead to a price premium as a positive consequence. The better a component supplier manages these consumer behavior relevant dimensions of InBranding effects, the higher the price premium benefit will be. There are still many options in the Branding toolbox for managers; Ingredient Branding is just one of them. Therefore it is very important to evaluate the offering and the management activities carefully.

Ingredient Branding Management Tools

The establishment of an Ingredient Branding strategy does not necessarily lead to business success; it is an ongoing process of continuous adjustment and learning. When Intel invested in its first campaign, the success was not secure at the beginning, and they are at another crossroads today. The management process is about creating value and Ingredient Branding is a special form of it. The process has to be monitored and the created brand equity measured.

Developing a brand is challenging and rethinking the outcome of the action is continuously necessary. However, instruments are needed which provide information about multiple success factors. Just focusing on brand equity is not sufficient. We need brand knowledge, awareness and preferences from the customer as well as information about sales development, key product categories, sales location, margin, turnover rates, etc.

A brand management tool needs to aggregate this information to bring it to the attention of the management so it can react to individual challenges immediately. Instruments that are applied and use standardized brand measurement systems are not really helpful. As demonstrated by the Ingredient Branding development stepladder, InBrands are continuously changing. Normally, they start as a B2B brand. After deciding to involve end users, the component supplier moves on to the other development stages. In each stage, the brand requires different management activities. Therefore, brand measurement has also to be flexible, in process.

In principle, we are talking about a continuous process of the following:

- Initiate and Integrate
- Manage and Exchange
- Evaluate and Control

In Fig. 100, this is displayed as a continuous InBrand management cycle. In the initiative and integration phase, the brand values have to be developed and defined; the strategy has to be determined and the visuals, logos, taglines all have to be developed or modernized. The customer experience of the InBrand has to be determined as well as the brand message to all customer segments. The partners have to be identified and the role in the value chain determined.

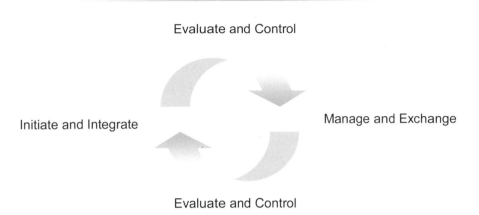

Fig. 100. Process flow of the InBranding management cycles

In the next phase, continuous brand management relies very much on the exchange of information between all partners. Joint benefit and joint process management is required. The brand value gains on the various sides of the joint value chain have to be established and continuously monitored. At the same time, the future developments have to be kept in mind and the current benefits have to be secured.

In the evaluation phase, the various facets of the InBrand have to be re-evaluated and the brand identity with the customer re-examined. Consider this as a continuous effort, which could be run through every year. With a clear understanding of the InBrand and its value, the brand owner can enjoy a well-managed brand.

To manage an Ingredient Brand means to steer through changing relationships and activities. The one, which produced business success, should be continued; and those that resulted in failure should be learned from. The life of an InBrand can be seen as a process with steps.

Moving from a B2B to a B2B2C brand requires determination and the vision that the final customer really benefits from the component in the final product. When the final customer starts asking for products with the ingredient, the chances are high that out of a not so highly valued B2B brand, a consumer brand can emerge. If the potential is high, this product configuration can be developed to a powerful InBrand, and may even evolve to a final consumer brand as we have seen in the case of Intel. NutraSweet was in a similar position, but after the patent rights expired, generic alternatives were available and their fortune went away.

InBrands are like all brands more than logos, taglines, slogans or commercials. InBrands deliver values. The brand mirrors wishes, dreams and desires; the customer identifies with them. To steer the Branding efforts through the various steps, a set of different information is needed to evaluate risk and opportunities.

For steering the Branding efforts through the development steps of an InBrand, we suggest a set of tools that have been proven in various applications. The tools offer clear steps for the management of the brand. This should include quantitative results (brand equity) and qualitative results (brand loyalty, brand recognition, etc.). We recommend using the tools during the whole life of the brand. This could over a time period of ten to fifty years.

With the analysis of the quantitative factors, you get the explanation of the ongoing development. Various layers of your cooperation could trigger the reasons for the change. If expected results could not be achieved modifications are needed to improve the performance.

7.2   Principles of Brand Evaluation

Many studies have been produced and numerous models investigated to make the complex interaction between the consumer and product manufacturer measurable. For many companies more than 50 % of the value of a company accrues to the brand as an asset. This is the result of a study by Professor Sattler from University of Hamburg.[13] This means that brand evaluation may well be the most important component in the information available for brand management. Business management research has concerned itself with this subject for more than half a century. The development of models and methods is an innovative process that is continually developing. The many different brand evaluation procedures are an indicator for the importance of this task at an academic and practical level. All evaluation approaches have the objective to establish generally recognized standards. However, this objective has not been reached, yet. The choice of the correct method for brand evaluation is solely dependent on the answer to the question: "For what purpose is the brand value required?" Key motives for brand evaluations are fusion, purchase or sale of brands, brand licensing, adjustment or expansion of brand portfolios, brand transfers, marketing resource allocation, control of brand growth and evaluation of management performance.[14]

This book does not aim to present a new preference model to explain customer behavior, but it wants to show a practical procedure for utilizing and measuring InBranding. In this context the references are previously confirmed models and examples. The success of a brand that also influences the company's success is revealed in the first place when determining the monetary value of a brand. In 2008, Interbrand determined a value of $61 billion[15] for the most valuable industrial brand in the world. They use their methodology for all kind of brand offering: consumer brands (B2C), industrial brands (B2B) and even InBrands (B2B2C). Like many of the existing brand evaluation models Interbrand started with a B2C approach and judged companies with B2B markets with the same approach, knowing that the conditions in these markets are very different. From a conceptual point of view these kinds of approaches carry a certain restriction and may lead to misinterpretation and non-appropriate management action. The Interbrand approach established itself as a measurement tool and is the most common instrument. With last year's measurements IBM was the largest B2B brand[16] with $59 billion brand equity, followed by Microsoft with $59 billion, and General Electric (GE) with $53 billion, which corresponds to more than 10 % of its market capitalization at the time.[17] For internal purposes GE is using a purely capital market-oriented brand evaluation method, because they wanted to use it as an asset in their balance sheet. GE stated an estimated value of more than $5 billion.

Intel and Microsoft as B2B2C companies have also been measured with the Interbrand evaluation instruments and ended up at impressive places 3 and 7 of the TOP 10 global brand list (see Table 13). However, a more dedicated instrument for managing In-Brands is needed. If brand evaluation is used as a strategic target measure in the company, and this requires a fundamental management decision, then management instruments must also be provided to enable detailed control. The brand effects at the customer stage can be used to measure the value.

Table 13. Top list of brand values for B2B companies

Turnover B2B > 95 %		Turnover B2B > 50 %	
Rank	Brand	Rank	Brand
7	Intel	2	IBM
23	Oracle	3	Microsoft
31	SAP	4	General Electric
44	Reuters	5	Nokia
47	Accenture	12	Hewlett-Packard
68	Caterpillar	27	HSBC
		37	J. P. Morgan
		42	Morgan Stanley
		59	Xerox
		99	Fedex

The components that can be used to determine the brand value according to Aaker can be divided into five categories:[18]

- Brand loyalty
- Familiarity of the name
- Assumed quality

- Additional brand associations

- Other brand advantages (patents, trademarks, sales channels, etc.)

Brand loyalty is defined by a company's fixed **customer base** that can be cost-effectively maintained. This is a consequence of lesser vulnerability to campaigns of the competition.

Consumers often associate attributes such as better quality or long-term market presence with well-known brand names. Hence the customer will often choose a well-known brand name over an unknown or lesser known one. The quality mentioned above, which customers expect from a branded article, exercises a direct influence on the decision to buy as well as to the brand loyalty. This means that higher prices in comparison to the competition can also be justified. Furthermore, such assumed quality by the customer can also be the starting point for expanding the brand since the new product will also then be associated with similarly positive quality expectations. Finally, the customer associations with the brand can also lead to a higher brand value. An example is the well-known positive side effects of a product such as Aspirin, which advertises that it prevents heart attacks. The areas of application for brand evaluation can be divided into in-house and cross-company areas. The following Table 14 shows the different areas of application.

Internally, the brand value is used on the one hand as a planning instrument and on the other as a control instrument for brand and

Table 14. Area of application of brand value and brand evaluation[19]

In-house	Cross -company

• **Brand value as planning instrument**
  - Allocation of marketing budget
  - Specified brand value as planning and target measure
 	
• **Brand value as control instrument**
  - Measure of success
  - Basis of remuneration
  - General evaluation instrument
	• **Price determination in brand acquisition**
	• **Determination of the level of license fees in:**
	  - Brand utilization
	  - Franchising
	
	• **Determination of the level of compensation for losses**
	• **Loan collateralization through the brand**
	• **External reporting and accounting**

product management. Thus specified brand values can be set as target measures and moreover, serve as measures of success on the control side. In the cross-company area of application, the brand value is mainly utilized in the acquisition of companies. In addition, it plays an important role as the basis for calculating license fees for franchising or brand utilization by third parties.

In order to enable the operationalization of the context in which brand function and brand value control take effect, we refer to the three key functions of brands. Both brands and InBrands should essentially fulfill the following basic functions:

- Intangible use (image)
- Information efficiency (time saving)
- Risk reduction (trust)

There are more than 30 different procedures that can be used to determine brand values. However, their results are sometimes contradictory. For example, in 2002, the brand value of Volkswagen was evaluated by **Interbrand** and **Semion**. Interbrand set the value at €7.6 m, while Semion specified a brand value of €18.8 m. This is only one example of major differences in determining brand values in practice.[20] However, a key element is how the success of a brand is influenced by brand management. A good example for successful brand management is NIVEA. This consumer goods brand started out as a skin lotion and has now a full assortment of cosmetics for women and for men. The active management of the brand led to an enormously increased shareholder return in subsequent years.

Now we begin to systemize the various brand evaluation methods. Of the many existing methods those of Interbrand, A. C. Nielsen and BBDO Consulting will be presented in detail. The brand evaluation methods are distinguished from each other according to input and result criteria. We will differentiate here between financially oriented, customer psychology and hybrid procedures.

The financially oriented procedures focus on values measured in monetary units for determining brand value. In contrast, the cus-

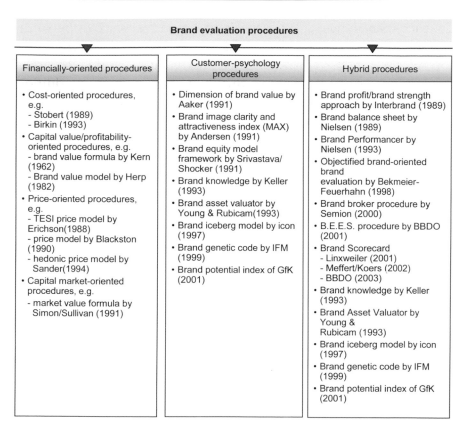

Brand evaluation procedures		
Financially-oriented procedures	Customer-psychology procedures	Hybrid procedures

• Cost-oriented procedures, e.g.
  - Stobert (1989)
  - Birkin (1993)
• Capital value/profitability-oriented procedures, e.g.
  - brand value formula by Kern (1962)
  - Brand value model by Herp (1982)
• Price-oriented procedures, e.g.
  - TESI price model by Erichson(1988)
  - price model by Blackston (1990)
  - hedonic price model by Sander(1994)
• Capital market-oriented procedures, e.g.
  - market value formula by Simon/Sullivan (1991)
	• Dimension of brand value by Aaker (1991)
	• Brand image clarity and attractiveness index (MAX) by Andersen (1991)
	• Brand equity model framework by Srivastava/ Shocker (1991)
	• Brand knowledge by Keller (1993)
	• Brand asset valuator by Young & Rubicam(1993)
	• Brand iceberg model by icon (1997)
	• Brand genetic code by IFM (1999)
	• Brand potential index of GfK (2001)
		• Brand profit/brand strength approach by Interbrand (1989)
		• Brand balance sheet by Nielsen (1989)
		• Brand Performancer by Nielsen (1993)
		• Objectified brand-oriented brand evaluation by Bekmeier-Feuerhahn (1998)
		• Brand broker procedure by Semion (2000)
		• B.E.E.S. procedure by BBDO (2001)
		• Brand Scorecard
		  - Linxweiler (2001)
		  - Meffert/Koers (2002)
		  - BBDO (2003)
		• Brand knowledge by Keller (1993)
		• Brand Asset Valuator by Young & Rubicam (1993)
		• Brand iceberg model by icon (1997)
		• Brand genetic code by IFM (1999)
		• Brand potential index of GfK (2001)

Fig. 101. Systematization of brand evaluation procedures[21]

tomer psychology procedures focus mainly on criteria of customer behavior, which are based on the observation of customers or the analysis of purchasing data. However, the relevant values are not expressed in monetary units.

Hybrid procedures combine the above-named categories so that the brand value can be expressed in monetary units. Fig. 101 gives an overview of the most important brand evaluation procedures and their allocation to one of the categories described. In all the procedures set out below, the aim is to determine a brand value in the sense of a real brand price.

The Interbrand model is a point evaluation model (scoring model), which is based on seven brand value factors as shown in Fig. 102.

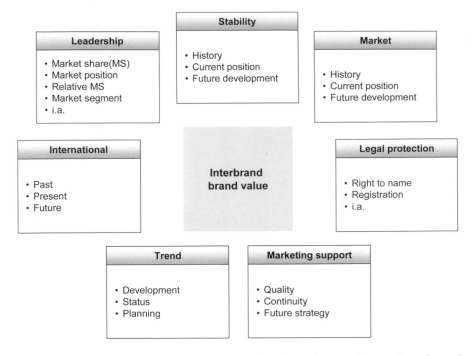

Fig. 102. Factors influencing the value of the brand according to Interbrand

The A. C. Nielsen Brand Performancer is a comprehensive system intended to determine the brand strength and brand value on the one hand, and on the other to give concrete recommendations for actions to steer and control the brand. To determine the brand value, only the **brand monitor** and **brand value system** components highlighted in Fig. 103 are required and are explained in greater detail below.

In the Brand Monitor, the strength of the brand is determined in comparison with the direct competition. Brand strength is characterized by four success factors:

- Market attractiveness (market volume, market acceptance)

- Assertiveness of brand (market share in terms of quantity and value)

- Commercial acceptance, distribution (technical reach)

- Degree of demand acceptance (scope of market familiarity)

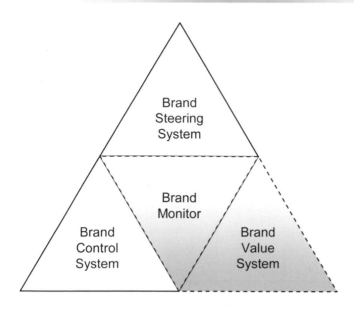

Fig. 103. Brand Monitor according to A. C. Nielsen

For these figures, the results are respectively shown in a weighted point's number from which the absolute and relative brand strength in comparison to the competition is calculated. The actual calculation of the **monetary brand value** in the **brand value system** is then undertaken through the total profit that would arise if the return on sales of the brand were used as a basis. The result, the so-called brand strength profit, is finally included in the managerial earning power formula. The procedure is very objective and transparent. The basic data can easily be acquired so that the brand evaluation can also be carried out discreetly in the own company. Moreover, third party and competitive brands can be evaluated.

The main points of criticism to be mentioned with regard to this procedure are the assumption of a constant return on sales and the infinite life of the brand. Furthermore, this approach does not include forecast data with the result that important influencing factors are not taken into account. Image factors are completely neglected in this procedure so that the influence on customer acceptance is not taken into account.

The **BBDO (brand equity evaluator)** from BBDO Consulting can be used both for monetary and non-monetary brand evaluation. Furthermore, it is possible to use this procedure for various brand evaluation reasons. The overview (see Fig. 104) shows the five components of the BBDO Brand Equity Evaluator:

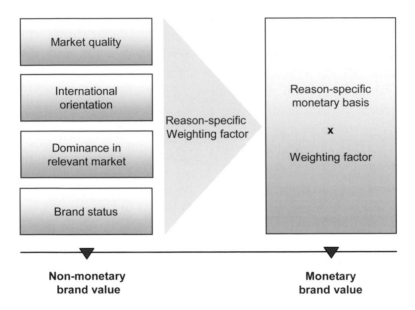

Fig. 104. Diagrammatic representation of the brand value calculation in accordance with BBDO[22]

The environment in which a brand moves is measured by means of market quality. Here the turnover development of the relevant market is used as an indicator for the sales potential of the brand. The international orientation factor, measured by the share of foreign turnover in relation to total turnover of the brand, provides an indicator for the capacity of the brand to develop globally. Dominance in relevant market expresses the relative turnover strength of the brand in relation to the competition.

Brand status describes the brand strength as well as the attractiveness of the brand as perceived by demanders. However, the status of a brand is not constant over time but is subject to internal and external influences. The monetary basis for the value potential of a brand is determined depending on the evaluation reason. This can either be the pre-tax profit or discounted cash flow values.[23]

In the subsequent calculation of the brand value, the components market quality, international orientation, dominance in relevant market and brand status are included in the total factor value with equal weight. This value is then used as weighing factor for the basic monetary component. Finally, the weighing factor and the monetary basis are used to calculate the monetary brand value. This model is primarily characterized by its adaptability to various evaluation reasons. The contributing components and their weight can be adapted to the specific evaluation situation. This enables the reason-specific determination of brand value that does justice to the purpose. However, as in the previous models, a subjective selection of the influencing variables by the experts cannot be excluded. In addition, there is no separation of brand and non-brand specific income for faster execution.

Brand Value with InBranding

The component manufacturers seek to escape the anonymity of their products by means of a brand policy, which transcends stages.[24] Suppliers attempt to gain advantage with regard to their direct customers by means of product improvements, innovation and additional services, as well as a higher level of supply quality and lower prices. An improved supplier-customer relationship is also intended to differentiate them from the competition. Nevertheless, this current brand strategy is increasingly reaching its limits.

In this context the **downstream process** stages such as processing firms, distribution middlemen and end users have hitherto been largely neglected. Taking these factors into account is necessary for a successful InBranding strategy since it can be assumed that the same importance accrues for InBrands through the strong development of the brand function. The development of the individual factors of the brand functions makes it possible to determine the brand relevance for the product segment concerned. The analyses of

our colleagues Prof. Backhaus and Prof. Meffert impressively demonstrated the importance of brand relevance for brand management, i.e., if a relative high brand relevance is determined for a
product area it is justified to assume that InBrands also have a
chance – both for the processing brand and for the accompanying
InBrand. From the perspective of the supply industry, Ingredient
Branding provides the opportunity to escape the easy substitution
of its products. Yet the majority of such companies still appear to
shy away from the effort and cost of an Ingredient Branding strategy. The following overview (see Fig. 105) shows the opportunities
and risks of an InBranding strategy for suppliers and OEMs. In order to realize the listed opportunities and to keep risks as low as
possible, three criteria of success must be assured:[25]

- Build-up and development of the brand value of the compo-
  nents
- Brand presentation and identification
- Assuring quality standards in the end product

In order to build up brand value through Ingredient Branding, one
must have a special product and use the brand as carrier. In a similar fashion to the brand value of other products, the factors of familiarity, image and relevance for the end user play an important
role with regard to the value of a brand.[26]

Fig. 105 shows the opportunities and risks of Ingredient Branding
for OEMs and suppliers.

The degree of competitive differentiation appears particularly important with regard to InBrands so that the product becomes more
difficult to substitute for the manufacturer of the end product.

A further prerequisite for an increase in brand value is the presentation and identification of the InBrand in the end product. A visible
brand symbol means that the end user has access to the product
and performance promises associated with the product. However,
the placement of such a "brand symbol" can only be achieved vis-

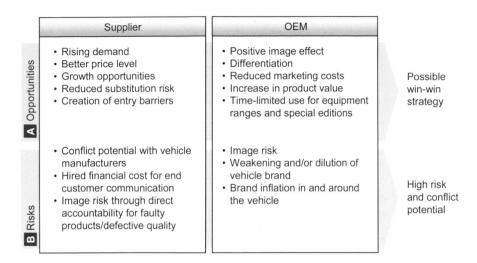

Fig. 105. Ingredient Branding – opportunities and risks

à-vis the manufacturer of the end product if it is possible to create added value through the InBrand which further adds to the benefit of the manufacturer's brand. In such a case the added value produces volume and price benefits for the end product manufacturer. Such synergy effects then produce competitive advantages, which are difficult for the competition to keep up. Strong component and manufacturer brands create further synergies from joint advertising campaigns and accompanying measures for the distribution middlemen.

The development of a sustained brand value is particularly difficult for InBrands and carries multiple dimensions since they always have a certain dependence on the end product. As it has frequently been emphasized, the quality of the end product also plays a decisive role here with regard to the image of the InBrand, since it can very quickly be destroyed by incidents. "From the perspective of the producer goods manufacturer, the question arises as to whether the anticipated result justifies the expenditure or use of the resources required for realization and whether the main product manufacturers can be persuaded to support such behavior. Along with the benefits or product appreciation, the main product manufacturer must also be shown the risks in the form of negative effects on his own brand or any dependency relationships."[27]

Development of an Evaluation Method for InBrands

As known from chapter 2, the component supplier offers a product to the OEM (B2B). The OEM uses the component to produce the end product and sells the end product to the end user (B2C). At the same time, the component supplier communicates advantages of the component for an end product to the end user (B2B2C). It is critical that Ingredient Brand evaluation captures the pull effect, resulting from the end user preference in this scenario. Most studies often focus solely on the OEM/end user stage and, as a result, success from the perspective of the component supplier at the B2B stage is overlooked. To appropriately allocate value to an Ingredient Branding strategy, it is necessary to include the network of all up-stream markets, beginning with the component supplier and culminating with the end customers. By taking this approach, it becomes necessary to broaden the analysis of exchange beyond dyads and include those exchanges that occur within larger networks of firms. In marketing, these sets of firms have been referred to as distribution channels, value chains, embedded markets, network markets, or, simply, networks[28]. The key to this perspective is that the firms are interrelated because they are all involved in bundling ingredients into final products or services for consumption by an end consumer and exchange in one dyad is affected by exchange in another dyad. This notion of interrelatedness has been the canter of many studies[29].

Constructs Related to Brand Equity

To measure brand equity at the B2C level, we build on four influencing factors of the brand. Aaker suggests an all-encompassing measurement of brand value.[30] We modify these to determine the advantages of carrying an end product with a branded ingredient. According to Aaker brand loyalty, trust, brand association and the recognized quality are factors, which build brand value (see Fig. 106).

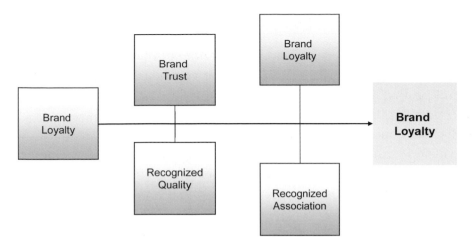

Fig. 106. Qualitative influence factors of the brand value

Brand Loyalty

Customer loyalty has been a major focus of strategic marketing planning and offers an important basis for developing a sustainable competitive advantage. The definition of brand loyalty by Jacoby and Chestnut is still used today. They discuss brand loyalty as being

(1) Biased (i.e., non-random)

(2) Behavioral response (i.e., purchase)

(3) Expressed over time

(4) By some decision-making unit

(5) With respect to one or more brands out of a set of such brands

(6) Function of psychological (decision-making, evaluative) processes[31]

Despite a multitude of definitions and measurements of brand loyalty it generally entails a strong commitment to a particular brand on the part of the consumer. Brand loyalty is thought to be an imported concept of marketing practitioners for a number of reasons. Dick and Basu suggest that brand loyalty favors positive word of mouth and greater resistance among loyal customers to competitive strategies.[32] It is widely considered that loyalty is one of the ways with which consumers express his/her satisfaction with the performance of the product or service received. Loyal consumers, compared to non-loyal consumers, will work harder to obtain that brand on each occasion, possibly by paying more attention to marketing activities such as advertising and promotion. Moreover, brand loyalty is a key determinant of brand choice and brand equity. Aaker notes that the brand loyalty of the customer base is often the core of a brand's equity.[33] If customers are indifferent to the brand and will buy with respect to features, price, etc., there is likely little equity. A big advantage of high loyal customers can be found in lower cost of holding customers. Brand loyalty can be measured by real customer behavior, their individual performance rating, the customers' satisfaction with a product and the sympathy for the brand.

Trust

Brand trust builds the core of brand value. Trust evolves from past experience and prior interaction, because its development is portrayed often as an individual's experiential process of learning over time. People trust a business based on their own past experience as well as by third party recommendations. Seen as multidimensional in the majority of marketing studies, trust is reported to be: involved in the acceptance of brand extension acceptance. It is fundamental to the development of loyalty and critical in maintaining successful agency-client relationships, as a component of brand equity. This is essential in building strong customer relationships, and is perhaps the single most powerful relationship-marketing tool available to a company. The impact of brand trust on brand value is manifold. To name only a few, the lower costs of communicating to trusting consumers instead of new ones, the reduced risk for future incomes and increased residual value as an effect of long-term brand image because of consumers brand trust. Moreover, a trusting consumer base is a strong argument for listing trails with retailers. Furthermore, only the existence of loyal consumer increases the awareness of the brand. However, trust is not easy to measure but it can be calculated by exploring the de facto customer behavior. The estimation of consumer satisfaction and affection to a brand can also be used as an indicator for brand trust.

Brand Awareness

Brand awareness is defined as the ability of possible consumers to remember that a special brand belongs to a special product. Based on that we can separate, there are several levels of brand awareness depending on the ease with which a consumer can recall the brand. Aided recall is insufficient to generate a consumer choice by itself, since the consumer is unable to generate a picture of the brand. The associative memory model would describe the strength of association between the brand and the situation as relatively weak. However, since the consumer can recognize the brand when confronted by it, marketing efforts may still have a positive effect. If consumers make decisions in the store for a group of products, recognition will be very important in shaping the purchase of those products. For measuring the brand value for the ingredient, another dimension is necessary. Customers need to recognize the branded component without the host product. They must notice the Ingredient Brand as a special component with a benefit for the whole product. This benefit must be linked to the component. Than the Ingredient Brand can have positive effects on the recognition as well as the assumption about the adopted quality. Methods to measure the brand awareness are recall-tests and recognition tests to find out the strength of awareness.

Recognized Quality

The recognized quality of a product or the ingredient is understood as the customer's assumption about the quality of product function compared to another product. At first, the recognized quality is an estimation about a product in the eyes of the consumer. Therefore, it can differ from the real quality of a product. We have to consider that the recognized quality of the end product can either be lower in consideration of the branded component as well as higher when first evaluated by the consumer. This factor is the answer to an important question for the OEM: Does the Ingredient Brand enhance the recognized quality of the end product or is my product devaluated by a weaker brand? To measure this, conjoint analysis or scanner data for the separation of the consumer preferences are used.

Brand Association

The underlying value of a brand name often is the set of associations, and its meaning for the people. Associations represent the basic for purchase decisions and for brand loyalty. Keller defined brand associations as the other informational nodes linked to the brand node in memory and contained the meaning of the brand for consumers.[34] Consumer-derived brand meanings are, in part, conveyed in the associations they make with the brand itself; and the associations also provide cues for information retrieval. Strong, positive associations help to strengthen brands and the equity that is carried into a leverage situation is affected by the types of associations made with the brand. Brand associations are anything about the likeability of a brand, and help in the formation of the brand's image. Brand image consists of the attributes and associations that consumers connect to a brand; they can be "hard", specific tangible, functional attributes of the brand, or "soft", emotional-based attributes of the brand such as trustworthiness or dullness. With the help of brand image, products can be differentiated from those of competitors even when the other product is physically 100% identical. Associations can be measured indirectly as well as directly. The direct questioning of consumers is relatively easy. However, an indirect approach is needed if it's expected that the consumer won't speak clearly and openly about his feelings and attitude.

Measuring Ingredient Brand Equity at the B2B Stage

As mentioned earlier, at the B2B stage brand equity provides value for the component supplier at the supplier-OEM stage. Value at the B2B stage is heightened when there is extraneous support from a consumer pull effect (because customers will demand end products containing the branded component). When an OEM demands the branded component in response to consumer pull effects, the final step of a successful Ingredient Branding strategy is achieved. Because this stage represents the point where component suppliers (who have initiated the Ingredient Brand strategy) can reap the most economic benefits, it is recommended that the measurement of brand equity is isolated at this stage.

Brand equity is derived from customer willingness to pay a price premium for a branded product when compared to the price of an identical unbranded product. The price premium, as a result of brand equity, becomes a source of value for the company. So the component supplier is able to ask for higher prices with a branded component compared with an identical component that is not branded. Conversely, it may sometimes be the case that increased sales of a component improves brand equity. In these situations, brand building is seen as an investment and increases in marketing expenditures; communication costs and other brand building activities should generate increased prices and/or sales. Based on previous studies, we define "revenue-premium" as the price premium multiplied by sales premium..

Data to measure price and sales premium are typically available from most companies via panel data. Another way to collect data is on the basis of individual survey and/or interview. Often, self-explicated models or conjoint analyses are used to find out the willingness to pay for a special branded product compared to an unbranded one.

OEMs pursue various goals when labeling components in their products. Differentiation from competitors, security from substitution, realization of price premiums, reduction of marketing costs or production/research/development costs are only a few possible advantages. However, these various advantages stem from the same source: consumer preference for an end product that contains the branded component. Extending these results, we argue that this preference becomes salient when consumers are asked to express their preference for an end product with a branded component versus an end product without the same branded component.

Value in the supplier-OEM dyad is of a qualitative nature because value in business-to-business markets such as these often manifests as "softer" factors such as awareness, trust, brand association or recognized quality. An OEM works between the component supplier and the end user. In this way, the OEM must manage both sets of relationships. As described above, the OEM derives financially based value from its end user customers, but in order to efficiently manage its supplier relationships and focus on its end user customers, it must be able to rely and depend on its suppliers. In other words, the OEM derives relationship-oriented value from its component supplier. This relationship oriented value assists the OEM in attaining the price premiums derived from Ingredient Brand equity at the OEM-end user stage. Component suppliers indirectly derive value from end user Ingredient Brand equity in other ways, such as increasing market power, increasing barriers to entry, shortening length of value chain, and improving brand position, among others. These have all been shown to positively influence willingness of a component supplier to initiate an Ingredient Brand strategy.

Measuring Ingredient Brand Equity at the B2C Stage

Measurement at the B2C stage is based on Aaker's brand valuation model.[35] The categories described above are used to illustrate the end consumer's brand understanding. The result is a qualitative brand profile that is as unique as each brand. Each category is operationalized for measuring the brand value from the consumer's perspective. The relativity of a concept such as "trust" is quite evident when considering its meaning across categories such as automotive, durable, or perishable products; explication of the meaning of "trust" should involve methodology that allows for such variations.

In order to further clarify this approach, let us consider "recognized quality". As demonstrated in previous studies, recognized quality is an important aspect to consider particularly in Ingredient Branding because it is often assumed that brands associated with high quality components have positive effects on the whole end product. With this approach the OEM can determine whether an Ingredient

Brand improves the whole recognized quality of an end product. If such positive effects exist, it is worthwhile to position an end product competitively by displaying the Ingredient Brand logo on the end product. This approach enables managers to utilize qualitative studies effectively, and for scholars of Ingredient Branding to generate a richer understanding of the phenomenon.

Ingredient Branding and the B2B2C Chain

In the B2B2C chain, both the component supplier and the end user are involved, and they each represent endpoints of the chain. An important assumption of Ingredient Branding in the B2B2C chain is that the component supplier undertakes the effort to communicate the benefits of a branded ingredient to the end user using instruments of the marketing mix. To determine the success of B2B2C marketing activities, Havenstein recommends using the willingness to pay price premiums.[36] However, most component suppliers implement an Ingredient Branding strategy expecting many advantages; including reducing the anonymity of a component, differentiating components from other competitors, and generating pull effects through the value chain by generating end user preference for the branded ingredient. However, measuring success on all these dimensions is difficult.

For this reason, it is recommended that "end user willingness to pay a price premium for an end product with the branded ingredient" is useful as a single index of success for the following reasons. First, it demonstrates that end users are aware of the component brand because they would not otherwise be willing to pay the price premium. Second, it demonstrates that end users are able to differentiate among competing component suppliers. More important, it demonstrates end users' ability to recall positive associations with the Ingredient Brand and use this recall to the benefit of the whole end product. Third, it demonstrates the positive accrual of a pull effect. From this point of view, a sales premium can also be seen as a price premium. Instead of higher sales, price can be increased. Extending the analysis to a broader realm of the B2B2C chain sheds light on otherwise "invisible" mechanisms in Ingredient Branding strategies.

For example, analysis of the OEM-end user stage as extracted from the B2B2C chain makes it difficult to isolate determinants of why the OEM embedded the branded component in its end product offering to the end user. However, investigating the end user's willingness to pay a price premium, along with the other mechanisms in the B2B2C chain does not constrain analysis to the OEM's procurement decisions. Instead, the analysis focuses on the motivations of the OEM to use the branded ingredient in an end product.

There is a wide range of instruments to measure willingness to pay for an end product embedded with an Ingredient Brand. The most prominent and well-established method is the conjoint analysis because it can be used to discover and compare varying attributes and sub-benefits. One of these sub-benefits may be the Ingredient Brand. As demonstrated above, it is a strong, attainable, and rigorous determinant of Ingredient Branding success.

This approach demonstrates the complex structure of an Ingredient Branding strategy by explicating how a branded component affects the multiple stages of exchange that exist among a component supplier, OEM, and end user. Giving attention to this network from the perspective of the component supplier allows an exploration of value that can be harnessed from the supplier's point of view. Building on existing marketing theory, this paper demonstrates that many questions remain unanswered and also demonstrates that the mechanisms of Ingredient Branding operate differently at each stage of the network. As a result, it highlights that assessing Ingredient Branding effects at multiple stages of the B2B2C chain requires varying types of measurement tools, data collection methods, and analysis techniques. These requirements demonstrate, on one hand, that each stage of Ingredient Branding requires various – perhaps contrasting – approaches to building brand equity at each stage (B2B vs. B2C and B2B2C Branding). On the other hand, they demonstrate that the component supplier's position and perspective relative to brand strategies are important in driving relevant, useful, and competitive brand and marketing theories. Fig. 107 shows measurement methods on the characteristic stages of Ingredient Branding.

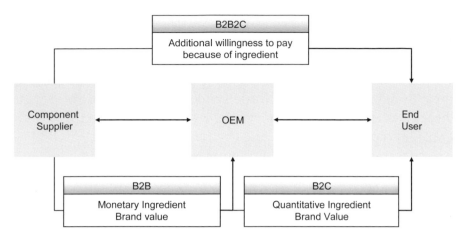

Fig. 107. Measurement methods on the characteristic stages of Ingredient Branding

In summary, the value of brand equity at each stage of the value chain should be considered independently and in combination with the other stages. Instruments for measuring Ingredient Branding success at multiple stages are summarized below:

1. B2B Stage: The level between the component supplier and the OEM is the most important point at which the component supplier can generate financial benefits. Here, a successful Ingredient Branding strategy reaps the benefits of a pull effect from the end user that drives the OEM to prefer the branded component over an unbranded one. Therefore, at this stage, it is recommended that a financially oriented measurement tool based on price premiums be used.

2. B2C Stage: From the perspective of a component supplier, the end user is distant and often out of immediate reach. However, Ingredient Branding is most successful when it can be fruitful at all levels of the B2B2C chain. In the B2C (or OEM-end user) stage, it is recommended that success be evaluated with a quantitative method from the perspective of the OEM.

3. B2B2C Stage: Analysis of the B2B2C chain is also quantitative, and is based specifically on end user willingness to pay a

price premium. For several reasons (such as Ingredient Brand awareness, differentiation, consumer's connection of positive brand understanding and initial point for pull effects), end user willingness to pay a price premium signifies successful Branding efforts from the perspective of the end user.

Appraisal of the Procedures

The two methods of brand evaluation chosen by us represent the variety of models and procedures used. Since the brand values and the calculation of the brand capital are determined by the situation and the purpose with a variety of targets, a decision must be taken in each situation as to which method is to be used.

In addition, there will always be the validity of the selected criteria and the subjectivity of the model components in the brand value measurement. However, the various diagnostic possibilities and the brand management process improve the security of steering and controlling the brand value through the use of recognized methods.

The possibility is then given to select the appropriate method for each specific case in the company. It is recommended – for reasons of comparability and consistency – to use the selected procedure over a sustained period. But there is fundamental freedom of choice if the user is aware of the advantages and disadvantages of the individual procedures. In individual cases, differing methods can also be used in parallel.

Brand evaluation will continue to pose a major challenge for every company management. A good approach would be to set up a body of experts of all those with an interest in the brand evaluation process and an economic interest, e.g. representatives from business administration, marketing research, management consulting, advertising agencies, brand evaluation institutes, as well as from the branded article industry to promote the development and the acceptance of standards.

In any event, a comprehensive and uniform brand evaluation model should be created in the near future which does not represent a new model but brings together the ideas in existing models and lies at the level of the combined brand evaluation models.

In summary, we can say that no model covers all requirements with regard to brand valuation; on the contrary, the best variant must be selected depending on the evaluation purposes and the available financial resources:

1. If the focus were on a financial evaluation of the brand value and its future potential, we would tend to recommend the Interbrand method.

2. If the focus is rather on the control and planning of instruments to improve brand value, then we recommend the Brand Scorecard or its variants.

The use of financially oriented methods often becomes necessary when companies are sold or taken over and they can be used at short notice. A Brand Scorecard requires two to three planning periods until it is fully implemented and can supply meaningful results.

A number of approaches have already been criticized, but irrespective of this, general problems relating to brand value measurement can be observed which have not yet been sufficiently clarified. The brand effects often extend over a rather long period. This means that the associated forecast problems are very large since the individual models mostly determine the going concern value. The procedures presented overwhelmingly assume that the brand value results solely from the perspective of the buyer. One last problem is represented by the concentration of current approaches largely from the consumer goods sector.

Business-to-Business brands in the form of InBrands have not so far been explicitly taken into account.[37] As a consequence, companies must themselves find the answer to the question "Which instrument is the best to measure the success of Ingredient Branding?" The answer would be: It depends on the purpose of the evaluation. For steering the Branding efforts through the development steps of an InBrand, we suggest a set of tools, which have been proven in various applications. The tool kit offers instruments for the management of the brand, including financial results (brand equity) and qualitative results (brand loyalty, brand recognition, etc.). We recommend maintaining the tool kit over the whole life of the brand. This could be over a time span from ten to fifty years.

As exemplified, brand equity has to be measured as a B2B and B2C endeavor. We recommend applying the price premium brand equity measurement. For this analysis in most of the existing cases, the data are available. However, you need the cooperation of your OEM of course; moreover, there could be more than only one OEM partner, so you have to measure with the help of all partners to get your total brand equity. The continuous measurement of the brand equity gives you increase or decrease of your overall value. The information to look out for is a positive or negative value change.

With the analysis of the quantitative factors, you get the explanation of the development. The reasons for the change could be triggered by various layers of your cooperation, maybe you improved the brand fit, or your push was more effective or the push of the OEM encouraged for customers to ask for more final products with your ingredient.

The way a company is aggregating this information depends very much on their constellation in the specific market. This is not an easy procedure and the instruments may look overwhelming for a B2B company starting to think of reaching out to the final customers. But the successful examples have shown such an approach is worth the investments.

An Ingredient Brand cannot be managed without analyzing the other partners, which are involved in the Branding process. These partners are linked together in the value chain. Typically the component supplier offers his product to many OEMs. These manufacturers produce a wide range of end products. In most cases, distributors and retailers are the next stages before the final product reaches the end user. All participants have an impact on Ingredient Branding. Successful management has to keep that in mind that value chains are complex and not easy to overlook, a requirement on a management tool is to bring management relevant insights about the value chain: "Who affects the value creation in which way?" and "who benefits from the brand?" are important questions for developing a suitable strategy. Because participation and benefit change in different stages and at different times, a method, which provides comparability, is needed once again.

As we have shown, push and pull are the basic principles of each Ingredient Branding strategy. The pull describes thereby the request of final products, which include the branded component. The stronger this effect is, the more influence the brand has on the OEM purchase decision process. A strong pull effect represents the success of all Branding activities. Therefore it has to be measured. Without information about these aspects, the management misses the knowledge of the impact of their Branding activities. In a similar way, the push effect describes the component supplier's power to persuade the OEM, as well as the end user, about the advantages of their product.

It is possible to measure the push by the communication activities. But then we care only about the spending for the Branding strategy. More important is the reaction we initiate with our Branding activities. A management tool should therefore capture the pull effect through the value chain. Starting at the end user, it should provide information about the strength of this effect, which reaches the component supplier. On the other hand, the push has to be quantified. Hereby, not only the communications spending is important. In this case, measuring is targeted to face the activities with their effect on the OEM and the end user.

Finally, a successful Ingredient Brand has to pay off. Therefore a management tool has to give answers about the brand equity. Brand equity brings a lot of information together. It describes the additional cash flow, which is achieved because the company runs an Ingredient Branding strategy. This value can be expressed in a figure over time or aggregated as net present value. However, it shows the value of the brand.

As we have demonstrated, Ingredient Branding is more complex than other Branding strategies. Because other downstream players are involved in the value creation process, the brand cares for brand relevant payments at different stages. Brand equity exists depending on the point of view at different stages in the value chain. When we talk about value creation with the Ingredient Brand, we are interested in various aspects of brand value. A management tool should also provide information about value through the whole value chain. Ingredient Branding is most successful in the cases in which this strategy brings benefit to all participants.

Creating a sustainable win-win situation is a guarantor for his or her own success. Component suppliers should therefore be not only interested in the value of the Ingredient Brand that it brings to them. The whole value creation for each participant must be kept in view.

We introduce an Ingredient Branding management tool, which fulfils these requirements. With this method, it becomes possible to give answers to management relevant questions on every stage in the development process. Moreover, this measurement model delivers information about different aspects of Ingredient Branding. It is not necessary to evaluate all information at every moment. Rather, this measurement can be used like a toolkit with the right instruments for management relevant questions.

If a company asks for the Ingredient Branding potential, we recommend the instrument "B2B potential" and "B2C potential". By evaluating these aspects, we get two blocks of information, which can be brought together in the red point of Fig. 108. The same company could be interested in the same time about the brand equity.

However with the tool for the B2B and B2C stages, we can already draw a picture of the brand equity. We can analyze the value for the component supplier as well as for the OEM. Therefore, we can ask not only for the brand value, we also get information about the distribution within the value chain. The red point provides in this case a picture of the brand equity and, if necessary, the value distribution and participation of all other players.

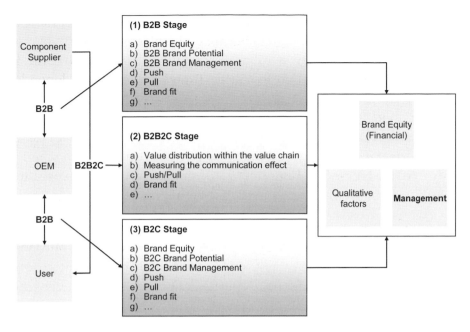

Fig. 108. Ingredient Branding measurement toolkit

The Ingredient Branding management toolkit is therefore a measurement, which provides relevant customized information for the management of Ingredient Brands. Because it is only one method, the results are comparable over a longer period of time.

They give the company a 360° perspective because they measure various important aspects (see Fig 109). These measurements could lead to a scorecard type analysis. If the brand management is executed in a fashion that considers all the four perspectives, we can talk about a "balanced scorecard".

This brand-balanced scorecard can be developed a bit further by each company and adapted to meet its own individual requirements. According to the motto "brand identity – you don't get it, you make it," this kind of approach is a continuous challenge for the management. In a certain sense, it is like a closed loop with no real beginning and no obvious ending. It is a continuous adaptation process to the changing needs of the customer and the requirements

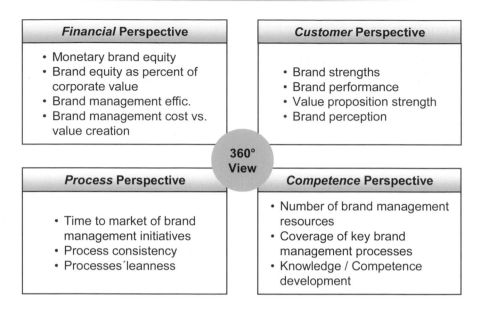

Fig. 109. Brand balanced scorecard for success management

of the partners. Many variables are continuously changing and each Ingredient Branding situation is different.

For every InBrand, we can state the following: once you have started the loop of creating, supervising and managing, the cycles become faster through the synergies and joint activities of the partner. This process can accelerate the brand benefits for the participants so that the chances for diluting the process get smaller. InBrands have great brand strength to survive the trends and economic cycle of industries and regions.

They also help to enhance the whole character of product groups or industries. They can change the perception of a product or an industry. With recognizable performance InBrands can change the world to be better. InBrands can become icons of the collective, global brand consciousness and develop trust in our increasingly complex world. They help to simplify the life of the customer and make life in general more enjoyable.

Summary

- The proper management of Ingredient Brands can create market-based assets, which leads to dependable sources of value creation.

- The basis for this future oriented asset lies in the ability and willingness of the customer to pay a price premium for a branded ingredient because it satisfies the customers functional and emotional needs.

- Certain processes typical of Ingredient Brand management are based on identifiable conditions, such as high functionality of the component to the final product.

- There are multifold effects between the partners in the value chain that have to be understood and managed according to the existing conditions and future expectations

- The relative brand power of an Ingredient Branding supplier has to be evaluated and managed in relation to expected goals.

- The execution of Ingredient Branding management depends very much on the intended brand development alternatives and the willingness of the component supplier to apply a B2B2C Branding concept.

- Existing examples have demonstrated that InBrand Management has five development steps, which open up new Branding dimensions for companies pursuing the Ingredient Branding concept.

- To manage InBrands, appropriate brand methods are needed. A multi-stage approach also suggests measuring the brand's success on the B2B, B2C and B2B2C level.

- An Ingredient Branding measurement toolkit is proposed to evaluate the financial aspects and qualitative factors of brand equity to control and improve the brand position.

- Many more Ingredient Branding applications can and will be implemented by using experiences from the demonstrated case studies and examples.

Notes

[1] Desai and Keller (2002); McCarthy and Norris (1999); Norris (1992); Rao, Qu, and Ruekert (1999); Venkatesh and Mahajan (1997); Havenstein (2004).

[2] Pfoertsch, W., and Chandler, J.D. „Why ingredient brands tmater: Understanding changing roles, and changing markets." *Journal of Business & Industrial Marketing* (2010) forthcoming.

[3] Iacobucci, Henderson, Marcati, and Chang (1996).

[4] Desai and Keller (2002).

[5] Baumgarth, (2001); Bugdahl, (1996).

[6] Shocker, Srivastava, and Ruekert, (1994).

[7] Note that we might also count in I-4 some of the negative effects that happen as the channel has alternatives to pick up products from other user/OEM's that incorporate the creator's ingredients.

[8] Dover, (1997); Hilton, (2003); Kleinaltenkamp, (2001).

[9] Digital Light Processing is the world's only all-digital display chip and a key ingredient in the best digital projectors available today. DLP technology uses an optical semiconductor to recreate source material with fidelity that analog systems cannot match. Ralph Oliva has particular insights, because he initiated that successful process of Ingredient Branding.

[10] Dover, (1997); Kotler and Pfoertsch (2006).

[11] Porter, M.E. *Wettbewerbsvorteile: Spitzenleistungen erreichen und behaupten.* 4th ed. Frankfurt/Main, New York, 1996, p. 12 and p. 453.

[12] Pfoertsch and Chandler (2010).

[13] Sattler, H. *Monetäre Bewertung von Markenstrategien für neue Produkte.* Stuttgart, 1997.

[14] Michael, B.M. *Werkbuch M wie Marke: Bausteine für ein erfolgreiches Brand Building. Anleitungen, Arbeitsmethoden, Fallbeispiele, Interviews.* Düsseldorf, 2003, Chapter 5.2, p. 5–6.

[15] Interbrand announcement see http://www.interbrand.com/best_global_brands.aspx.

16 The absolute share of the B2B orientation of the Interbrand listed companies can be determined by an analysis of their sales channels see Pfo-
ertsch/Schmid (2005): p. 92. GE had also B2C products including major appliances and related services for products such as refrigerators,
freezers, electric and gas ranges, cook-tops, dishwashers, clothes
washers and dryers, microwave ovens, room air conditioners and
residential water system products. These products are distributed
both to retail outlets and direct to consumers, mainly for the replacement market, and to building contractors and distributors for new in-
stallations. Lighting products include a wide variety of lamps and
lighting fixtures, including light-emitting diodes. Electrical equipment and control products include lighting and power panels, switch-
gear, and circuit breakers. Products and services are sold in North
America and in global markets under various GE and private label
brands. This segment revenues were less than 6% of consolidated
sales revenue ($11m out total $180m).

17 General Electric Company: Company Report, Nov. 2004.

18 Aaker, David A. (1992), p. 31.

19 Sattler (1995), p. 669.

20 www.markenlexikon.com, seen 10.01.2010.

21 Gerpott, J.; Thomas, S. (2004), p. 396.

22 Klein-Boelting, U., and Murad-Aga, T. „Markenbewertung für das
Controlling." *Marketingjournal* (2003): 39–41.

23 Ditto, p. 40.

24 Simon/Sebastian (1995), p. 42ff.

25 Haller (2001), p. 21ff.

26 Simon/Sebastian (1995), p. 42ff.

27 Havenstein (2004), p. 117; also Overview, p. 85–91.

28 Coughlan et al. 2001; Vargo and Lusch 2004; Wathne, Biong and Heide
2001; Frels, Shervani and Srivastava 2003; Wilkinson 2001.

29 Wathne and Heide 2004; Achrol, Reve and Stern 1983; Bagozzi 1975.

30 Aaker (1991, 1992).

31 Jacoby/Chestnut (1978).

32 Dick/Basu (1994).

33 Aaker (1991).

34 Keller (1993).

35 Aaker (1991).

36 Havenstein ((2004).

37 Baumgarth (2001), p. 240–244.

CHAPTER 8

Perspectives of Successful InBranding

With the introduction of a new brand strategy, companies face both risks and opportunities. Establishing a brand with an Ingredient Branding strategy can enhance the **brand awareness** and the **image** of the product, but it comes with a considerable investment if companies want to have a recognizable reputation and an individual brand personality. Any company considering such an approach has to be aware of the **financial investment** and **management resources** they must put in, in order to have a successful result. Yet even despite these financial requirements, a large number of companies have opted for Ingredient Branding concepts in the last twenty years. Since the importance of branding in general as well as customer sophistication in specific increased,[1] the decline of relative importance of consumer brands has created a great opportunity for InBrands. This was impressively demonstrated in various consumer industries, in Haverstein's[2] and other empirical analysis (see Fig. 110).[3]

In a recent conducted research we could prove that InBrands that were able to establish quality perception and have positive performance recognition create a positive impact on the willingness of a customer to pay a price premium. This was tested by Ingredient Brands with strong and weak final product brands. In both cases a price premium was justified, and led to tangible benefits for the OEM[4]. Strong Ingredient Brands include advantages for component suppliers as well. They give them a better marketing position compared with the OEM. The OEM is interested in **strong Ingredient**

P. Kotler and W. Pfoertsch, *Ingredient Branding: Making the Invisible Visible*,   331
DOI 10.1007/978-3-642-04214-0_8, © Springer-Verlag Berlin Heidelberg 2010

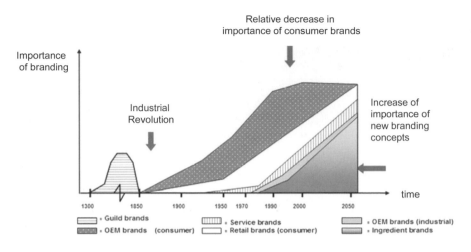

Fig. 110. Development of the brand concept projected by Havenstein[5]
Havenstein (2004)

Brands to achieve a higher price premium that increases his profits so he will prefer component suppliers who have established strong brand recognition. This way, the component supplier can increase his sales. Moreover, he could use the line of arguments from Ingredient Brands to the price premium to benefit partly from the price premium as well by demanding higher prices for the branded component. So the main advantage of Ingredient Brands for the OEM is a higher profit caused by the price premium, the main advantage for the component supplier are higher sold quantities and higher negotiated prices for the branded component.

Since 1950, the importance of brands has increased in general and since 1990, Ingredient Brands have played a much bigger role. This was so significant that even accountants needed to acquaint themselves with this concept.[6] Using a key word searching (KWS) methodology has resulted in 71,700 hits in 2009 (on google.com), compared to just 2,900 in 2006. Everyday new applications appear in various industries, in particular the automotive and consumer electronic industry, but also for wellness and care products, food and cosmetic industries. By establishing a single product or making a new innovation, companies broaden their scope by becoming part of larger product offerings.

It is not always the supplier who feeds the brand enrichment, but also the producer of the final product or the retail partner. Home Depot, the large do-it-yourself store chain, is consciously looking for products with antibacterial protection to give their customers more options and new product choices. Similar approaches were used by Sainsbury supermarket when they offered kitchen appliances and utensils with Microban antibacterial protection. ALDI, the super discount stores offers no-name winter clothes with 3M Thinsulate insulation fibers for increased comfort in cold weather.

Crucial to all of these efforts, though, is both the promise and the fulfillment of that promise, so that the quality of the offered ingredient is superior to the non-branded ingredient. When a company promises the customer by using a sticker, logo, or product explanation that the delivered product has an invisible extra benefit for the customer, it is imperative that they make sure that the customer really experiences it. This is not particular to Ingredient Branding, but to Branding and marketing in general. If it is not proven, the customer will not be willing to pay the extra price premium. Customers are quick to move away from non-proven product features.

Since we know that it takes a long time to establish a brand image, consolidated efforts are necessary to be successful. The knowledge of the product image has to stay and has to travel from customer to customer, something that takes time. When companies promote a final product, the product can be touched and experienced to prove its promised functionality. With an ingredient offering, the differences of the component must be recognized during the consumption of the product. Ingredient Branding marketing is very similar to service marketing, where the actual product could only be experienced during the service offering. That is why the establishment of the image of the ingredient is so important. A Brand claims help to establish the better recognition of the component performance.

This image can also be shattered by the end product performance if the end product has any manufacturing defects. This happened with the outdoor jacket from Columbia, which seriously affected Gore-Tex, the component manufacturer. Because the customer has consciously chosen this product due to the ingredient, such disasters affect the ingredient supplier directly. Therefore, the supplier has to be very careful in selecting its partner OEMs.

In a regular B2B relationship, customer selection is driven by factors such as profitability, sales growth, etc. If a company intend to Ingredient Branding, quality considerations of the final product become more important. This may be the reason why Caterpillar Inc. is expanding its diesel engine production in China with an additional brand, Perkins engines. They do not want to sell Caterpillar engines to Chinese equipment suppliers, but with Perkins, they have a secondary brand, that fits the current market environment. Perkins, an independent British diesel engine manufacturer has been putting the Perkins logo in form of grill badges on tractors, harvesters, loaders, etc., since 1949.

For managing Ingredient Brands, component suppliers need clarity about the impact of brand functions and brand relevance for each end product. The different functions vary in each individual case and have to be evaluated appropriately. Starting with the brand function characteristics, companies have to decide where they want to position their brand in relation to the competition. For example, Perkins puts emphasis on durability versus power output. This criterion explains the benefits and the risks of early breakdowns to the final user of heavy construction equipment, and the component manufacture Perkins guarantees with its brand for this kind of performance.

Establishing trust, performance, quality, and security for the end user creates the difference. By establishing the image benefits to the end user, the former B2B becomes a B2B2C brand where risk reduction, though important, is not the ultimate choice as in B2B. Intel managed to convince the end user about the image benefit of their microprocessors the same way as Lycra, Splenda, NutraSweet, Shimano, Bose and Gore-Tex did. Understanding the brand functions and determining their extent to the final user is an important exercise companies have to go through when they want to reach out to final customers. The reason for this is that if you continue to rely on information efficiency and risk reduction in your Branding efforts, you will not reach the important requirements of the final customer:

to benefit from the component in the product he buys, to improve his image through the products and components. Even the highly branded Apple Mac Book Air uses Dual Core Intel Processors to convince the user about its product benefits.

In addition, the brand relevance has to be determined. It does not make sense to push Branding efforts when the category the product is in does not have any relevance to the customer. Aaker[7] offers a definition and a model to determine brand relevance. Relevance for a brand occurs when three conditions are met:

- A product or service category or subcategory — defined by some combination of attributes, applications, user groups, or other distinguishing characteristics — exists or emerges.

- There is a perceived need or desire on the part of a customer segment for the category or subcategory.

- The brand is in the set that the segment considers being material to the product category or subcategory.

To better understand relevance and the concept of product categories and ingredients, Aaker suggests considering a simple model of customer-brand interaction adapted for Ingredient Brands (see Fig. 111).

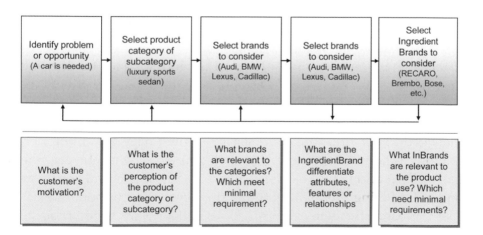

Fig. 111. Key questions adapted from Aaker (2004)

The judgment of the brand relevance for the Ingredient Brand determines heavily the further direction of any Branding activities and the financial commitment.

Through the creation of a brand identity, the chances for substitution diminish. The branded component is of high relevance to the customer and can create benefits for him, even when different final products are competing with the same ingredient. Gore-Tex offers membranes to various outdoor clothing retailers such as Mammut, The North Face, etc, all offering the ingredient, but according to end customers, the preference for Gore-Tex is what makes their purchasing decision.

The more Branding relevance could be found for the ingredient, the higher the chances are for success. As a result, there is a chance for customer preference to increase. The Branding potential for ingredients depends very much on the specific performance advantages they create in the final product. Only the end user can judge this. In addition, the functional advantages through the ingredient are also important. Putting this in perspective, the monetary value of the ingredient in relationship to the value of the total has to be considered. There is no threshold set, but when you calculate the value relationship of a microprocessor and a computer, we see a range from 1:5 to 1:10 and similar relationships you could find in other In-Branding constellations.

For determining the brand relevance for a future Ingredient Brand product or service offering, all relationships in the value chain have to be considered. It starts with the relationship of the supplier (B2B) and continuing to the relationship to the final user (B2B2C). Each relationship can be evaluated by the three major brand dimensions:

- Information efficiency
- Risk reduction, and
- Performance benefit

By evaluating these dimensions though various factors on the B2B and B2B2C brand relevance, the area of relevance and the amount of relevance can be determined for a future product offering. The factors in the B2B area are: Recognition of the brand, differences in quality, number of decision makers, and competition. In the B2C area the factors are: Recognized importance of the component, performance advantage of component, symbolic value added, consumer quality orientation, evaluation competence and number of OEMs.

Out of the aggregation of these two factors, the potential for B2B and B2B2C brand relevance could be determined and only if both factors are considered to be high a recommendation for an Ingredient Branding concept could be justified. In a series of analysis various industries have been examined and clear recommendation could be achieved[8]. The principle of such an approach is displayed in Fig. 112.

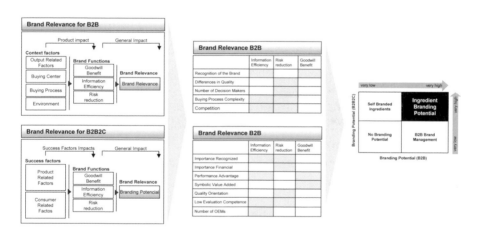

Fig. 112. Ingredient Brand relevance analysis

The Branding potential for component suppliers is an important prerequisite for any investment into the InBrand. With the start of the investment and the used management time, new entry barriers can be established to hinder other competitors from entering. By positioning the brand in the minds of the customer, the chances increase to develop a justification for price premiums. Many examples have demonstrated this.[9]

This development will also have an impact on the improvement of the company brand equity. At this moment, we would like to come back to the Ingredient Branding development steps and remind the reader that there could be a limit to any InBranding activity if the component supplier delivers the product to all of the product providers in the category. The Fiesco-Effect will take the potential for differentiation away. Companies that have reached this position can move on to the development of the final product. However, only a few companies have achieved the last step in developing Ingredient Brands. These steps are also an instrument to determine company's current achievements and evaluate future prospects. In relationship to the implemented brand management, various effects can be selected to move up the development stepladder.

InBrands are creating benefits for everyone; they can improve the lives of many and the whole community. To summarize it: InBrands are more (as all brands) than logos, taglines, slogans or commercials. They deliver values, union whishes, dreams and devices, the customer identifies with them, thus discover attributes. As authors offering this book, we hope that we could provide you valuable information for your brand development process and for the increased economic success of your brand investments.

Summary

- Ingredient Brands have found ample applications in our current business world and have become an accepted brand management concept.

- It is projected that the increase of importance of Ingredient Brands will continue in the future.

- Based on the principle functions of brand management, InBrands have the chance to increase customer satisfaction and to improve the financial and image function of companies.

- A thorough customer-brand interaction is needed to achieve successful brand management.

- Before establishing a future InBrand, an Ingredient Brand relevance analysis is required before investing into the brand.

- Continuous InBrand management is required to keep an InBrand afloat.

- A major goal for successful InBrand management is the control and expansion of the price premium throughout the value chain.

- With a brand balanced scorecard system, many aspects of the InBrand implementation can be managed.

- Further InBranding applications in many industries are expected to be implemented in the future.

Notes

[1] Swysten, J. „Business drives and brand responses." May 2003.

[2] Havenstein (2004), p. 9.

[3] Rid, J., and Sigurdsson, N. „Ingredient branding: A strategy option? A comparative case study of Intel, Gore-Tex, Bosch, and Autoliv." Postgradutate dissertation, Stockholm, January 2004.

[4] Pfoertsch, W., Linder, C. and Scheel, H. „Price premium enhancement through a brand in a brand." Working paper Pforzheim University, 2009.

[5] Havenstein (2004), p. 9ff.

[6] Chorafas, D.N. *Strategic business planning for accountants: Methods, tools and case studies:* CIMA Publishing, 2006.

[7] Aaker (2004).

[8] Berkowitsch, N. „Ingredient branding wirkt!" Diplom thesis, Pforzheim, 2006.

[9] See also Havenstein (2004).

About the Authors

Philip Kotler is the S. C. Johnson & Son Distinguished Professor of International Marketing at the Kellogg School of Management, Northwestern University, Evanston, Illinois. He received his Master's Degree at the University of Chicago and his PhD Degree at MIT, both in economics. He did post-doctoral work in mathematics at Harvard University and in behavioral science at the University of Chicago.

Professor Kotler is the author of: Marketing Management: Analysis, Planning, Implementation and Control, the most widely used marketing book in graduate business schools worldwide. He also published Principles of Marketing; Marketing Models; Strategic Marketing for Nonprofit Organizations; The New Competition; High Visibility; Social Marketing; Marketing Places; Marketing for Congregations; Marketing for Hospitality and Tourism; The Marketing of Nations; Kotler on Marketing, Building Global Biobrands, Attracting Investors, Ten Deadly Marketing Sins, Marketing Moves, Corporate Social Responsibility, Lateral Marketing, and Marketing Insights from A to Z. He has published over one hundred articles in leading journals, several of which have received best-article awards.

Professor Kotler was the first recipient of the American Marketing Association's (AMA) "Distinguished Marketing Educator Award" (1985). The European Association of Marketing Consultants and Sales Trainers awarded Kotler their prize for "Marketing Excellence".

He was chosen as the "Leader in Marketing Thought" by the Academic Members of the AMA in a 1975 survey. He also received the 1978 "Paul Converse Award" of the AMA, honoring his original contribution to marketing. In 1989, he received the Annual Charles Coolidge Parlin Marketing Research Award. In 1995, the Sales and Marketing Executives International (SMEI) named him "Marketer of the Year".

Professor Kotler has consulted for such companies as IBM, General Electric, AT&T, Honeywell, Bank of America, Merck and others in the areas of marketing strategy and planning, marketing organization and international marketing.

He has been Chairman of the College of Marketing of the Institute of Management Sciences, a Director of the American Marketing Association, a Trustee of the Marketing Science Institute, a Director of the MAC Group, a former member of the Yankelovich Advisory Board, and a member of the Copernicus Advisory Board. He has been a Trustee of the Board of Governors of the School of the Art Institute of Chicago and a Member of the Advisory Board of the Drucker Foundation. He has received honorary doctoral degrees from the Stockholm University, University of Zurich, Athens University of Economics and Business, DePaul University, the Cracow School of Business and Economics, Groupe H. E. C. in Paris, the University of Economics and Business Administration in Vienna, Budapest University of Economic Science and Public Administration, and the Catholic University of Santo Domingo.

He has traveled extensively throughout Europe, Asia and South America, advising and lecturing many companies about how to apply sound economic and marketing science principles to increase their competitiveness. He has also advised governments on how to develop stronger public agencies to further the development of the nation's economic well being.

In 2008, the Wall Street Journal listed him as the 6th most influential person on business thinking, and in 2009 Forbes named him number 9 of "**The 10 Most Influential Business Gurus**", up from number 11 in 2007.

Waldemar Pfoertsch holds the position of Professor for International Business at the Pforzheim University, and he is Associate Professor of Marketing at CEIBS, China Europe International Business School, Shanghai. He was Visiting Professor at the Executive MBA Program of the Liautaud Graduate School of Business, University of Illinois at Chicago and the Illinois Institute of Technology (IIT Chicago), In addition, he was an on-line tutor for MBA Program In-ternational Management University Maryland College Park and at the Steinbeis University in Berlin.

He received two Master Degrees (economics & business administration) and his Doctorial Degree in social science at the Free University Berlin. He did his post-doctoral work in industrial planning at the Technical University Berlin.

His latest publications cover the areas of B2B marketing, brand management, Ingredient Branding and globalization of Chinese brands. He published various books about Internet marketing: Living Web and Internet Strategies. He also published several articles in Chinese, German and English language on international management issues.

Professor Pfoertsch has consulted for such companies as Daimler, HP, IBM, and many medium-sized corporations in Europe, Asia and North America in the areas of international marketing and brand management. He is on the advisory board of various companies and non-profit organizations.

His other teaching positions have been at the University of Cooperative Education Villingen-Schwenningen, Visiting Associate Professor at Kellogg Graduate School of Management, Northwestern University and Lecturer for Strategic Management at Lake Forest Graduate School of Management.

Prior to his teaching appointments, he was a management consultant for international consulting companies. In this position, he traveled extensively throughout Europe, Asia and North America working with companies in developing international strategies. His earlier positions include being an economic advisor to the United Nations Industrial Development Organization (UNIDO) where he supported the ministry for trade and industry in Sierra Leone (West Africa) on how to develop internationally competitive industries. He also worked for many years in the automation industry, serving automotive companies.

Bibliography

Aaker, D. A. "Value of brand equity." *Journal of Business Strategy* 13 (1992): 27–33.

Aaker, D. A. *Management des Markenwerts.* Frankfurt a. Main, 1992.

Aaker, D. A. "The power of the branded differentiator." *MIT Sloan Management Review* 45 (2003): 83–87.

Aaker, D. A. *Brand portfolio strategy.* New York, 2004.

Aaker, D. A. *Managing brand equity: Capitalizing on the value of a brand name.* New York, 1991.

Aaker, D. A., and Joachimsthaler, E. *Brand leadership.* New York, 2002.

Achrol, R. S., Reve, T., and Stern, L. W. "The environment of marketing channel dyads: A framework for comparative analysis." *Journal of Marketing* 47 (1983): 55–67.

Anderson, J. C., and Narus J. A. *Business market management: Understanding, creating, and delivering value.* 2nd ed. New Jersey, 2004.

Andrews, S. M. "Invista will tout Teflon at showtime." *Furniture Today,* December 15 2003.

Backhaus, K., and Voeth, M. *Industriegütermarketing.* 8th ed. Munich, 2007.

Backhaus, K., and M. Voeth, eds. *Handbuch Industriegütermarketing: Strategien, Instrumente, Anwendungen.* Wiesbaden, 2004.

Bagozzi, R. P. "Marketing as exchange." *Journal of Marketing* 39 (1975): 32–39.

Bartlett, C. A., Ghoshal, S., and Birkinshaw, J. M. *Transnational management: Text, cases, and readings in cross-border management.* 4th ed. Boston, 2004.

Baumgarth, C. "Ingredient branding: Markenpolitik für Produktionsgüter." In *Tagungsband zur 1. Kunststoff-Marketing-Tagung,* edited by H. Breuer and D. E. Willich, 1998.

Baumgarth, C. "Ingredient branding: Begriffe, state of the art & empirische Ergebnisse." Working paper, 1998.

Baumgarth, C. "Ingredient branding: Markenkonzept und Kommunikationsumsetzung." Working paper, 1999.

Baumgarth, C. *Markenpolitik: Markenführungen – Markenwirkungen – Markencontrolling.* Wiesbaden, 2001.

Bekmeier-Feuerhahn, S. *Marktorientierte Markenbewertung.* Wiesbaden, 1998.

Belz, C., and Kopp K.-M. "Markenführung für Investitionsgüter als Kompetenz- und Vertrauensmarketing." In *Handbuch Markenartikel,* edited by Manfred Bruhn. Stuttgart, 1994

Berkowitsch, N. "Ingredient branding wirkt!" Diplom thesis, Pforzheim, 2006.

Bremner, B. "Shimano – The Tour de France's other winner: Japan's leading bike parts maker is also ahead of the pack. But it can't afford to coast." *Business Week,* Aug. 9, 2004.

Breuer, H., and Dolfen E., eds. *Tagungsband zur 1. Kunststoff-Marketing-Tagung.* Willich, 1998.

Bruhn, M. *Marketing, bases for study and practice.* Wiesbaden, 2004.

Bruhn, M. "Die zunehmende Bedeutung von Dienstleistungsmarken." In *Erfolgsfaktor Marke,* edited by R. Köhler, W. Majer, and H. Wiezorek. München, 2001.

Bruhn, M. *Die Marke: Symbolkraft des Zeichensystems.* Bern, 2001.

Bruhn, M., ed. *Handbuch Markenartikel: Anforderungen an die Markenpolitik aus Sicht von Wissenschaft und Praxis.* Stuttgart, 1994.

Bugdahl, V. "Ingredient branding: eine Markenstrategie für mehrere Nutznießer." *Markenartikel* 58 (1996): 110–113.

Chorafas, D. N. *Strategic business planning for accountants: Methods, tools and case studies:* CIMA Publishing, 2006.

Clef, U. *Die Ausgezeichneten: Die Unternehmenskarrieren der 30 Deutschen Marketingpreisträger.* Munich, 2002.

Collins, J. *Good to great. Why some companies make the leap...and others don't.* New York, 2001.

Collins, J., and Porras, J. I. *Built to last. Successful habits of visionary companies.* New York, 1994.

Coughlan, A., Anderson, E., Stern, L. W., and El-Ansary, A. *Marketing channels.* 6th ed. New Jersey, 2001.

Deichsel, A., and Henning M., eds. *Jahrbuch Markentechnik 2006/2007.* Frankfurt a. M., 2006.

Delaney, B. "Splits with Giant, Specialized." *Bicycle Retailer & Industry News* 14 (2005).

Desai, K. K., and Keller, K. L. "The effects of ingredient branding strategies on host brand extendibility" *Journal of Marketing* 66 (2002): 73–93.

Dick, A. S., and Basu, K. "Customer loyalty: toward an integrated conceptual framework." *Journal of Academy of Marketing Science* 22 (1994): 99–113.

Dickerson, M. "Shimano to recall 2.5 million bicycle cranks." *Los Angeles Times,* July 10, 1997.

Diller, H. "Preis- und Distributionspolitik starker Marken vor dem Hintergrund fortschreitender Handelskonzentration." In *Erfolgsfaktor Marke,* edited by R. Köhler, W. Majer, and H. Wiezorek. Munich, 2001.

Donath, B., ed. *Customer value: Moving forward − back to basics,* 1997.

Dover, J. "Adding value through the „intel inside" brand." In *Customer value: Moving forward − back to basics,* edited by B. Donath, 1997.

Dwyer, D. M., Hodder, K. I., and Honey, R. C. "Perceptual learning in humans: Roles of preexposure schedule, feedback, and discrimination essay." *Quarterly Journal of Experimental Psychology* 57B (2004): 245–259.

Foremski, T. "Fishing gear maker floats a helpful idea." *Financial Times (London),* February 3, 1999.

Frels, J. K., Shervani, T., and Srivastava, R. K. "The integrated networks model: Explaining resource allocations in network markets." *Journal of Marketing* 67 (2003): 29–45.

Friedland, J. "Components of success: Japanese bicycle-parts maker Shimano eyes China." *Far Easter Economic Review,* November 18, 1993.

Galvin, P., and Morkel, A. "The effect of product modularity on industry structure: The case of the world bicycle industry." *Industry and Innovation* 8 (2001).

George, R. *When the parts become greater than the whole: Fueling growth through ingredient branding,* 2002.

Gerpott, T., and Thomas, S. E. "Markenbewertungsverfahren: Einsatzfelder und Verfahrensüberblick." *Wirtschaftsstudium* (2004): 394–400.

Haller, T. "Ingredient branding." *Textil Zeitung,* August 16, 2001, pp. 21 ff.

Harrison, C. "Big battle over big-screen." *The Dallas Morning News,* May 2, 2005.

Havenstein, M. *Ingredient branding: Die Wirkung der Markierung von Produktbestandteilen bei konsumtiven Gebrauchsgütern.* Wiesbaden, 2004.

Hillyer, C., and Tikoo, S. "Effect of co-branding on consumer product evaluations." *Advances in Consumer Research* 22 (1995).

Hilton, J. "Ingredient branding update: examining ingredient branding as a strategy for growth." *Nutraceuticals World* 6 (2003): 68–73.

Homburg, C., and Krohmer, H. *Marketingmanagement.* Wiesbaden, 2003.

Iacobucci, D., Henderson, G., Marcati, A., and Chang, J. "Network analyses of brand switching behavior." *International Journal of Research in Marketing* 13 (1996): 415–429.

Ibara, Y. "Hub Company in the Global Bicycle Industry." Morgan Stanley Dean Witter, July 18, 2001, p. 14

Isely, P., and Roelofs, M. R. "Primary market and aftermarket competition in the bicycle component industry." *Applied Economics* 36 (2004).

Jacoby, J., and Chestnut, R. W. *Brand loyalty measurement and management.* New York, 1978.

Janiszewski, C., and Osselaer, S. M. J. van. "A connectionist model of brand-quality associations." *Journal of Marketing Research* 37 (2000): 5–20.

Jeltsch, M. "Auto 2010: Eine Expertenbefragung zur Zukunft der Automobilindustrie." Accenture-Studie, 2001.

Johnson, B., and Crumley, B.. *Euro RSCG acquires global role at intel,* March 18, 1996 *Advertising Age (*March 18, 1996).

Kalmbach, R., and Kleinhans, C. "Zulieferer auf der Gewinnerseite." *Automobil-Produktion* (2004): 4–8.

Kapferer, J. N. *Reinventing the brand. Can top brands survive the new market realities?* London, 2001.

Kasper, E., Klar, J., Renner, D., and Specht, S. "Ingredient branding: Bedeutung des InBranding für Automobilzulieferer." Unpublished working paper January, 2005.

Kaul, P. "Swarovski cuts new branding strategy to counter fakes." *The Financial Express,* April 26, 2004.

Keller, K. L. "Conceptualizing, measuring, and managing customer-based brand equity." *Journal of Marketing* 57 (1993): 1–23.

Keller, K. L. "Measuring brand equity." In *Handbook of marketing research: Dos and don'ts,* edited by R. Grover and M. Vriens. Beverly Hills, CA, 2006.

Keller, K. L., ed. *Strategic brand management: Building, measuring, and managing brand equity.* Upper Saddle River, NJ, 1998.

Keller, K. L. "Brand knowledge structures." In *Strategic brand management: Building, measuring, and managing brand equity,* edited by K. L. Keller. Upper Saddle River, NJ, 1998.

Kemper, A. K. "Ingredient branding." *Die Betriebswirtschaft* 57 (1997): 271–274.

Kerber, R. "Bicycles: Bike maker faces a tactical shift." *The Wall Street Journal,* October 12, 1998.

Kleinaltenkamp, M. "Ingredient branding: Markenpolitik im Business-to-Business-Geschäft." In *Erfolgsfaktor Marke,* edited by R. Köhler, W. Majer, and H. Wiezorek. Munich, 2001.

Klein-Boelting, U., and Murad-Aga, T. "Markenbewertung für das Controlling." *Marketingjournal* (2003): 39–41.

Kohlbrenner, M. "Branding from the inside out" http://www.kolbrenerusa.com/blog/index.php/2008/04/14/branding-from-the-inside-out/ seen June 4, 2008

Köhler, R., W. Majer, and H. Wiezorek, eds. *Erfolgsfaktor Marke.* Munich, 2001.

Koppelmann, U. *Produktmarketing: Entscheidungsgrundlage für Produktmanager.* Stuttgart, 1989.

Kotler, P., and Keller, K. L. *Marketing Management.* 13th ed. New York, 2008.

Kotler, P., Andersen, G., Wong, V., and Saunders, J. *Principles of marketing.* 4th ed. London, 2004.

Kotler, P., and Bliemel, F. *Marketing-Management: Analyse, Planung, Umsetzung und Steuerung.* Stuttgart, 1999.

Kotler, P., and Pfoertsch, W. *B2B brand management: Building successful business brands.* Heidelberg, New York, 2006.

Lang, N. "Wild things." *Marketing Computers,* May 1, 1992.

Leuthesser, L., Kohli, C., and Suri, R. "2+2=5?: A framework for using co-branding to leverage a brand." *Journal of Brand Management* 11 (2003).

Leven, W. "The power of industrial branding (Maidenhead Microbrews: The scope of branding, in: Kotler, P.; Keller K., (2006): Marketing Management 12e, Upper Sattle River, p. 275

Linxweiler, R. *BrandScoreCard: Ein neues Instrument erfolgreicher Markenführung.* Gruß-Umstadt, 2001.

Ludwig, W. F. „Branding erobert auch die Investitionsgüterindustrie." *Markenartikel (2000):* 16–25.

Ludwig, W. F. "Ingredient branding: Markenpolitik im Business-to-Business-Geschäft." In *Erfolgsfaktor Marke,* edited by R. Köhler, W. Majer, and H. Wiezorek. Munich, 2001.

Luger, A. E., and Pflaum, D. *Marketing: Strategie und Realisierung.* Munich, 1996.

Malaval, P., and Bénaroya, C. *Strategy and management of industrial brands: Business to business products and services.* Boston, 2001.

Mauborgne, R. A., and Kim, W. C. "Blue ocean strategy: How to create uncontested market space and make the competition irrelevant." 2004.

McCarthy, M. S., and Norris, D. G. "Improving competitive position using branded ingredients." *Journal of Product & Brand Management* 8 (1999): 267–285.

McQueen, M. P., and Spencer, J. "U.S. orders new China toy recall: Aqua dots are pulled off shelves after reports of children falling ill." *Wallstreet Journal,* November 8, 2007.

Meffert, H. *Marketing: Grundlagen marktorientierter Unternehmensführung.* 9th ed. Wiesbaden, 2000.

Michael, B. M. *Werkbuch M wie Marke: Bausteine für ein erfolgreiches Brand Building. Anleitungen, Arbeitsmethoden, Fallbeispiele, Interviews.* Düsseldorf, 2003.

Mitchell, A. "Get ready for a brand new battle." *Marketing Week,* September 25, 1994.

Moon, Y. "Inside intel inside." Harvard Business School case No. 11, 2002.

Moore, J., and Gore, W. L. "Dry goods." 2005, http://www.baselinemag.com/article2/0,1397,1817356,00.asp.

Morris, B. "The brand's the thing." *Fortune Magazine,* March 4, 1996.

Muehr, D. "Branding für Automobilzulieferer." PLEX Studie No. 07, 2001, www.plexgroup.com/cox_www/images/publications/path6/PLEXst udie_01_07_automotive.pdf.

Mundy, M. E., Dwyer, D. M., and Honey, R. C. "Inhibitory associations contribute to perceptual learning in humans." *Journal of Experimental Psychology* 32 (2006): 178–184.

Norris, D. G. "Ingredient branding: A strategy option with multiple beneficiaries." *Journal of Consumer Marketing* 9 (1992): 19–31.

Odrich, B. "A productive partnership." Schott online magazine Solutions, 2007, http://www.schott.com/magazine/english/info103/si103_05_rinnai.html?PHPSESSID=91.

Ogg, E. "HDTV's evolving alphabet soup: LED, OLED, LCD, DLP, CNET news." October 11, 2007.

Ohnemus, L., and Jenster, P. "Corporate brand thrust and financial performance: An examination of strategic brand investments." *International Studies of Management and Organization* 37 (2007): 84–107.

Oliva, R., Srivastava, R., Pfoertsch, W., and Chandler, J. "Insights on ingredient branding." Unpublished working paper, 2007.

Pepels, W. *Handbuch moderne Marketingpraxis.* Düsseldorf, 1993.

Peters, T., and Waterman, R. H., JR. *In search of excellence.* New York, 1982.

Pfoertsch, W. and Chandler, J. D., "Structure as strategy: Linking buyer-seller relationships and networks." Working paper submitted to The Logic of Science and Service Conference January 2008 Honolulu.

Pfoertsch, W., and Chandler, J. D. "Why ingredient brands matter: Understanding changing roles, and changing markets." *Journal of Business & Industrial Marketing* (2010) forecoming.

Pfoertsch, W., Linder, C. and Scheel, H. "Price premium enhancement through a brand in a brand." Working paper Pforzheim University, 2009.

Pfoertsch, W, and Mueller, J. Die Marke in der Marke Bedeutung und Macht es Ingredient Braning, Springer Verlag Heidelberg, 2006

Pfoertsch, W., and Schmid, M. *B2B-Markenmanagement: Konzepte – Methoden – Fallbeispiele.* Munich, 2005.

Pfoertsch, W., ed. *Living Web: Erprobte Anwendungen, Strategien und zukünftige Entwicklungen im Internet.* Landsberg, 1999.

Pfoertsch, W. *Mit Strategie ins Internet.* Nuremberg, 2000.

Pfoertsch, W. Ingredient Branding für Automobilzulieferer, Marketing Management Bulgaria (2004).

Pinar, M., and Trapp, P. S. "Creating competitive advantage through ingredient branding and brand ecosystem: The case of turkish cotton and textiles." *Journal of International Food & Agribusiness Marketing* 20 (2008): 29–56.

Porter, M. E. *Wettbewerbsvorteile: Spitzenleistungen erreichen und behaupten.* 4th ed. Frankfurt/Main, New York, 1996.

Powell, E. "The great technology war." 2003, http://www.projectorcentral.com/lcd_dlp.htm.

Quelch, J. "„Blank" inside: Branding ingredients." *Harvard Business School Working Knowledge,* October 10, 2007.

Rao, A. R., Qu, L., and Ruekert, R. W. "Signaling unobservable product quality through a brand ally." *Journal of Marketing Research* 36 (1999): 258–268.

Reifman, S., and Murphy, A. D. "America's largest private companies." *Forbes,* March 11, 2008.

Renno, D., and Huebscher, M. *Glas-Werkstoffkunde.* 2nd ed. Stuttgart, 2000.

Rid, J., and Sigurdsson, N. "Ingredient branding: A strategy option?: A comparative case study of Intel, Gore-Tex, Bosch, and Autoliv." Postgradutate dissertation, Stockholm, January 2004.

Rooney, J. A. "Branding: A trend for today and tomorrow." *Journal of Product and Brand Management* 4 (1995): 48–55.

Ruebenthaler, K. "Marketing in der technischen Glasindustrie." In *Handbuch Industriegütermarketing: Strategien, Instrumente, Anwendungen,* edited by K. Backhaus and M. Voeth. Wiesbaden, 2004.

Saloner, G., Chang, V., and Shimano, T. "Shimano and the high-end road bike industry." Stanford University case study CASE: SM-150, 2006.

Sattler, H. *Monetäre Bewertung von Markenstrategien für neue Produkte.* Stuttgart, 1997.

Sattler, H. "Markenbewertung." *ZfB* 65 (1995): 663–682.

Sattler, H. "Praxis von Markenbewertung und Markenmanagement in deutschen Unternehmen." In *Industriestudie,* edited by Pricewaterhouse-Coopers. Frankfurt a. M., 1999.

Schlager, E. "Glas: Ein schwer durchschaubarer Stoff." 2004, www.go.de/index.php?cmd=focus_detail&f_id=181&rang=1.

Schmaeh, M., and Erdmeier, P. "Sechs Jahre „Intel Inside"." *Absatzwirtschaft* (1997): 122–129.

Shocker, A., Srivastava, R., and Ruekert, R. "Challenges and opportunities facing brand management: An introduction to the special issue." *Journal of Marketing Research* 31 (1994): 149–158.

Sibert, J. R., and Frude, N. "Bittering agents in the prevention of accidental poisoning: Children's reactions to denatonium benzoate (Bitrex)." 1854387 (P,S,E,B) *Arch Emerg Med,* 1991 Mar 8, pp. 1–7.

Simon, H., and Sebastian, K. -H. "Ingredient Branding: Reift ein neuer Markentypus?" *Absatzwirtschaft* 45 (1995): 42–48.

Simonin, B. L., and Ruth, J. A. "Is a company known by the company it keeps?: Spill-over effects of brand alliances on consumer brand attitudes." *Journal of Marketing Research* 35 (1998): 30–42.

Srivastava, R. K., and Shocker, A. D. "Brand equity: A perspective on its meaning and measurement." Technical working paper 91 – 124, 1991.

Stacherl, R. *Das Glaserhandwerk.* Renningen, 2000.

Starling, S. "Branding: The vital ingredient for marketing success." June, 2002.

Swysten, J. "Business drives and brand responses." May 2003.

Taylor, R., and Karl, U. "Product variety, supply chain structure, and firm performance: Analysis of the U.S. bicycle industry." *Management Science* 47 (2001).

Temporal, P. "Case study: Intel corporation's re-branding." 2009, http://www.temporalbrand.com/publications/articles-260806.shtml.

Trinquecoste, J. F. "Pour une clarification théorique du lien marketing-stratégie." *Recherche et Applications en Marketing* 14 (1999): 59–80.

Vargo, S. L., and Lusch, R. F. "Evolving to a new dominant logic for marketing." *Journal of Marketing* 68 (2004): 1–17.

Venkatesh, R., and Mahajan, V. "Products with branded components: An approach for premium pricing and partner selection." *Journal of Marketing Science* 16 (1997): 146–165.

Vickers, G. "Graham Vickers explains how a Japanese cycle component maker is having a growing impact on the high quality bicycle market." *Design Week,* April 19, 1987.

Vitale, R. P., and Giglierano, J. J. *Business to business marketing: Analysis and practice in a dynamic environment,* 2002.

Voigt, K. "Your life: The interview: Pedal power." *Asian Wall Street Journal,* November 28, 2003.

Voelckner, F., and Sattler, H. "Empirical generalizability of consumer evaluations of brand extensions." Research paper No. 25, 2005.

Vucurevic, T. "Die GORE-TEX® Marke: Eine Komponente wird zum Kaufgrund." In *Jahrbuch Markentechnik 2006/2007,* edited by A. Deichsel and H. Meyer. Frankfurt a. M., 2006.

Wathne, K. H., Biong, H., and Heide, J. B. "Choice of supplier in embedded markets: Relationship and marketing program effects." *Journal of Marketing* 65 (2001): 54–66.

Wathne, K. H., and Heide, J. B. "Relationship governance in a supply chain network." *Journal of Marketing* 68 (2004): 73–89.

Webster, F. E., and Wind, Y. *Organizational buying behavior,* 1972.

Wedepohl, K. H. *Glas in Antike und Mittelalter.* Stuttgart, 2003.

Wilkinson, I. "A history of network and channels thinking in marketing in the 20th century." *Australasian Journal of Marketing* 9 (2001): 23–53.

Willhardt, A. B., and Baumbach, R. "Ingredient branding: Herausforderung für die Markenführung der Automobilzulieferindustrie." 2004.

Worm, S., and Durme, J. van "An empirical study of the consequences of co-branding on perceptions of the ingredient brand." Proceedings EMAC 2006 Conference.

List of Ingredient Brands

Company	Ingredient Brand	Product Function	Logo
Chemicals			
Bayer AG	Makrolon	Polycarbonate	
Microban	Microban	Anti-bacterial chemical compounds	
Johnson Matthey's Fine Chemicals	Bitrex	Bittering agent	
Sanitized AG	Sanitized	Antimicrobial additives	
Cognis Corporation (Henkel)	Cognis	Speciality chemicals for wellness & sustainability	
Alcantara Spa	Alcantara	Synthetic leather	
Sika	Sika	Specialty chemicals	
Hoechst	Hostalen	Polyolefins	

BASF	Indanthren	Synthetic vat dyes	
	Luran	Plastics	
Owens-Corning Fiberglas Corporation	Fiberglas	Products from glass fibers	
Brand Association Stainless Steel Germany	Edelstahl rostfrei	Stainless steel	
WMF	Cromargan	Special stainless steel	
Evonik	Plexiglas	Performance Polymers	PLEXIGLAS®

Dietary Supplement

NutraSweet Company	NutraSweet	Natural sweetener	
McNeil Nutritionals, LLC	Splenda	Natural sweetener	
Cargill Inc.	CoroWise	Naturally Sourced cholesterol reducer	
	HFT	Omega 3 food ingredients	
	Oliggo	Natural soluble fibers	

	Xtrend	Starch and sweetener	
	Maltidex	Natural sweetener	
	IsoMaltidex	Natural sweetener	
	Treha	Multi-functional, non-reducing carbohydrate	
	Barliv	Barley beta fiber	
	Truvia	Natural sweetener	
	Zerose	Natural sweetener	
Südzucker	Isomalt	Natural sweetener	
	Beneo	Inulin and oligofructose	
Alfa Aesar	Xylit	Natural sugar alcohol	
OceanSpray Cranberries, Inc	OceanSpray	Cranberry	
Z Trim Holding	Z-Trim	Fat replacement	

P&G	Olean	Fat replacement	
Solae Company	Solae	Soy products	
	Prolisse	Soy protein	
Perdue products	Senokot	Natural laxative	
WBANA	Wild Blueberries	Antioxidant	

Systems

Sun Microsystems	Java	System software	
Dolby Laboratories	Dolby	Sound system	
THX Inc.	THX	Sound system	
Microsoft	Vista	Operating system	
	Media room	Media system	
DivX Networks Inc.	DivX	Media system	

Cable & Wireless	Cable & Wireless	Telecom systems	CABLE & WIRELESS
Realtek Semiconductor Corp	Realtek	Multi-media systems	REALTEK

Fibers			
The Woolmark Company (Australian Wool Innovation)	Woolmark	Natural wool	WOOLMARK
Invista	Cordura	Performance fabric	CORDURA
	Coolmax	Performance fabric	COOLMAX
	Stainmaster	Carpeting	STAINMASTER
	Cordura	Carpet fiber	CORDURA
	Antron	Carpet fiber	Antron carpet fiber
	Lycra	Elastic fiber	LYCRA
	Supplex	Micro fiber	supplex
	…and others		

Reliance Industries Ltd.	Trevira	Micro fiber	**Trevira**
SympaTex Technology GmbH	SympaTex	Laminate	SYMPATEX
W. L. Gore & Associates	Gore-Tex	Laminate	GORE-TEX
	Windstopper	Laminate	WIND STOPPER
DuPont	Teflon	Multiple applications	Teflon
	Nomex	Thermal protection	DuPont NOMEX
	Kevlar	Brand fiber	DUPONT Kevlar.
	Corian	Surface materials	DUPONT corian
	…and others		
NatureWorks	Ingeo	Biopolymer & fibers	ingeo
Diolen Industrial	Diolen	Polyester yarn	**Diolen**
Nano-Tex Inc.	Nanotex	Textile enhancements	NANOtex

Thai Acrylic Fiber	Amicor	Intelligent fiber	Amicor⁺

Glass			
Schott	Schott Optics	Optical lenses	SCHOTT
	Schott Ceran	Glass ceramic cook tops	SCHOTT CERAN®
Zeiss AG	Zeiss	Optical lenses	ZEISS
Schneider Kreuznach	Schneider	Optical lenses	Schneider KREUZNACH
Kodak	Kodak	Optical lenses	Kodak
Leica Cameras	Leica	Optical lenses	Leica
Swarovski	Crystallized elements	Crystal glass	CRYSTAL LIZED SWAROVSKI ELEMENTS

Bicycle Components			
Shimano Products	Shimano	Bicycle gears	SHIMANO
Campagnolo S.r.l.	Campagnolo	Bicycle gears	Campagnolo
SRAM Corporation	SRAM	Bicycle gears	SRAM.

	Rockshox	Bicycle components	
	Avid	Bicycle components	
	Truvavtiv	Bicycle components	
Formula	Formula	Bicycle components	
Salomon SAS	Mavic	Wheel-sets	
Race Face Performance Products	Raceface	Mountain bike components	
Easton Sports	Easton	Bicycle components	
DT Swiss	DT Swiss	Bicycle components	
MAGURA Bike Parts GmbH & Co. KG	Magura	Bicycle components	

Automotives

Deutz	Deutz	Diesel engines	
ThyssenKrupp	Bielstein	Shocks	

Torsen Traction	Torsen	Permanent 4 wheel drives	
Continental AG	VDO	Automotive components	
Brembo	Brembo	Brakes	
ZF AG	ZF	Automotive components	
Perkins Engines	Perkins	Diesel engines	
Recaro GmbH & Co. KG	Recaro	Car seats	
TomTom NV	TomTom	Navigation systems	
Chevron	Techron	Fuel additive	
ABT	ABT	Design service	
PININFARINA	PININFARINA	Design service	
Robert Bosch GmbH	Bosch	Automotive components	
	ABS	Anti-block break system	

	ESP	Electronic stabilization-program	
Cummins Engines	Cummins	Diesel engines	
Goodyear Tires	Goodyear	Tires	
Rotax	Rotax	Small engines	
Audi	Quattro	Permanent 4 wheel drives	
Cadillac	Northstar	V8 engines	Northstar
Kuka AG	Kuka	Industrial robots and factory automation equipment and services	
Fanuc	Fanuc	Automation controls	
Siemens	Sinumeric	Automation controls	
Webasto	Webasto	Heatings	
SIRIUS	Sirius	Satellite radio	

Audio & TV Components			
JBL	JBL	Sound systems	JBL
Bosch	Blaupunkt	Radio and Hifi	BLAUPUNKT Bosch Group
Bose	Bose	Sound systems	BOSE
TI	DLP	Projection systems	DLP TEXAS INSTRUMENTS
Sony	Trinitron	TV monitors	Trinitron

Computer Components			
Intel Corporation	Intel	Processors	intel
	Centrino	Processors	intel Centrino Duo
	Xeon	Processors	intel Xeon
	Core	Processors	intel Core 2 Duo
	Pentium	Processors	intel Pentium D

AMD	ATI	Graphic cards	
AMD	AMD	Processors	
AMD	Athlon	Processors	
MSI Technology	MSI	Motherboards	
NVIDIA CORPORATE	nVIDIA	Graphic cards	
Brokat Technologies AG	Brokat	Security	
ASUSTeK Computer Inc.	Asus	Motherboards	
Universal ABIT	Abit	Motherboards	
Giga-Byte Technology Co., Ltd.	Gigabyte	Motherboards	
Samsung Group	Samsung	Memory	
Kingston Technology Company, Inc.	Kingston	Memory	
Seagate Technology	Maxtor	Hard Drives	

	Seagate	Hard Drives	
LG Electronics	LG	DVD Drives	
Samsung Group	Samsung	DVD Drives	
Toshiba Corporation	Toshiba	DVD Drives	
Pioneer Corporation	Pioneer	DVD Drives	
Hitachi, Ltd.	Hitachi	DVD Drives	
Payment Systems			
Visa	Visa	Payment Systems	
MasterCard	MasterCard	Payment Systems	
ZKA	EC Card	Payment Systems	
UnionPay	UnionPay	Payment Systems	
Packaging			
Tetra Pak	Tetra Pak	Packaging systems	

SGS	SGS	Packaging systems	
SIG	CombiBlock	Packaging systems	
Innovative Components			
3M	Vikuiti	Enhancement films and projection components	
	Scotchlite	Reflective material	
	Scotchguard	Paint protection	
	Filtrete	Water filtration system	
	Thinsulate	Insulation	
	Twaron	Para-aramid fiber	
Truma Gerätetechnik	Truma	Power supply/heating for recreational vehicles	
Services			
Les Mills	Les Mills	Fitness program/system	
Billy Blanks	TaeBo	Fitness program/system	

| Lufthansa | Lufthansa Cargo | Air transportation systems | |

Aircrafts

| Boeing | Boeing | Airplane | |
| Airbus S.A.S. | Airbus | Airplane | |

Standards

US EPA	EnergyStar	Use less energy, save money, and help protect the environment	
SATA-IO	Sata	Serial Advanced Technology Attachment	
USBIF	USB	Universal serial bus	

Internet Addresses

3M	www.3m.com
ABT	www.abt-sportsline.de
Airbus	www.airbus.com
Alcantara	www.alcantara.com
AMD	www.amd.com
Asus	de.asus.com
Audi	www.audi.de
AZO	www.azo.de
BASF	www.basf.com
Bayer AG	www.bayer.de
Bilstein	www.bilstein.de
Binder	www.binder-magnete.de
Bitrex	www.bitrex.com
Boeing	www.boeing.de
Bosch	www.bosch.de
Bose	www.bose.de
Brembo	www.brembo.com

Cable & Wireless	www.cable-and-wireless.de
Cadillac	www.cadillaceurope.com
Campagnolo	www.campagnolo.com
Chevron	www.chevron.com
Cognis	www.cognis.com
Corning	www.corning.com
Cummins	www.cummins.com
Cycle Shimano	cycle.shimano-eu.com
Deutz	www.deutz.de
DivX	www.divx.com
DLP	www.dlp.com
DLP	itsthemirrors.com
Dolby	www.dolby.com
DT Swiss	www.dtswiss.com
DuPont	www2.dupont.com
Easton	www.eastonsports.com
Edelstahl Rostfrei	www.edelstahl-rostfrei.de
Fanuc Robotics	www.fanucrobotics.de
Gigabyte	www.gigabyte.de
Goodyear	eu.goodyear.com
Google	google.com
Gore	www.gore-tex.de

Harman/Becker	www.harmanbecker.com
Hitachi	www.hitachi.de
Hoechst	www.hoechst.com
Intel	www.Intel.com
Invista	www.invista.com
Java	www.java.com
Kendrion	www.kendrion.com
Kingston	www.kingston.com
Kodak	www.kodak.de
Kuka	www.kuka-ag.de
Label Online	www.label-online.de
Leica	www.leica-camera.de
LG	de.lge.com
Maestro	www.maestro.ch
Makrolon	www.makrolon.de
Markenlexikon	www.markenlexikon.com
Marketing-Verein	www.marketingverein.de
MasterCard	www.mastercard.com
Microban	www.microban.com
Microsoft	www.microsoft.com
MSI	www.msi-technology.de
nVidia	www.nvidia.de

Onpulson	www.onpulson.de
Perkins	www.perkins.com
Pininfarina	www.pininfarina.de
Pioneer	www.pioneer.de
Plexiglas	www.plexiglas.de
Raceface	www.raceface.com
Realtek	www.realtek.com.tw
Recaro	www.recaro.de
Rotax	www.rotax.com
Salomon	www.salomonsports.com
Samsung	www.samsung.de
Sanitized	www.sanitized.com
Schneider Kreuznach	www.schneiderkreuznach.com
Schott	www.schott.com
Seagate	www.seagate.com
SGS	www.de.sgs.com
Siemens	www.siemens.de
SIG	www.sigallcap.ch
Sika	www.sika.com
Simon Kucher & Partner	www.simon-kucher.com
Sirius	www.siriusitc.ch
Sony	www.sony.de

Sram	www.sram.com/de
Swarovski	www.crystallized.com
SympaTex	www.sympatex.de
Tetra Pak	www.tetrapak.de
Thoma	www.thoma-magnettechnik.de
Tomtom	www.tomtom.com
Torsen Traction	www.torsen.com
Toshiba	www.toshiba.de
Trevira	www.trevira.de
Truma	www.truma.com
VDO	www.vdo.de
Visa	www.visa.de
Webasto	www.webasto.de
Wind Stopper	www.windstopper.de
Wirtschaftslexikon 24	www.wirtschaftslexikon24.net
WMF	www.wmf.de
Zeiss	www.zeiss.de
ZF	www.zf.com

Company/Brand Index

C

Subject Index